TAX SECRETS
OF
MILLIONAIRE
REAL ESTATE
INVESTORS

TAX SECRETS
OF
MILLIONAIRE
REAL ESTATE
INVESTORS

RICHARD T. WILLIAMSON, ESQ.

Dearborn™
Trade Publishing
A **Kaplan Professional** Company

This publication is designed to provide accurate and authoritative information in regard to the subject matter covered. It is sold with the understanding that the publisher is not engaged in rendering legal, accounting, or other professional service. If legal advice or other expert assistance is required, the services of a competent professional should be sought.

Vice President and Publisher: Cynthia A. Zigmund
Acquisitions Editor: Mary B. Good
Senior Project Editor: Trey Thoelcke
Interior Design: Lucy Jenkins
Cover Design: Design Alliance
Typesetting: Elizabeth Pitts

Published by Dearborn Trade Publishing
A Kaplan Professional Company

05 06 07 10 9 8 7 6 5 4 3 2 1

Library of Congress Cataloging-in-Publication Data

Williamson, Richard T.
   Tax secrets of millionaire real estate investors / Richard T. Williamson.
     p. cm.
   Includes index.
   ISBN 0-7931-9362-1
  1. Real estate investment–Taxation–Law and legislation–United States. I. Title.
   KF6535.W54 2005
   343.7305'246–dc22

                                  2004015643

Dearborn Trade books are available at special quantity discounts to use for sales promotions, employee premiums, or educational purposes. Please call our Special Sales Department to order or for more information at 800-621-9621 ext. 4444, e-mail trade@dearborn.com, or write to Dearborn Trade Publishing, 30 South Wacker Drive, Suite 2500, Chicago, IL 60606-7481.

Dedication

To Michelle, my wife of eight years and still my best friend and soul mate. Each time I look back at my life and think or wish I had done things differently, I realize that if I had, I might not have ever met Michelle. With that in mind, I regret nothing because no change would be worth that risk.

To Christina, my daughter and friend, who, at 21 years of age, has come so far already and still has her whole life ahead of her. Watching her grow to the intelligent and articulate woman she has become has been a true gift in my life. Her recent accomplishments have filled me with a type of pride I have never known before.

To Rebecca, my ten-year-old daughter, who has a whirlwind level of energy and excitement for life that is a wonder. To me, she is a star softball and basketball player and she constantly surprises me with glimpses of the high school and college athlete she may yet become. Her energy and enthusiasm is highly contagious and I am very thankful to feel just a little younger because of it.

CONTENTS

Preface   xiii
Acknowledgments   xv

PART I
REAL ESTATE TAX BASICS

1. INTRODUCTION   1

Income Taxes Are Not the Same as Capital Gains Taxes   1
What Are Capital Gains?   2
Capital Gains Tax Repeal   3

2. ESTIMATING CAPITAL GAINS TAXES   7

The Basics   7
Understanding Recapture of Depreciation   9
Estimating Your Tax Liability   11

3. DEALER VERSUS INVESTOR   15

What Is a Property Dealer?   16
What Is a Property Investor?   16
Why Does It Matter If You Are a Dealer or an Investor?   17
How Millionaire Real Estate Investors Avoid Being
   Labeled Dealers   22
Statutes and Case Law   24

4. THE BENEFITS OF DEPRECIATION   27

Understanding How Depreciation Shields You from Taxes   30
Maximizing Your Depreciation   31

5. COST SEGREGATION LIVES AGAIN   35

What Is Cost Segregation?   35
Cost Segregation Studies   36
The Four Basic Considerations   38
When Is the Best Time to Do a Cost Segregation Study?   39

6. PASSIVE INVESTMENT RULES AND EXCEPTIONS   43

Understanding the Passive Loss Rules   43
The Exception for Active Participation   44
The Exception for Real Estate Professionals   47
Understanding the Material Participation Requirement   49
Carrying Forward Unused Losses   52
Disposing of an Entire Passive Property Interest   52
Passive Loss Rules Summary   53

PART II
TAX DEFERRAL AND AVOIDANCE STRATEGIES

7. TAX-FREE EXCHANGES   55

Introduction   55
How Exchanges Work   56
Advantages of 1031 Exchanges   59
1031 Exchange Requirements   68
Using Qualified Intermediaries   73
Time Requirements of Selecting the Replacement Property   76
Avoiding Potential Problems   80
Holding Period Requirements   83
Splitting Up Partnerships and Joint Ventures   85
Recharacterizing Property to Qualify for Exchanges   87
Exchanges between Related Parties   89
Primary Residence Issues in Exchanges   89
The Future of 1031 Exchanges   94

8. REVERSE EXCHANGES   95

Reverse Exchange Opportunities   96
Legal Status and Costs Involved   97

9. BUILD-TO-SUIT EXCHANGES   103

How a Built-to-Suit Exchange Works   104
Strict Timelines   107
Financing Issues   107
Insurance Issues   108
Summary   108

10. TENANT-IN-COMMON EXCHANGES   109

Introduction to Triple Net or TIC Offerings   109
Revenue Procedure 2002-22   111
How TIC Property Investments Are Structured   114
How a 1031-to-TIC Exchange Works   114
Selecting the Right Tenant-in-Common Property   115

11. USING INSTALLMENT SALES   119

Introduction to Installment Sales   119
How Installment Sales Work   120
Advantages of Installment Sales   121
Disadvantages of Installment Sales   123
Balancing the Risk   129
Structuring the Deal   133
Prepayment Penalties   136
How and When the Taxes Are Paid   140

12. HYBRIDS—COMBINING TAX STRATEGIES   147

The Best of Both Worlds—Combining an Installment Sale
    with an Exchange   147
Legal Status and Possible Complications   148
Other Combinations to Consider   152

13. PRIVATE ANNUITY TRUSTS   153

What Is a Private Annuity Trust?   153
A Millionaire's Tax Secret   155
A Specialty Plan Tool   156
Both Estate and Capital Gains Tax Advantages   157
Structure and Implementation   159
Transfer and Sale of the Property   162
Maximizing the Tax Deferral   163
Reinvestment within the Trust   164

Private Annuity Trusts Inveseting in Commercial Annuities   164
Installment Sale or Private Annuity Trust? Sometimes Both.   166
Trust Investing—Keeping It in Your Family   167
Legal Formalities and Requirements   169
Private Annuity versus an Installment Sale   173
Summary and Frequently Asked Questions   174
Where to Get More Information about Private Annuity Trusts   177

14. CHARITABLE REMAINDER TRUSTS   179

Introduction to Charitable Remainder Trusts   179
Stream of Income Illustration   180
How the Immediate Income Tax Deduction Works   182
Philanthropic Advantages   184
How the Trust Structure and Property Sale Works   184
Charitable Remainder Trust Types   187
Legal Requirements   190
Disadvantages   194
Ways to Solve the Family Inheritance Issue   195
Charity Selection Considerations—What If You Change
   Your Mind?   199
Where to Get More Information about Charitable Remainder
   Trusts   199

PART III
OTHER TAX ADVANTAGES

15. PRIMARY RESIDENCE EXCLUSIONS   201

What Is the Primary Residence Exclusion?   201
What Property Qualifies as a Primary Residence   202
How the Required Two-Year Time Period Is Calculated   203
Exceptions to the Two-Year Requirements   205
The New "Unforeseen Circumstances" Rules   207
How to Calculate a Partial Exclusion   208
Fractional Exemption Use for Investment Property   208
Investment Property Converted to a Primary Residence   210
Recapture of Depreciation   211
Home Office Tax Issues   212

16. STEPPED-UP BASIS   215

What Is a Stepped-Up Basis   215
Stepped-Up Basis on Jointly Owned Property   218
Filing for a Step Up in Basis   221
Using Fair Market Value to Your Advantage   221
Summary   228

17. USING YOUR IRA TO BUY REAL ESTATE   229

Yes, You Can Use Your IRA to Invest in Real Estate   229
How It Works   231
IRAs—Tax-Free versus Tax-Deferred   232
Where to Start—The Self-Directed IRA   233
How to Buy Real Estate within Your Self-Directed IRA   235
Self-Dealing and Other Prohibited Transactions   235
Unrelated Business Income Tax (UBIT) Issues   236
Summary   237

Conclusion   239
Appendix A—Form: 45-Day Identification of Replacement
   Property   241
Appendix B—Revenue Procedure 2000-37   243
Appendix C—Revenue Procedure 2002-22   251
Glossary   263
Recommended Advisors   271
Index   273

PREFACE

"The avoidance of taxes is the only intellectual pursuit that still carries any reward."

John Maynard Keynes

Real estate investment has created more millionaires than all other types of investments combined. That statement has probably never been truer than in today's booming real estate market. More and more, property investment is becoming recognized as one of the most stable, predictable, and controllable ways to build wealth and plan for retirement. However, as in most investments, what you don't know can hurt you financially. Making *great* property investments usually involves good timing, available resources, knowledge of the market, and a little luck. But it doesn't take *great* property investments to make you wealthy, just *good* ones.

One aspect that all real estate investments have in common is taxes. Whether you are Donald Trump or the mom-and-pop rental property owner, you have at least one silent partner in your investments, the federal government via taxation. In fact, because there are only a few states that have no income taxes, most of us actually have two silent partners, the state government and the federal government.

Like most partnerships, when profits are made, each of the partners wants their share. Conversely, if there is a loss from an investment, our "tax partners" are kind enough to allow us to reduce their share on other investments by using losses to offset other gains. Unfortunately, unlike traditional partnerships, we don't get to choose whether we want to have partners, so it's best just to acknowledge that some portion of all profits made will have to be shared with our silent partners via taxes. The question then becomes what or how much is their share and when do we have to pay it to them.

Every time a piece of real estate changes hands there are tax consequences. The two primary tax considerations on the sale of investment property are capital gains and recapture of depreciation. Between the two, state and federal taxes can be as much as a full one-third of the profit on the sale of a property. Not surprisingly, most property investors are always on the lookout for ways to avoid or defer these taxes. Here's a quote I ran across that seems to sum up the state of mind of a lot of investors:

> *"I don't know what to do or where to turn in this taxation matter. Somewhere there must be a book that tells all about it, where I could go to straighten it out in my mind. But I don't know where the book is, and maybe I couldn't read it if I found it."*
>
> Warren G. Harding

In 18 years of real estate and law practice, I have never come across any such book, but in *this* book I am going to try to give you a straightforward, nontechnical look at some of the various possible ways to deal with capital gains taxes. We are also going to look at some taxation tricks and traps of owning real estate and the different types of taxation tools used by millionaire real estate investors in building wealth. You are going to find tax techniques that range from the simple to the sophisticated along with real world examples and a look at the pros and cons of each.

ACKNOWLEDGMENTS

The one thing every author probably learns while writing a book is that the work is not possible without the encouragement and assistance of people around you. With that in mind, I would like to thank my wife and my daughter for tolerating all the nights and weekends I spent closed up in my office working.

I was fortunate to have the assistance and input from a number of other professionals. I would like to give credit and my sincere thanks to the following people:

- *Ed Dowd.* Ed is a broker and investment property specialist with Coldwell Banker Real Estate in Long Beach, California. Ed's contributions were critical because sometimes things seem right "on paper," but not in the "real world." Ed generally knows the difference. His wealth of real-world experience was tapped many times for the examples and explanations given herein.
- *Matthew Crammer.* Matt is an accountant and financial planner with Crammer Accountancy in Downey, California. As always, Matt has been very supportive and generous with his time. He has been a sounding board and helped with editing some of the technical aspects of the manuscript's rough draft. Matt also

made valuable suggestions for improving the accounting examples and explanations. His accounting expertise was essential for the examples and illustrations throughout the book.

- *Michelle Williamson.* Michelle is a real estate broker in Long Beach, California. Michelle spent long hours editing and proofreading. As always, her suggestions and feedback were some of the most important factors in completing the manuscript. If you find this book clear and easy to read, the credit belongs to Michelle.

- *Paul Flores.* Paul is the former Chief Deputy Director Tax Collector for Lake County, California. When I was nearing the final days of writing, Paul was generous enough to thoroughly read the manuscript in a very short period. His perspective was very much appreciated.

- *Anette Kerr.* Anette is not a broker or accountant or lawyer. She didn't add to the text of this book or proofread the copy, but her assistance was just as necessary and just as appreciated as anyone who did. Anette is my paralegal and assistant. She has the very difficult job of trying to protect me from the daily interruptions and distractions that threaten to absorb all of my time. How she manages that while juggling all the other tasks I ask of her is truly amazing. Anette, you are appreciated more than you know.

CHAPTER 1

Introduction

"The Government that robs Peter to pay Paul can always depend upon the support of Paul."

George Bernard Shaw

Income Taxes Are Not the Same as Capital Gains Taxes

When the average person thinks of taxes, they usually think of *income* taxes. However, the tax system in the United States is not based on taxing *income*. Instead, our tax system is based on taxing *increases in wealth*. The subtle difference in this terminology is very important because taxing all forms of increases in wealth allows the taxation of all income sources rather than just the earnings we take home from work. So, in addition to income taxes we also have taxes on gifts, interest income, debt forgiveness, capital gains, and even death (estate taxes). All of these things represent increases in wealth according to the IRS and are taxed in one manner or another. Both income tax and gift tax is scaled to essentially provide that the more you make/give, the higher the percentage of tax you will pay. Likewise, estate taxes as a percentage are higher in larger estates. Taxing debt forgiveness is an odd but necessary concept in the eye of the IRS. If debt forgiveness was not taxed, companies could circumvent *income* taxes by simply paying their employees wages with "loans" each month and simply forgiving the debt at the end of the year. It's a simple example of tax planning creativity, but it makes the point that simply focusing on earnings would be insufficient. The majority of this book will focus on capital gains taxes. Capital gains are actually given a preferential tax treatment in that the applicable tax is based on a flat rate. At the time of this writing, the long-term federal capital gains tax rate is 15 percent, which is the lowest it has been in 45 years.

There are also state taxes to consider. Each state sets its own rules as to how they will tax capital gains. In some states there are no state capital gain taxes, but in most there will be some tax liability due upon the sale of an appreciated property. Additionally, each state has its own rules about capital gains tax deferral. Most states mirror the federal taxation rules and guidelines, but not all. It is important to understand that the focus of this book will be on federal taxation and those states—California, for example—that mirror the federal rules. I suggest you see your local tax advisor regarding your specific state's taxation of capital gains.

As previously mentioned, true *income* tax is scaled to tax larger incomes at higher percentage rates. The capital gains tax, however, is a flat 15 percent rate. More important, capital gains taxes, unlike ordinary income taxes, can be deferred indefinitely and in some situations eliminated completely. In the next section, we are going to look at what types of wealth increases are categorized as capital gains.

What Are Capital Gains?

The IRS definition of a capital asset is just about everything you own whether it is used for personal purposes or for investment. Examples it gives include your home, household furnishings, and stocks or bonds held in your personal account. After the tax changes of 2003, the IRS now categorizes capital gains in two basic ways, short term and long term.

If you hold the asset for more than one year before you dispose of it, your capital gain is long term. If you hold it for one year or less, your capital gain will be considered short term. That seems fairly straight-forward, but as you will see in later chapters, that one-year mark is not the deep line in the sand that it appears to be. For our purposes in this chapter, however, we will pretend that we can actually count on that one-year differentiation. Why does it matter? It matters because the tax difference between the two can be staggering on large gains. Long-term capital gains are taxed at that flat 15 percent as mentioned above, but short-term capital gains are taxed at ordinary income tax rates.

When you sell a capital asset, the difference between the amount at which you sell it and your basis is a capital gain or a capital loss. In the case of real estate investments, most people take depreciation and make improvements to the property over time so the basis of the property changes each year. In a normal property investment situation, there are two forces at work creating a gain on the property. First, appreciation increases the fair market value of the property; and second, depreciation taken on the property over the years correspondingly reduces the property's basis adding another component, recapture of depreciation, which is taxable when the property is eventually sold. See Figure 1.1.

Capital Gains Tax Repeal

The idea of having the capital gains tax eliminated sounds appealing, but most millionaire real estate investors like it just the way it is. That may sound strange, but not when you really think about it. Remember, the focus of the IRS is taxing increases in wealth, not wages. The flat 15 percent capital gains rate is one of the lowest taxes available. If you had $100,000 of *income* in a year, your tax rate would be

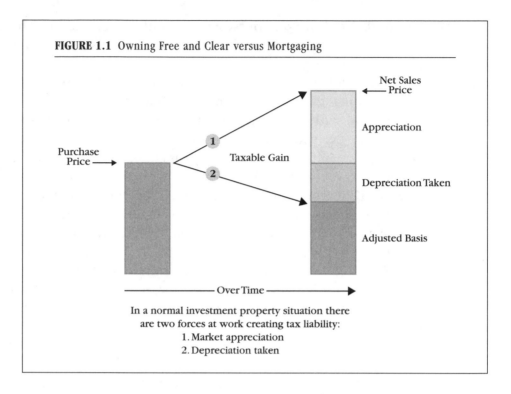

FIGURE 1.1 Owning Free and Clear versus Mortgaging

In a normal investment property situation there
are two forces at work creating tax liability:
1. Market appreciation
2. Depreciation taken

approximately 30 percent. A taxable *gift* of $100,000 would be taxed
at approximately 37 percent. A taxable *estate* inheritance would be
taxed at approximately 37 percent. So what's so bad about a 15 percent flat rate tax on capital gains? Of course, *zero* tax would be better,
but that's just not realistic given the IRS's mission to tax "increases in
wealth."

Another reason the current capital gains tax is good is because it
allows for planning. If you know that the taxable consequence of selling a capital asset is going to be the same now as it will be in the future, you are more able to do intelligent tax planning. Most capital
assets have a built-in variable—the resale market. Real estate values
have cycles just like any other investment. Anyone who has held real
estate for more than ten years can tell you there are market highs and
lows. The last thing investors need to compound the uncertainty and
risk is a variable tax environment. In one worse-case scenario, it is

possible that politicians eliminate the capital gains tax to get votes, but the next administration decides the "increase in wealth" should be taxed at the (higher) ordinary income tax rates. Few people are comfortable with the idea of politicians messing around with tax rates that are already the lowest they have been in a half-century. Stability and certainty in an investment or business environment encourages additional investment by allowing intelligent growth planning.

Additionally, the present capital gains system can be used to build wealth. The capital gain you make from a real estate investment can be deferred when trading property investments. You cannot sell your mutual funds in a high market and reinvest the money in other Wall Street products without "cashing out," paying the taxes due, and then buying the replacement investment with after-tax dollars. With real estate capital gain, however, you can sell (through a 1031 exchange) an investment property in a high market and buy another using the *untaxed* dollars from sale of the first investment. This is a millionaire real estate investor's best friend.

☛ **Example:** George is an insurance agent, he bought a triplex ten years ago for $100,000 and its current value is $220,000. He would like to open his own insurance office and has found a perfect office building for sale at $300,000 that he wants to buy. George sells his triplex under the provisions of a 1031 tax-deferred exchange and purchases the office building replacement property. George is able to fully defer any capital gains tax or recapture of depreciation. George operates his insurance company for 15 years and is ready to retire. He would like to move to another state and buy an income-producing investment property there. The office building value has grown to $500,000 and the 12-unit apartment building he would like to buy is priced at $550,000. Again, George uses a 1031 exchange to sell the office building and purchases the 12-unit apartment building, and he is able to completely defer all capital gains and recapture of depreciation.

There is no limit to the number of times you can use a 1031 exchange to "trade up" without incurring any tax liability. The key is that the current IRS regulations allow this continuing deferral on *capital gains* but not on any other types of *increases in wealth.* The ability to defer capital gains through a 1031 exchange was a hard-fought-for right that had to been pounded out in the courts and forced upon the IRS through legislative mandate over a period of 20 to 30 years. This wealth-building tool now works extremely well and any changes to the capital gains tax rules can only do it harm.

In summary, the idea of eliminating the capital gains tax sounds great, but at what real cost? At best, it is unrealistic to think that the IRS's concept of taxing increases in wealth is going to allow big gains from investments to flow to individuals tax-free.

Even if there were a tax reform that eliminated the capital gains tax as currently defined, the increase in wealth *is* going to be taxed in some other way. When you take into consideration the current flat 15 percent rate, the now-existing certainty for planning, and the present ability to defer capital gains for wealth building, you start to appreciate the current real estate capital gains tax system.

> *"Tax reform is taking the taxes off things that have been taxed in the past and putting taxes on things that haven't been taxed before."*
>
> Art Buchwald

CHAPTER 2

Estimating Capital Gains Taxes

"The hardest thing to understand in the world is the income tax."

Albert Einstein

The Basics

Understanding the tax secrets or tax alternatives used by millionaire real estate investors starts with understanding how real estate investments are taxed. Before you can make an intelligent choice of which tax tools to use, you have to start by knowing the extent of the taxes. Any one particular method of deferring or eliminating taxes might seem like too much trouble at a $10,000 tax savings, but at a $50,000 tax savings it might be much more tolerable, and at a $100,000 tax savings it might seem the ideal solution. In fact, the extent of your tax liability will usually dictate how open-minded you are in exploring options. With that in mind, it makes sense to start with a discussion about how you can estimate your own taxes on the sale or taxable transfer of an investment.

To estimate your tax liability on the sale of a property, you have to know what the gain will be. The gain on a property is the difference between the net sales price and the adjusted basis on the property. The adjusted basis of a property is:

> Original Purchase Price
> \+ Purchase Expenses
> \+ Capital Improvements
> − Depreciation Taken
> _____
> Adjusted Basis

This information is usually calculated each year when you are filing your tax returns on a particular investment property; so most people just call their tax preparer and ask. You can use the amount of yearly depreciation from a previous tax return to come up with a pretty good estimate.

Once you have your adjusted basis on the property, estimating the capital gain is fairly straightforward:

> Sales Price
> − Sales Expenses
> − Adjusted Basis
> _____
> Capital Gain

Your capital gain on a property is usually going to be made up of two components—actual gain and recapture of depreciation. So, before you can estimate the actual tax on the gain, you need to know how much of the gain will be considered recapture of depreciation. We have already covered the basic tax rate for capital gains, so if you have never taken any depreciation on the property (usually only land) you can generally estimate your taxes as simply 15 percent of your capital gain (plus state taxes). However, if you are like most people, you have taken the available depreciation on the property over the years thereby reducing your adjusted basis (see Figure 2.1). As such, your tax estimate will need to take into account the higher tax rate on

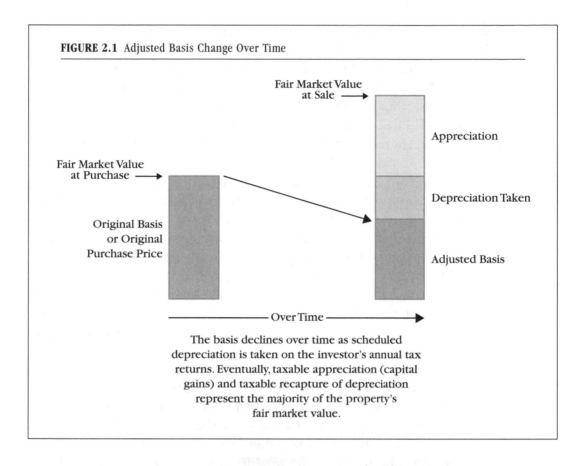

FIGURE 2.1 Adjusted Basis Change Over Time

Fair Market Value at Sale ⟶

Appreciation

Fair Market Value at Purchase ⟶

Depreciation Taken

Original Basis or Original Purchase Price

Adjusted Basis

⟵ Over Time ⟶

The basis declines over time as scheduled depreciation is taken on the investor's annual tax returns. Eventually, taxable appreciation (capital gains) and taxable recapture of depreciation represent the majority of the property's fair market value.

the recapture of the depreciation portion of the gain. Chapter 4 will look at maximizing the available depreciation on real estate investments, but for the purposes on this chapter our focus will be on recapturing whatever depreciation was actually taken.

Understanding Recapture of Depreciation

Prior to 1997, capital gains tax and recapture of depreciation were taxed at the same rate. The 1997 tax changes reduced the tax on both capital gains and recapture of depreciation, but not by the same amount. The capital gains rate was reduced from 28 percent to 20 percent, but the recapture of depreciation was only reduced to 25 percent. Then in 2003, the capital gains rate again was reduced; this time to 15 percent. Everyone initially celebrated the capital gains rate reductions, but a closer look showed that in almost all real estate situations, a significant portion of the gain would be recapture of depreciation and therefore still taxed at the 25 percent rate instead of the celebrated 15 percent rate.

The recapture of depreciation consideration is very important because many property investors do not think in terms of "adjusted basis." The average property investor owns one or two rental properties, usually rental houses, rental condominiums, or small multi-family buildings. Most of these people have taken significant depreciation over the years and are appalled when they find out how that will impact their capital gains picture. Worse, in some cases, market values have fluctuated and the current value is approximately what they paid originally for the property, but because the adjusted basis is low the tax liability is high.

☛ **Example:** Hal bought a fourplex 15 years ago. When he bought it, the real estate market was strong and getting better. For a few years after he bought the property, the value continued to increase, but then real estate values declined sharply. Hal was literally unable to sell the property for a number of years without taking an unacceptable loss, so he held it through the bad times and now the values have come back up. Hal has managed the property for 15 years and he no longer wants to be a landlord. Because the values are now back to where they were, Hal figures he can get his money out. Let's say he paid $300,000 and can now sell it for $320,000. After selling expenses, Hal figures he will net the $300,000 he originally paid for it. However, Hal has taken the allowable depreciation each year on his taxes and his adjusted basis currently stands at $190,000. While Hal has no true gain because he is selling the property for approximately what he paid for it, he will still have to pay taxes on the recapture of depreciation. In this example, the recapture of depreciation is $110,000 taxed at 25 percent or a federal tax liability of approximately $27,500 (plus state taxes).

As you can imagine, anyone in a similar situation to that of the example above is going to deeply resent having to pay any taxes at all. It's usually perceived as an insult added to the injury of bad investment timing. But is it really? Don't get me wrong, I don't usually take the IRS's side on many things, but in this instance there was a significant benefit. In the example above, if Hal is normally in the 30 percent tax bracket for income tax purposes, he was able to use that depreciation deduction over the years to shield himself from $33,000 in income taxes. So, actually he would be $5,500 ahead. Okay, that doesn't really make it any better but it is at least a silver lining in the dark cloud.

In any case, recapture of depreciation is taxed at a higher rate so it is a crucial factor when estimating taxes.

Estimating Your Tax Liability

It does not take a CPA to estimate the potential tax liability on the sale of real estate. The math is fairly straightforward, but you will need to know the three key factors previously described: the adjusted basis, the total depreciation taken, and the expected net sales price. From there, you will be able to estimate what portion will represent capital gain and what portion will be taxed at the higher recapture of depreciation rate. Let's look at how this works through a couple of simple examples.

☛ **Example 1:** Richard has an apartment building he purchased ten years ago for $500,000. During the ten years of ownership he has deducted $148,000 in depreciation and made $100,000 in property improvements. His adjusted basis would be as follows:

Purchase Price	$500,000
Plus Improvements	$100,000
(through the years)	
Less Depreciation	($148,000)
Adjusted Basis	$452,000

If Richard sells this investment property for $1 million, the tax calculation would be:

Sales Price	$1,000,000
Adjusted Basis (from above)	($452,000)
Taxable Capital Gain	$548,000
Taxes	
Tax on the Recapture	
of Depreciation	
($148,000 at 25%)	$37,000
Capital Gain	
($400,000 at 15%)	$60,000
Total Federal Tax	$97,000

☛ **Example 2:** Bette has a rental property she has owned for 15 years. She originally paid $200,000 for the property and it now has an *expected sales price* of $300,000. She has been depreciating the property for the full 15 years and her *total depreciation taken* to date is $100,000. Her *adjusted basis* is now $100,000. Setting aside selling expenses, if she sells the property, her taxable gain would be $200,000 (sales price less adjusted basis; $300,000 – $100,000 = $200,000). See Figure 2.2.

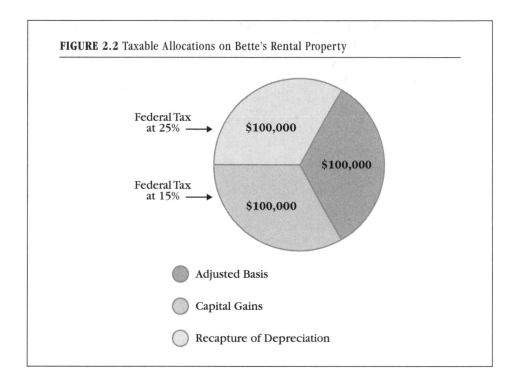

FIGURE 2.2 Taxable Allocations on Bette's Rental Property

Federal Tax at 25% → $100,000

Federal Tax at 15% → $100,000

$100,000

● Adjusted Basis

○ Capital Gains

○ Recapture of Depreciation

One-half of the total gain on Bette's property is represented by recapture of depreciation and is taxed at the 25 percent rate and the remaining capital gain would be taxed at 15 percent. Thus, on the sale of this property, if the taxes were not deferred, Bette would owe $40,000 in federal taxes.

In the second example above, it is easy to see that the tax consequences of selling Bette's property will be significant. If this property was located in California or another state with similar state tax rates, the total state and federal taxes could be approximately $58,600 ($40,000 federal plus $18,600 state).

As a side note, if you buy in to all the political rhetoric about eliminating federal capital gains taxes, remember, recapture of depreciation is still going to be taxed at 25 percent and state capital gains taxes will still apply. So, if Bette's property was located in California, for example, even with *full* elimination of federal capital gains tax, there would still be approximately $43,600 in tax liability because of the tax on recapture of depreciation and state's capital gains taxes.

Okay, now that we have investment property capital gains and recapture of depreciation basics out of the way, we have to look at another possible way the IRS taxes real estate transactions. In Chapter 3, we will look at the taxation on "dealer property."

Dealer versus Investor

"I'm proud to pay taxes in the United States; the only thing is, I could be just as proud for half the money."

Arthur Godfrey

One of the more difficult tax secrets that millionaire real estate investors have to learn is the dealer versus investor distinction and how to steer clear of being labeled a dealer. The amount of tax you pay and the tax advantages available to you in a given real estate investment may change drastically depending on whether the IRS labels you an investor or a dealer. Investor versus dealer status is one of those areas of real estate tax law that can truly drive you nuts trying to figure out. If you sell multiple properties in any single tax year or a few properties over the course of two or three years, you may find yourself at risk of being labeled a dealer. Unfortunately, there is no real distinction test or recognized "number of properties sold" criterion that determines whether a person has crossed a line into dealer status. You may come across real estate agents or accountants who will tell you that if you sell less than three or five (or whatever number) properties per year that you will not be considered a dealer. Unfortunately, this

15

street wisdom or rumor is not based on fact. There is nothing in the tax code or in case law that sets any definitive number of properties as a dividing line between dealer and investor status. This ambiguity, compounded with possible severe tax consequences, has caused more than a few sleepless nights for real estate investors in the past. With this in mind, this chapter will try to shed some light on dealer versus investor status issues and offer some possible ways to avoid potential problems.

What Is a Property Dealer?

A real estate dealer is a person who is involved on a regular basis in the development, improvement, and advertisement of property for sale. Subdividers and developers are almost always labeled dealers. However, even if you are not a subdivider or developer, you may be labeled a dealer if your real estate activities rise to the level of a trade or business in which your property investments appear more like inventory to be sold rather than long-term investments.

What Is a Property Investor?

Unlike a dealer, a property investor is a person who generally holds real estate for appreciation and/or cash flow from rental activities.

But doesn't everyone invest in real estate with the hope that it will appreciate? Yes, but the IRS says there are two categories of real estate investment and for the sake of clarity lets call them "buy-to-sell" (dealer) properties and "buy-to-hold" (investor) properties.

Why Does It Matter If You Are a Dealer or an Investor?

Our tax rules favor the investor over the dealer. An investor files a Schedule E for investment properties and a Schedule D for reporting profits from the sale of an investment property. These Schedule D profits qualify for capital gains tax rates, currently at 15 percent for federal taxes, and are not considered income from employment. A dealer, however, is forced to report operations and profits from the sale of his or her buy-to-sell real estate on a Schedule C as ordinary income and expenses. That's a bad thing because, generally speaking, ordinary income tax rates are higher than capital gains tax rates. Let's take a look at an example of the difference.

☛ **Example:** Let's say two people, Joe and Danny, buy two similar investment/rental properties. Both are single-family homes and both have a purchase price of $300,000. Now let's say that both Joe and Danny make $20,000 in improvements to their properties and the market value of each of the properties grows to $420,000 in 18 months (hot market). At that time both properties are sold. Let's assume both Joe and Danny collected rent and depreciated their respective properties on their tax returns. Let's further assume this is Joe's first investment property, but Danny has bought and sold four or five other similar houses in the last few years.

The tax situation for Joe looks fairly straightforward. He has made the investment a capital asset by keeping it for more than 12 months and his intention was to buy to hold. He will have some amount of recapture of depreciation tax to deal with, but the gain on the property will be federally taxed at the long-term capital gains rate (currently 15 percent). As such, Joe's federal taxes on the gain will be approximately $15,000.

Danny, on the other hand, may have very different results. If the IRS decides to label Danny as a real estate dealer a couple of things happen. First, any depreciation Danny has taken on the property will be disallowed. Second, all of the profit on the sale of the property will be taxed at federal ordinary income rates (currently as high as 35 percent). Third, the profit from the sale, now relabeled ordinary income, will trigger self-employment taxes that can be as high as 14.5 percent. As such, Danny would owe as much as $39,000 on the gain plus whatever self-employment taxes may be triggered.

Obviously, there's a huge difference in the tax consequences between Joe and Danny. To make matters even worse, we really need to expand the example to consider the way these things can quickly get out of control in the real world.

☞ **Example:** Using the same facts as above, let's assume both Joe and Danny decided not to cash out their investments but instead do 1031 exchanges into other properties. Moreover, let's say that Danny has been doing exchanges all along selling one fixed-up property and exchanging into the next fixer-upper.

In Joe's case there's no problem. As a property *investor,* Joe can do a tax-deferred exchange into another property as long as he conforms to ordinary 1031 exchange requirements.

Danny, on the other hand has got a big problem. If the IRS labels Danny a property *dealer* things can get really ugly. Keep in mind that Danny won't be reporting the fact that he has done his most recent exchange until it is completed and he is doing his taxes for that calendar year. Also, keep in mind that IRS audits don't happen instantly. It might be a year or two after he files his taxes before the IRS gets around to auditing Danny. If the audit does result in Danny being labeled a real estate dealer, the IRS will disallow his exchange triggering immediate taxes, self-employment taxes, plus interest and possible penalties in cases of willful neglect or fraud.

To make matters worse, if Danny is labeled a dealer, the IRS will surely be basing their dealer determination partially on the number of properties Danny has sold in recent years. In the facts of our example, Danny had bought and sold four or five other similar houses in the few years preceding and done exchanges with those as well. The IRS will likely disallow each of Danny's previous exchanges triggering, in each case, more immediate taxes, interest, and any self-employment taxes not paid in those previous years.

Hopefully, you are starting to see the potentially dire consequences of being labeled a real estate dealer. Okay, you get the point. So how many properties can you sell before being labeled a dealer? There are rumors of a "three properties a year" rule or "six properties a year" rule. However, the fact is that there is no written set-number rule; not in the tax rules/regulations and not in the tax court case decisions.

All right, so then how long do you have to hold a property to be sure you won't be labeled a dealer when you sell it—one year, two, five? No one knows. None of those time periods are a barrier to being labeled a dealer. There are no set rules.

Okay, if there is no set number of sales and no set holding period in the regulations, how does the IRS label a person a dealer? Everything hinges on your *intent* at the time you buy the property. If you purchased the property with the intent of holding it for income and appreciation benefits, you are an investor. If, instead, you purchased the property with the intent of reselling it, you are a dealer. Right about now your brain should be saying . . . wait a second, everyone buys a property with the intent of eventually reselling it for a profit. Yes. I agree. Nevertheless, this is the distinction the IRS and the courts use to differentiate between an investor and a dealer.

Okay, so how does the IRS know what your intent was at the time you bought the property? How are they going to climb into your head and know what you were thinking when you bought the property? Well, the fact is they don't have to. In law, there is this concept called "burden of proof." Usually, the burden of proof rests on the asserter, meaning that the person that makes an assertion has the responsibility of proving it. For example, if you are charged with a crime, it's the prosecutor's burden to prove it. If someone sues you, they have the burden of proving you did something wrong. In both of these examples, if the person with the burden of proof fails to "prove it" they lose their case or lawsuit. With the IRS, however, many times the burden of proof is shifted to the taxpayer. This means that all the IRS has to do is assert that your intent was to resell the property and *you* have the burden of "proving" it's not true. If you fail to prove that you actually intended to hold the property for income and appreciation, you lose.

As you can imagine, this dealer versus investor issue leads to a lot of tax court litigation and appeals. Okay, so what do the courts use as criteria to determine if a person is a dealer or an investor? Unfortunately, the court decisions are almost as ambiguous as the IRS's definition. Courts usually look to other court decisions to see how a determination has been made in the past. However, in one case, one court actually reviewing the other courts' decisions stated that the dealer versus investor issue was "engulfed in a fog of decisions with gossamer-like distinctions, and a quagmire of unworkable, unreliable, and often irrelevant tests." [*U.S. v. Winthrop, 417 F.2d 905, 906 (5th Cir. 1969).*] Yes, that pretty much sums it up. Anyway, over time a list of criteria has emerged that the tax courts will apply on a case-by-case basis. The courts have consistently held that no single factor is controlling in any given case and that each case must stand on its own set of circumstances. With that said, here are some of the factors the courts use in determining dealer status.

- How long the property was held. Properties held for less than two years appear more like dealer property.
- The number of sales by the taxpayer in that year. Although this is very important, there is no definitive number. Even one sale can be considered dealer property if the intent was to resell rather than to invest.
- The types of improvements made to the property. The more extensive the improvements, the more likely the property was intended for resale.

- The purpose of acquiring the property
- The amount of income from the property sales compared to taxpayer's other income
- Extent and nature of efforts to sell the property. Constant advertising and control agents are seen more like the characteristics of a dealer.
- The subdivision and development of the property
- The use of a business office to sell the property

You may think some of these factors would be present whether a property was bought to sell or bought to hold. I would agree. Nevertheless, these are the factors the tax court uses in trying to determine if a person's actions add up to a pattern of regular, frequent, and continuous sales. If so, being labeled a dealer is almost a certainty.

Because the courts have stated that a determination must be made on a property-by-property basis, it is possible a taxpayer can be considered a dealer with respect to some properties and an investor with respect to others. This is a very important concept because many people with mostly buy-to-hold properties run across good fixer-uppers occasionally that they buy simply to fix up and sell. The danger is, if a person does too many of these buy-to-sell properties the IRS may decide to label them a dealer. If so labeled, there is a significant chance that the IRS will lump all of your buy-to-hold properties into the dealer category as well. You may be able to cure the taint on your buy-to-hold property by meeting the burden of proof on a property-by-property basis, but this is definitely not a predicament in which you want to find yourself. Remember, a real estate dealer is not entitled to depreciation, so if the IRS says you are a dealer, you may face losing any depreciation write-offs you have taken not just on your buy-to-sell properties but also buy-to-hold properties. Obviously, if the IRS disallows your previously taken depreciation, you will probably be facing potentially considerable back taxes and interest.

How Millionaire Real Estate Investors Avoid Being Labeled Dealers

There is no magic, foolproof way to avoid being labeled a dealer if you look and act like a dealer when buying and selling a lot of properties. However, if you are the person who does the occasional fix-and-flip or subdivision, *and also* has buy-to-hold properties, there are ways to protect yourself from having the IRS label *all* your properties as dealer properties. The secret is to understand and use separate entities.

Most sophisticated investors would immediately agree that it is wise to use differing entity types to separate your real estate dealer-like activities from other real estate investments. Besides holding property in your own name, there are three basic entity types commonly used for real estate: corporations (usually S corporations), limited liability companies (LLCs), and limited partnerships (or family limited partnerships). Setting aside any discussion of the asset protection characteristics of these entity choices, let's just focus on their suitability for separating real estate investments.

- *S Corporation.* An S corporation is generally considered the best entity for buy-to-sell (dealer) type of properties. Because of the way dealer properties are taxed, a corporation offers the benefit of the profits being passed through to the investor as profits of the corporation rather than self-employment earnings. That's an important consideration when you remember that the profits from the sale of dealer-type property in an individual's name are considered ordinary income and may trigger self-employment tax. Those same profits to an S corporation are ordinary income to the corporation, but S corporations pay no income taxes directly. Instead, the design of the S corporation is that all profits pass through to the shareholders as profits from the corporation—not self-employment earnings. With no self-employment earnings, there are no self-employment taxes.
- *Limited Liability Company.* An LLC is generally considered the best entity choice for buy-to-hold (investor) type proper-

ties. The structure of an LLC is not all that different than an S corporation. An LLC does not pay taxes directly, rather, profits from the LLC pass through to the owners. However, the profits from an LLC may create self-employment tax issues. As such, the LLC is preferred for the buy-to-hold properties where profits are considered and taxed as capital gains.

- *Limited Partnership.* Limited partnerships and family limited partnerships are considered best for buy-to-hold properties for the same reasons stated above for LLCs. The main difference between an LLC and a limited partnership is the well-established protection offered to the limited partners. Generally speaking, an LLC would be more appropriate for an individual or husband and wife who own a couple of investment properties. A limited partnership would be more appropriate for a larger group of owners with passive investors.

Although the use of S corporations, LLCs, and limited partnerships in real estate investment is becoming common, the vast majority of investment properties are still held in the names of the individual owners. However, if you are one of those people doing fix-up-and-sell-type investments or subdividing and you also own long-term investment properties, you would be wise to separate your real estate activities by use of separate entities.

Incorporating an S corporation or forming an LLC or limited partnership is no longer difficult. If you are already fairly well versed on business entities, there are services right on the Internet that can do the job for you quickly and inexpensively. One Internet-based company my clients have used in the past is http://www.mycorporation.com. If instead, you think you might need or want a little more guidance, most small business or real estate attorneys will set up your entity for you and point you in the right direction for less than $1,000. That fee will be money well spent if you need to segregate your buy-to-sell ventures from your buy-to-hold investments.

In summary, the dealer versus investor issue is one that causes a lot of anxiety for people who find themselves selling properties that might fit into the dealer property category. The bottom line is that real estate *dealers* get stuck with the highest tax rates and self-employment tax, they can't take depreciation, and they can't use any of the tax advantages normally associated with tax deferral on real estate investments. Real estate *investors,* on the other hand, get one of the lowest tax rates, have no self-employment tax, can write off depreciation, and get to use 1031 exchanges and installment sales.

Statutes and Case Law

Because of the importance and relative ambiguity of this topic, this will be one of the few chapters that will include case citations. If you find yourself in a position where you think you may be seriously at risk of being labeled a real estate dealer, you will want to do further research by taking a look at these case decisions and comparing your own situation to the set of facts in a given case. The full text of these cases is available on the Internet or at your local law library. As you'll see from the quick summary of these reviews, there is no clearly defined line of when a person becomes a dealer. Each case cited below has a specific set of facts associated with the taxpayer's situation. The facts in your situation may seem close, but remember, this is an area of law where even identical sets of facts may result in completely different court decisions. These are by no means the only cases on this issue, but the ones here will be sufficient to get you started.

- The courts are pretty much in agreement that a pattern of regular, frequent, and continuous sales coupled with substantial development activity will almost certainly be characterized by the IRS and the courts as dealer activity. See *Biedenharn Realty Co., Inc. v. U.S., 526 F.2d 409 (5th Cir. 1976), cert. denied, 429 U.S. 819 (1976), Achong v. Comr., 246 F.2d 445 (9th Cir. 1957), and Gault v. Comr., 332 F.2d 94 (2d Cir. 1964).*

- No single factor is controlling in any given case. *Biedenharn Realty Co., Inc. v. U.S., 526 F.2d 409 (5th Cir. 1976)*.
- The fact that one court case reached one conclusion on a given set of facts is not necessarily indicative of a similar result by the same or another court on essentially the same facts. *Scheuber v. Comr., 371 F.2d 996 (7th Cir. 1967)*.
- The Fifth Circuit has indicated that frequency of sales is the most important determining factor. *Biedenharn Realty Co., Inc. v. U.S., 526 F.2d 409 (5th Cir. 1976), cert. denied, 429 U.S. 819 (1976)*.
- Taking the case note above one step further, the court in the following case found the property in question to be dealer property *solely* based on the factor of sales frequency. *Suburban Realty Co. v. U.S., 615 F.2d 171 (5th Cir. 1980), cert. denied, 449 U.S. 920 (1980)*.
- Property primarily held for sale is dealer property. The term *primarily* means "of first importance" or "principally." *Malat v. Riddell (1966) 383 US 569, 16 L Ed 2d 102, 86 S Ct 1030*.

Property is not dealer property if it is held for investment because it has income-producing potential, is offered by the taxpayer for lease but not actively for sale, is held for a significant period of time, and is exchanged for another income-producing property that was later leased out rather than sold. *George M. Bernard, supra.* See also *Margolis v. Commissioner (9th Cir. 1964) 337 F.2d 1001, 1005*.

CHAPTER 4

The Benefits of Depreciation

"If you are truly serious about preparing your children for the future, don't teach them to subtract . . . teach them to deduct!"

Fran Lebowitz

One of the great advantages of real estate investment is the ability to take depreciation on a property. The benefit of depreciation is that it can shield you from taxes on paper while providing a real dollar cash flow. Depreciation is a way of accounting for the costs associated with any tangible asset used in a business or for investment, and that has an expected useful life of more than one year. The one-year period is considered the line between assets you write off in a fiscal year and capital assets which must be depreciated. Capital assets have an initial cost and are expected to eventually wear out. Conceptually, depreciation is an expense that represents the yearly depletion or use of the life or cost of purchasing the asset. The IRS assigns the depreciation schedule that must be followed for different types of assets.

As an example, let's look at a business that purchases a vehicle. Over time, the wear and tear of using the vehicle necessitates its replacement. So, if the IRS says that this particular asset, the vehicle, has a useful life of five years, then the business will depreciate or expense the vehicle on paper over that five-year period of time. The theory is that the business gets to write off that portion of the vehicle actually used or "consumed" in each of the five years.

The concept works the same with real estate. There are two basic recovery periods for real estate assets: residential real estate which the IRS has determined as a useful life of 27.5 years, and commercial real estate with a useful life of 39 years.

Depreciation in the case of real estate is a fiction. In most cases, real estate appreciates in value, not declines. However, that's not always true. A warehouse or industrial structure may actually have to be replaced because of wear, tear, and/or obsolescence. In that case, the 39-year useful life assigned to commercial property by the IRS might well be too long a period. However, residential real estate like apartment buildings or rental houses rarely has to be replaced or rebuilt after 27.5 years of use.

For most real estate investment scenarios, depreciation is a planned for, and relied upon, tax advantage. However, there are occasional situations where an investor might not want to take the depreciation on an investment property. Unfortunately, in those unique situations, the investor is simply not given a choice. The IRS says you *will* take the allowable depreciation on residential and commercial real estate investments. Yes, depreciation is mandatory. If an investment property is sold and the investor did not take the allowable yearly depreciation, the IRS will tax the profits on the sale as if the depreciation had been taken and was being recaptured. Why? Maybe it's because recapture of depreciation is taxed at the higher (25 percent) rate. Here's how IRS Publication 527 puts it:

> *Claiming the correct amount of depreciation.* You should claim the correct amount of depreciation each tax year. Even if you did not claim depreciation that you were entitled to deduct, you must still reduce your basis in the property by the full amount of depreciation that you could have deducted.

Again, in most real estate investment situations, depreciation is a big advantage and is part of the planned cash flow. Okay, so how much depreciation do we get on any particular investment? That will depend on two things: your basis (or adjusted basis) in the property and the land-to-improvements ratio on the property. The land-to-improvements ratio is how much the land is worth in relation to the total price of the property. You can't take depreciation on land, so it must be subtracted from the total purchase price of the investment to establish the value of the improvements that will be depreciated. Why can't you depreciate land? Unlike buildings or other improvements, land never wears out. So, we have to subtract the value of the land as a nondepreciable portion of the investment. With the land value subtracted, we now know what amount to depreciate. From there, it will depend on the type of real estate investment—residential or commercial.

DEPRECIATION METHODS

There are three ways to figure depreciation. The depreciation method you use depends on the type of property and when it was placed in service. For property used in rental activities, you use one of the following.

- MACRS (modified accelerated cost recovery system) for property placed in service after 1986
- ACRS (accelerated cost recovery system) for property placed in service after 1980 but before 1987
- Useful lives and either straight-line or an accelerated method of depreciation, such as the declining balance method, for property placed in service before 1981

Source: IRS Publication 597

At one time, there were also different types of depreciation methods to be considered. Prior to 1986, under the accelerated cost recovery system (ACRS), the cost of an investment in real property could be written off over 19 years, using the 175 percent declining balance method of depreciation. This accelerated method allowed a larger proportion of the investment cost to be written off in the earlier years of the depreciation. That's long gone. Now all real estate depreciation is done on the modified accelerated cost recovery system (MACRS) and straight-line method. Meaning that, for the most part, real estate depreciation schedules evenly allocate the expense over either the 27.5-year for residential or 39-year depreciation schedule for commercial property.

Understanding How Depreciation Shields You from Taxes

To help understand how depreciation works in a real estate investment, we need to create a basic example property for discussion.

☛ **Example:** James buys a four-unit apartment building (a fourplex). The purchase price is $400,000. Let's say James's basis in this case is the cost or purchase price of the property. James estimates the fair market value of the land and improvements at $125,000 for land and $275,000 for depreciable improvements.

Using the example above, the available depreciation for James would be $275,000. Each year James would be able to deduct $10,000 of depreciation on Schedule E of his tax returns. James would be able to do this for 27.5 years. The net effect of having this depreciation is to offset profits otherwise made on the property. So, for example, if James's fourplex nets $15,000 a year after repairs, maintenance, and other expenses, the first $10,000 of that net income would be tax-free because the scheduled $10,000 of depreciation would offset that amount. Now this is a very simple example and there are lots of factors that go into the income and expenses of a rental property, but for the purposes of understanding how simple depreciation works, this example is useful.

It is important to understand that depreciation is an expense on paper only. It's an accounting fiction, meaning that James in the above example did not actually have to pay out $10,000 and hopefully James's property did not actually decline in value by $10,000. So, the net effect of James's $10,000 yearly depreciation write-off is to shield him from taxes on the first $10,000 of profits made in rental income from his property.

If you use this simple example as a starting place and imagine that James doesn't own just one rental property but rather has five similar properties, you can see how depreciation can have a significant impact on your tax-free income. Unfortunately, in the real world, investors rarely have this type of a positive cash flow on a newly purchased building. In fact, most investment property, if properly leveraged, is going to show at least a paper loss for the first years. So, the question becomes, what can we do with this depreciation if it's not shielding a rental income from the property? We're going to discuss the rules of active versus passive use of rental property losses later in this book, but first, we'll look at ways to maximize the depreciation available to you.

Maximizing Your Depreciation

How much depreciation you can claim on a given real estate investment will depend on what type of real estate investment you have—residential or commercial—and how you allocate the improvements-to-land ratio and your adjusted basis on the property. For example, let's say you buy a $1 million residential rental property. You will need to decide how much of the $1 million purchase price represents the purchase of land. The remainder of the purchase price represents the improvements to the land and the amount upon which your depreciation schedule will be based. So, how do you figure out how much to allocate to land? The guidance from IRS Publication 527 is:

> If you buy buildings and your cost includes the cost of the land on which they stand, you must divide the cost between the land and the buildings to figure the basis for depreciation of the buildings. The part of the cost that you allocate to each asset is the ratio of the fair market value of that asset to the fair market value of the whole property at the time you buy it. If you are not certain of the fair market values of the land and the buildings, you can divide the cost between them based on their assessed values for real estate tax purposes.

I can't recall any time in the past where an investor has actually looked to the tax assessor's allocation in determining how the investor wanted to make the allocation on his or her own property. Many of the clients I've talked to over the years have no idea how the allocation of land to improvements was made on their property. In most cases, they simply had an accountant prepare their tax returns and the accountant used whatever ratio he or she felt was appropriate. Unfortunately, this isn't always the best approach because it sometimes results in an overly aggressive or overly conservative depreciation schedule. Fortunately, the IRS doesn't seem too concerned about challenging any improvement ratio an investor uses as long as it is reasonable. From the publication quote above, the IRS does require the ratio be based on the fair market values of the land and the buildings. Realistically, however, the IRS is not going to know what the fair market values of the land and the buildings would be on any given investment and they simply don't have the time or manpower to audit these situations. Likewise, most investors don't really know what the fair market value of buildings would be in relation to land on a given investment. Sure, most investors can do a guesstimate, but the fact is there is no fast and easy way to establish fair market values in these situations. Obviously, on a $1 million real estate investment, assigning a very low number like $25,000 to the land value would seem unreasonable and might draw the attention of the IRS. Likewise, a very high value assigned to land with a very small value assigned to the improvements for the purposes of depreciation might also seem unreasonable. Setting aside these types of extremes, it is unlikely that the IRS would challenge any reasonable allocation you make in establishing your depreciation schedule on a given investment. So, ignoring your county tax assessor's allocation and instead claiming a 50-50 ratio, or 60-40, or 70-30, or whatever other ratio you would like to use is probably not going to cause any problems.

For most investors, deciding what initial ratio to use to establish their depreciation schedule is where the tax strategy discussion would end. However, for the more sophisticated investor, there is much more to depreciation than just assigning the standard land-to-improvements ratio. The next chapter will discuss the little-known, and not widely used, depreciation tax secret called cost segregation.

CHAPTER 5

Cost Segregation Lives Again

"We have a tax code that favors those with the best accountants."

Shane Keats

What Is Cost Segregation?

Cost segregation is an accounting method used to divide up the components of improvements made to a property. Cost segregation's purpose is to identify those elements or improvements to real estate that qualify for a shorter depreciation schedule. Unlike traditional real estate depreciation thinking, the concept of cost segregating is that some portion of the improvements to real property should be depreciated over five-, seven-, or 15-year periods. Cost segregation was used extensively prior to 1986. However, the 1986 tax revisions were perceived as an end to the benefits of cost segregation. The concept of cost segregation was revived again in 1997 when the tax court ruled that a taxpayer could depreciate certain "special use components" of a building over a shorter life than the overall building structure. The court ruled that these special use components of buildings could be depreciated over five-, seven-, or 15-year lives rather than the standard 39-year or 27.5-year depreciation schedules. [*Hospital Corp. of America, et al. v. Commissioner, 109 TC 21 (1997).*] This court decision is significant because it is the first to allow a post-1986 property investor to depreciate portions of a real estate investment faster that the standard straight-line 27.5-year or 39-year schedules. Accelerating depreciation increases the cash flow and return on investment in the early years of owning the property. In this landmark case decision, Hospital Corporation of America successfully argued that portions of a newly constructed hospital building were more like personal property than they were like structural components of the building. The court agreed and found that improvements, such as carpeting, television wiring, landscaping, secondary electrical systems, and more could be depreciated faster.

Since the Hospital Corporation of America case was decided, cost segregation has gained wider acceptance and is moving more into mainstream accounting techniques for sophisticated investors.

Cost Segregation Studies

Although the IRS has acquiesced to the tax court decision in the Hospital Corporation of America case, they have not issued any guidance on what types of improvements qualify for the shorter five-, seven- or 15-year depreciation schedules. From this lack of guidance, a number of engineering and architectural firms have evolved into providing "cost segregation studies." These studies analyze and identify the nonstructural elements and exterior improvements that qualify for a shorter depreciation schedule. The main purpose of having a cost segregation study is to allow property investors to reclassify as much of the property improvements as possible. A cost segregation study also provides documentation supporting the reclassification. In the case of an audit, a well-documented cost segregation study may be essential.

FIGURE 5.1 Modified Accelerated Cost Recovery System

Type of Property	Life
Computers and their peripheral equipment	5 years
Office machinery, such as typewriters, calculators, and copiers	5 years
Automobiles	5 years
Light trucks	5 years
Appliances, such as stoves and refrigerators	5 years
Carpets	5 years
Furniture used in rental property	5 years
Office furniture and equipment, such as desks and files	7 years
Any property that does not have a class life and that has not been designated by law as being in any other class	7 years
Roads	15 years
Shrubbery	15 years
Fences	15 years
Residential rental property (buildings or structures) and structural components such as furnaces, water pipes, and venting	27.5 years

Source: IRS Publication 527

Some examples of property improvements that may qualify for a five-year or seven-year depreciation schedule would be: movable wall partitions, appliances, wall coverings, heating equipment, ventilation systems, and security systems. Examples of improvements that may qualify for a 15-year depreciation schedule include: landscaping, roads, walkways, walls, outdoor lighting, driveways, and parking lots.

As mentioned earlier, the IRS has not put forth any on-point guidance as to what components of a rental property will qualify for shorter depreciation schedules. Nevertheless, a look at the standard MACRS depreciation schedule in Figure 5.1 would appear to be insightful.

What types of properties benefit most? In cost segregation circles, the conventional wisdom is that certain properties can benefit more than others from having a study done. Generally speaking, the properties that benefit the most are specialty properties like office buildings, restaurants, medical facilities, and specialized manufacturing facilities. Properties that would benefit the least would include primary structure properties like a tilt-up concrete warehouse. Apartment buildings, smaller commercial properties, and mixed-use properties usually fall somewhere in between.

The Four Basic Considerations

There are four basic considerations that should be explored before deciding to do a cost segregation study:

1. Can you actually benefit from accelerated tax depreciation on your real estate investment? It may seem that the answer to this would always be a resounding yes. However, that's not always the case. For example, if your property does not provide a positive cash flow at this time there would be little use in accelerated depreciation unless that depreciation could offset income from other sources. So, in the case of a property without a positive cash flow, there would be little benefit from a cost segregation study.
2. Was your property purchased, constructed, or expanded after 1986? If not, the property may not qualify for real characterization of depreciation.
3. How long do you plan on keeping the property? If the property will be kept for less than three years, the cost of having a study done may not be well balanced with the tax benefits gained over such a short period time.
4. What is the value of the property? Most firms that do cost segregation studies suggest that a property must be worth over a million dollars to make the expense and effort involved in the study worthwhile.

These four considerations are not the only relevant issues, but they are foundational matters that can determine whether the concept of doing a cost segregation study should be explored further.

When Is the Best Time to Do a Cost Segregation Study?

Some people would say that no time is a bad time to increase the cash flow on a property. That may be true, but how much effort it takes to complete a study and how much IRS attention an investor draws when they recharacterize a portion of their property makes the time strategy an issue. Obviously, the best time to do a cost segregation study is when the buildings are constructed or when there are significant improvements made to the property. This is mainly because the study can be accomplished during the architectural and engineering planning phase. Moreover, if the study is completed at the same time the improvements are constructed, the varying depreciation schedules set out in the first tax return for the property will seem more consistent with the new improvements or development. Be that as it may, cost segregation studies can also be well worthwhile for fully built properties being acquired and for restructuring depreciation characteristics of a property already owned. In addition, cost segregation studies are also recommended for high-value inherited property due to the stepped-up basis (see Chapter 16).

While there may be strategic advantages to timing for these studies, I would have to agree with those who say there is no bad time to increase depreciation if it improves the cash flow on an investment.

☞ **Example:** Let's say you acquire an office and manufacturing building. The total purchase price is $2.5 million. Of that amount, $500,000 represents the cost of the land. The conventional real estate and accounting perspective would then be that $2 million would be depreciated using the standard 39-year depreciation schedule. The yearly depreciation for each of those 39 years would be approximately $51,282.

Now let's say that at the time the investment was pur-chased a cost segregation study was completed showing that 10 percent of the improvements qualified for a five-year de-preciation schedule and 20 percent of the improvements qualified for a 15-year depreciation schedule. As such, the yearly depreciation for this property would now be $40,000 for the five-year improvements, $26,667 for the 15-year im-provements, and approximately $35,897 for the 39-year structures. Added together, the total depreciation on this in-vestment would now be approximately $102,564 per year in the first five years, $62,564 in years six through 15, and ap-proximately $35,897 for years 16 through 39.

It is fairly common that a cost segregation study can reclassify 20 to 40 percent of the improvements qualifying for five-, seven-, or 15-year depreciation schedules. As you can see from the above example, the results can be dramatic. Some investors feel the cost segregation method of depreciation represents a considerable windfall and should be considered for all buildings and significant tenant improvements placed in service after 1986.

Making the situation even more appealing is the Jobs and Growth Act of 2003. This legislation was intended to stimulate the national economy. Under this act, businesses are offered a first-year *bonus* de-preciation deduction equal to 50 percent of the adjusted basis on qual-ified property. Qualified property is basically any business property purchased, constructed, or improved that has a useful life of 20 years or less and was acquired or improved after September 11, 2001, but be-fore September 11, 2004. If you fit in this category, the bonus depreci-ation due to you would be considerable. In the previous example, the additional bonus depreciation is well over $100,000. For those of you who qualified for this bonus depreciation but failed to take advantage of it, it's not too late. See your accountant for more information.

Okay, so what's the bad news? Like everything else, there are some downside factors. The following are some points that need to be considered:

- *The expense of the study.* Depending on the size of the real estate investment, the cost of a cost segregation study can be pretty steep. In many cases, the benefits may far outweigh the costs involved. Nevertheless, due consideration should be given to the cost of a study in relation to the expected benefits.
- *Sales tax issues.* The classification of real property improvements to a shorter personal property depreciation schedule may trigger some potentially negative sales tax aspects. Along those same lines, but on the other hand, some states have favorable tax treatment for real property and a reclassification may result in a loss of those tax benefits.
- *Recapture of depreciation issues.* Real estate is considered Section 1250 property and has a recapture of depreciation tax rate of 25 percent. Portions of a real estate investment reclassified to a shorter depreciation schedule are usually recharacterized to Section 1245 property. Section 1245 property has a potentially higher recapture of depreciation rate.
- *Future 1031 exchange issues.* The provisions of IRC 1031 require tax-deferred exchanges be made of like-kind property. The effect of cost segregating is to reclassify a portion of real estate as personal property to get the shorter depreciation schedule. In 1031 exchanges almost all domestic real estate is considered like-kind to all other domestic real estate. However, if a portion of a property is recharacterized as personal property it may have to meet a much more stringent like-kind test to qualify in a tax-deferred exchange. The net effect may be that some portion of an otherwise fully tax-deferred exchange may end up being taxable because of how the property was characterized.

In summary, cost segregating has the potential to accelerate the depreciation you can take and improve your cash flow in the early years, but it is not for all real estate investors. The more extensive your real estate investments, the more significant the benefits would be. However, like all tax strategies, the cost segregation benefits need to be considered along with the potential problems and costs of implementation.

CHAPTER 6

Passive Investment Rules and Exceptions

"Today it takes more brains and effort to make out the income tax form than it does to make the income."

Alfred E. Neuman

Understanding the Passive Loss Rules

Prior to 1986, real estate investment had an additional advantage . . . sheltering other income. The pre-1986 rules allowed an investor to use the on-paper (depreciation) losses to shelter real dollar income from other unrelated sources. Prior to 1986, high-income earners, doctors, lawyers, business owners, and the like invested heavily in real estate as a way to generate losses which could then be used to shield or offset portions of their non–real estate income from taxes. Those same pre-1986 rules also allowed a real estate investor to take accelerated depreciation on properties, which just added to the yearly write-offs and, thus, the desirability of real estate investment for those high-income earners.

In an attempt to end what the IRS saw as abusive tax sheltering of income, the Tax Reform Act of 1986 was enacted, having a major impact on real estate investment. The Tax Reform Act of 1986 added Internal Revenue Code Section 469, which limits a taxpayer's ability to deduct or write off losses from any business in which the taxpayer does not materially participate. The act specifically targeted real estate by including the language "any rental activities" in the definition of passive activity.

Okay, so what does that mean? It means, as a general rule, a taxpayer now cannot deduct losses from real estate investments in which he or she does not materially participate unless there is reported passive income on the tax return against which to offset the losses. In addition, losses from passive activities cannot offset nonpassive income such as wages, salaries, or *other* nonpassive income from sole proprietorships, partnerships, or entities in which the taxpayer materially participates.

Like most general rules in taxation, however, there are usually exceptions. In this case, there are two exceptions (actually three, but only two worth talking about). The first exception, the active participation exception, is for persons with adjusted gross incomes of less than $150,000; the second is an exception made for real estate professionals.

The requirements for both of these exceptions are often misquoted in news articles and on the Web. Fortunately, this is one topic where the IRS's own publication provides good (and understandable) information. The following two explanations summarize the points from IRS Publication 527.

The Exception for Active Participation

If you or your spouse actively participated in a passive rental real estate activity, you can deduct up to $25,000 of loss from the activity from your nonpassive income. This special allowance is an exception to the general rule disallowing losses in excess of income from passive activities. Similarly, you can offset credits from the activity against the tax on up to $25,000 of nonpassive income after taking into account any losses allowed under this exception.

If you are married, filing a separate return, and lived apart from your spouse for the entire tax year, your special allowance cannot be more than $12,500. If you lived with your spouse at any time during the year and are filing a separate return, you cannot use the special allowance to reduce your nonpassive income or tax on nonpassive income.

The maximum amount of the special allowance is reduced if your modified adjusted gross income is more than $100,000 ($50,000 if married filing separately).

☛ **Example:** Jane is single and has $40,000 in wages, $2,000 in passive income from a limited partnership, and a $3,500 passive loss from a rental real estate activity in which she actively participated. $2,000 of Jane's $3,500 loss offsets her passive income. The remaining $1,500 loss can be deducted from her $40,000 wages.

Active Participation

You actively participated in a rental real estate activity if you (and your spouse) owned at least 10 percent of a rental property and you made management decisions in a significant and bona fide sense. Management decisions include approving new tenants, deciding on rental terms, approving expenditures, and similar decisions.

☛ **Example:** Mike is single and had the following income and losses during the tax year:

Salary	$42,300
Dividends	$ 300
Interest	$ 1,400
Rental loss	($ 4,000)

The rental loss resulted from the rental of a house Mike owned. Mike had advertised and rented the house to the current tenant himself. He also collected the rent payments, which usually came by mail. All repairs were either done or contracted out by Mike. Even though the rental loss is a loss from a passive activity, because Mike actively participated in the rental property management, he can use the entire $4,000 loss to offset his other income.

Maximum Special Allowance

If your modified adjusted gross income is $100,000 or less ($50,000 or less if married filing separately), you can deduct your loss up to $25,000 ($12,500 if married filing separately). If your modified adjusted gross income is more than $100,000 (more than $50,000 if married filing separately), this special allowance is limited to 50 percent of the difference between $150,000 ($75,000 if married filing separately) and your modified adjusted gross income.

Generally, there is no relief from the passive activity loss limits if your modified adjusted gross income is $150,000 or more ($75,000 or more if married filing separately).

Modified adjusted gross income. This is your adjusted gross income from IRS Form 1040, figured *without* taking into account:

- Taxable Social Security or equivalent tier 1 railroad retirement benefits
- Deductible contributions to an IRA or certain other qualified retirement plans
- The exclusion allowed for qualified U.S. savings bond interest used to pay higher educational expenses
- The exclusion allowed for employer-provided adoption benefits
- Any passive activity income or loss included on Form 8582
- Any passive income or loss or any loss allowable by reason of the exception for real estate professionals discussed earlier

FIGURE 6.1 Phase-Out of $25,000 Passive Activity Loss Deduction

Adjusted Gross Income	Maximum Allowable Passive Loss
$100,000 or less	$25,000
$110,000	$20,000
$120,000	$15,000
$130,000	$10,000
$140,000	$ 5,000
$150,000 or more	$ 0

- Any overall loss from a publicly traded partnership (see Publicly Traded Partnerships, PTPs, in the instructions for Form 8582)
- The deduction for one-half of self-employment tax
- The deduction allowed for interest on student loans
- The deduction for qualified tuition and related expenses

In summarizing the IRS info, it is most important to understand that if you have more passive losses from real estate than you have passive income and you can show active participation, you can get up to $25,000 to offset other income. However, your available deduction of $25,000 will phase out as your income rises. You'll lose $1 of the deduction for every $2 that your adjusted gross income rises above $100,000. Once your AGI hits $150,000 or more, the write-off is completely phased out (see Figure 6.1).

The Exception for Real Estate Professionals

Rental activities in which you materially participated during the year are not passive activities if for that year you were a real estate professional. Losses from these activities are not limited by the passive activity rules.

For this purpose, each interest you have in a rental real estate activity is a separate activity, unless you choose to treat all interests in rental real estate activities as one activity.

Real Estate Professional

You qualify as a real estate professional for the tax year if you meet both of the following requirements:

1. More than half of the personal services you performed in all trades or businesses during the tax year were performed in real property trades or businesses in which you materially participated.
2. You performed more than 750 hours of services during the tax year in real property trades or businesses in which you materially participated.

Do not count personal services you performed as an employee in real property trades or businesses unless you are a 5 percent owner of your employer. You are a 5 percent owner if you owned (or are considered to have owned) more than 5 percent of your employer's outstanding stock, or capital or profits interest.

If you file a joint return, do not count your spouse's personal services to determine whether you met the preceding requirements. However, you can count your spouse's participation in an activity in determining if you materially participated.

Real property trades or businesses. A real property trade or business is a trade or business that does any of the following with real property:

- Develops or redevelops it
- Constructs or reconstructs it
- Acquires it

- Converts it
- Rents or leases it
- Operates or manages it
- Brokers it

Material Participation

Generally, you materially participated in an activity for the tax year if you were involved in its operations on a regular, continuous, and substantial basis during the year. (We will look at this requirement in more detail below.)

Participating spouse. If you are married, determine whether you materially participated in an activity by also counting any participation in the activity by your spouse during the year. Do this even if your spouse owns no interest in the activity or files a separate return for the year.

Choice to Treat All Interests as One Activity

If you were a real estate professional and had more than one rental real estate interest during the year, you can choose to treat all the interests as one activity. You can make this choice for any year that you qualify as a real estate professional. If you forgo making the choice for one year, you can still make it for a later year.

Understanding the Material Participation Requirement

In the previous two IRS considerations, there were two participation standards: active participation and material participation. The two are not the same. You can meet the active participation standard by simply doing things like approving new tenants, deciding on rental terms, and approving expenditures. The requirements for material participation, on the other hand, are much more demanding. IRS Publication 925 sets out the material participation requirements as follows:

> For purposes of the passive activity rules, you materially participated in the operation of this trade or business activity during 2003 if you met *any* of the following seven tests:
>
> 1. You participated in the activity for more than 500 hours during the tax year.
> 2. Your participation in the activity for the tax year was substantially all of the participation in the activity of all individuals (including individuals who did not own any interest in the activity) for the tax year.
> 3. You participated in the activity for more than 100 hours during the tax year, and you participated at least as much as any other person for the tax year. This includes individuals who did not own any interest in the activity.
> 4. The activity is a significant participation activity for the tax year, and you participated in all significant participation activities for more than 500 hours during the year. An activity is a "significant participation activity" if it involves the conduct of a trade or business, you participated in the activity for more than 100 hours during the tax year, and you did not materially participate under any of the material participation tests (other than this test).
> 5. You materially participated in the activity for any five of the prior ten tax years.
> 6. The activity is a personal service activity in which you materially participated for any three prior tax years. A personal service activity is an activity that involves performing personal services in the fields of health, law, engineering, architecture, accounting, actuarial science, performing arts, consulting, or any other trade or busi-

ness in which capital is not a material income-producing factor.

7. Based on all the facts and circumstances, you participated in the activity on a regular, continuous, and substantial basis during the tax year. But you do not meet this test if you participated in the activity for 100 hours or less during the tax year. Your participation in managing the activity does not count in determining if you meet this test if any person (except you) (a) received compensation for performing management services in connection with the activity or (b) spent more hours during the tax year than you spent performing management services in connection with the activity (regardless of whether the person was compensated for the services).

Participation by Your Spouse Counts

IRS Publication 925 allows your spouse's participation during the tax year to be counted as your participation. This applies even if your spouse did not own an interest in the property and whether or not you and your spouse file a joint return.

Participation as an Investor Does Not Count

Work you do as an investor in an activity is not treated as participation unless you are also directly involved in the day-to-day management or operations of the activity. IRS Publication 925 says work done as an investor includes:

- Studying and reviewing financial statements or reports on the activity
- Preparing or compiling summaries or analyses of the finances or operations of the activity for your own use

- Monitoring the finances or operations of the activity in a non-managerial capacity

Carrying Forward Unused Losses

So what do you do if you have passive losses and don't qualify for either the active participation exception or the real estate professional exception to the passive losses rules? Well, unused passive losses can be carried forward to offset passive income generated in future years. These losses that are not deductible because there was insufficient passive income to offset are often referred to as "suspended losses." You can carry suspended losses forward indefinitely and can use them as deductions against passive income in later years when the property shows a greater income.

Disposing of an Entire Passive Property Interest

Suspended losses can also be used when the passive investment property is sold in a fully taxable disposition. A fully taxable disposition is one that is an arm's-length sale of the interest to an unrelated third party. However, if you dispose of a passive activity to a related party you will not be able to deduct any suspended losses until that person disposes of the interest to an unrelated person.

There are three primary rules that apply when disposing of entire passive investment property interest:

1. Losses on an entire disposition of a passive property activity and its suspended losses can offset active income from all sources.
2. Gains on an entire disposition of a passive property can be used to offset suspended losses from other passive activities.

3. The disposition must be to an unrelated party. Family, lineal descendants, ancestral descendants, siblings, spouses, and half-blood relatives are all considered "related parties."

Passive Loss Rules Summary

The 1986 tax revisions made it much more difficult to use losses from real estate investments to offset other sources of income. Under the rules today, the best-case scenario is to qualify as a real estate professional with material participation in your investment activities. If you can qualify, the passive loss rules will not limit your ability to use losses to offset income from other sources.

The next best position to be in is to qualify for the $25,000 in passive loss write-offs by actively participating in your real estate investments.

Finally, even if you can't qualify for either exception to the passive loss rules, you will still get the benefit of your write-offs, but not until the property becomes profitable beyond its depreciation, or until you dispose of the property in a fully taxable sale.

Tax-Free Exchanges

"A person doesn't know how much he has to be thankful for until he has to pay taxes on it."

Author Unknown

Introduction

Like-kind or 1031 exchanges are perhaps the best known and most commonly used tax deferral tool for real estate. Just about every experienced real estate agent has been involved in an exchange at some time. Exchanges go by a lot of different names like 1031 exchange, Starker exchange, tax-free exchange, tax-deferred exchange, trading properties, delayed exchange, like-kind exchange, and more. All of these names describe the same thing—an exchange of property and tax deferral under the provisions of Internal Revenue Code Section 1031.

The original exchanges were true exchanges in that the owner of a property truly "traded" one for another. As you might imagine it was pretty difficult to find two property owners who wanted each other's properties and agreed upon the fair market values of each. So in the early development of the property exchange concept, there was not widespread use. In 1967 and 1969, two court cases, both called *Starker v. U.S.,* were decided. From those cases, the legal authority to do a "delayed" exchange was created. It was these two cases that gave the 1031 deferred exchange the street name or nickname "Starker exchange." As a result of the Starker cases, property owners had the ability to sell one property after which they had up to six months to purchase another property and still have the transactions considered an exchange for tax deferral purposes. The IRS initially had a difficult time with this concept of a "delayed" exchange. Their position was that if the seller of a property had any period of time in which he or she was in receipt of the proceeds from the sale, then it was not truly an exchange but rather a sale (triggering taxes) and a subsequent purchase. The IRS's main concern was not in the time allowed, but the receipt of funds. To make everyone happy, the court in the Starker cases allowed the exchanger extended time to find and purchase a replacement property, but agreed with the IRS's position that there could be no actual or constructive receipt of funds by the seller or the taxes would be triggered. From these cases, a new segment of the real estate industry sprang to life—the "qualified intermediary" or "accommodator." The job of a qualified intermediary or accommodator is to facilitate and document 1031 exchanges by receiving the proceeds of the sale under the terms of an exchange agreement and then applying those funds at the direction of the exchanger for the acquisition of the replacement property.

How Exchanges Work

Today, 1031 exchanges are accomplished with very little effort on the part of the buyer and seller. Most of the paperwork is handled quickly and smoothly in the background by qualified intermediaries or accommodators and then channeled through escrow/title companies or closing agents to the buyer and seller of each property for signatures.

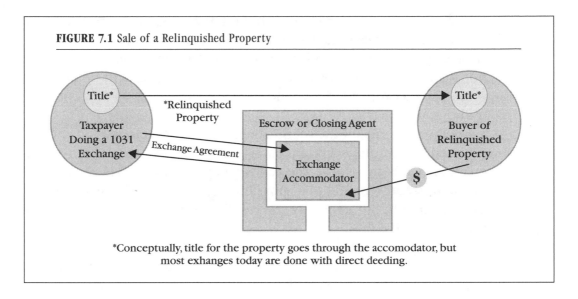

FIGURE 7.1 Sale of a Relinquished Property

*Conceptually, title for the property goes through the accomodator, but most exhanges today are done with direct deeding.

If you are the seller/exchanger, the process of selling the relinquished property goes like this:

- List your property for sale with your chosen real estate agent making sure it is understood you intend to do a 1031 exchange for another property.
- When you get an offer, your agent will include a counteroffer provision that states the "buyer agrees to cooperate with seller's 1031 exchange."
- Open escrow, and then choose your accommodator (your real estate agent or escrow/title agent can give you names of companies in your area).
- You will be signing an "exchange agreement" with your accommodator through escrow along with the other customary escrow paperwork.
- On the close of escrow, your proceeds will be transferred to your accommodator's trust fund on your behalf and held there until you begin the process of buying your replacement property.

As you can see from Figure 7.1, the selling portion of the exchange is fairly straightforward. There are, of course, some variations to the simple example above and there are also "simultaneous" exchanges, but for the most part, the above sequence of events will be how the relinquished property side of the exchange will go in 95 percent of all traditional exchanges today.

Once the sale on the relinquished property is completed and the proceeds are in the accommodator's trust account, the taxpayer/exchanger needs to acquire the replacement property. There are time lines and requirements that must be followed which we will cover more in depth, but generally the purchase of the replacement property will go like this:

- The taxpayer/exchanger will identify potential replacement properties following the IRS rules (discussed below).
- Negotiate the purchase agreement, being sure to include a provision that the seller of the replacement property will cooperate with the 1031 exchange.
- Open escrow and have the purchase contract earnest money deposit transferred from the accommodator's trust fund to the escrow or closing agent's account.
- The taxpayer/exchanger would then continue along the purchase process like normal, doing inspections, arranging financing, etc.
- When all is ready to close, the accommodator transfers the balance of the exchange funds to the escrow or closing agent who then closes the transaction.

Once again, Figure 7.2 is a simple example, but it does show how most replacement property transactions occur today. Left out of both examples above are the requirements and formalities that must be followed to ensure your 1031 exchange conforms to IRS requirements. We will look at the requirements and formalities in depth later in this chapter, but right now let's take a look at the advantages of doing an exchange.

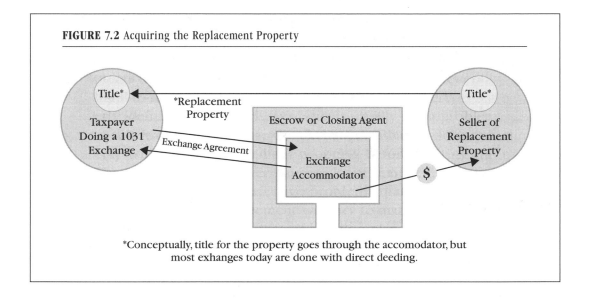

FIGURE 7.2 Acquiring the Replacement Property

Title*

Taxpayer Doing a 1031 Exchange

*Replacement Property

Exchange Agreement

Escrow or Closing Agent

Exchange Accommodator

$

Title*

Seller of Replacement Property

*Conceptually, title for the property goes through the accomodator, but most exhanges today are done with direct deeding.

Advantages of 1031 Exchanges

Full, Indefinite Capital Gains Tax Deferral

The most important advantage of 1031 exchanges is the fact that you can defer all capital gains *indefinitely*. The other deferral tools available (installment sales and private annuity trusts) allow a deferral "period" that begins when the property is sold or traded for the private annuity and ends when the note or annuity payments are made. Although installment sales and private annuity trusts can postpone the payment of taxes for an extended period, they still are only a "scheduled" deferral of a capital gain. On the other hand, 1031 exchanges do not create deferral "periods," but rather, allow you to continue to "roll" your real estate profits into other properties as many times as you want without recognizing any taxable gain. There is no limit to the number of times you can do a 1031 exchange in your lifetime. So a person could (and many do) start out with a small rental property early in life, 1031 exchange the property up into successively larger rental properties every five to ten years, and end up with a substantial amount of income property at retirement.

The fact is that if you never sell an investment property without exchanging it into another, you will never have to pay taxes on your real estate capital gains during your lifetime. Then, when you die, your heirs will be entitled to receive a "stepped-up" basis on the investment property you leave them and will escape paying taxes on the capital gains you deferred throughout your life.

Building Wealth

One of the more common reasons for doing 1031 exchanges is building wealth. As mentioned in the previous section, it is fairly common to find people parlaying real estate investments into successively larger real estate investments over their lifetime. It is not hard to understand a plan where an investor exchanges every few years to double the size of the investment.

☛ **Example:** A couple in their 30s buys a small four-unit apartment building with the idea of gradually increasing their real estate investment. Their plan is to hold the property for ten years and gain equity through appreciation and mortgage reduction. At the ten-year mark, they plan to sell the property and use that increased equity as the down payment to buy two four-unit apartment buildings. They intend to do the same thing every ten years until they retire at age 70. According to their plan, at age 40 they will own two four-unit buildings, at age 50 they will own four four-unit buildings, and at age 60 they will own eight four-unit buildings. According to their plan, at age 70 they could double the number of rental units again. Instead, they intend to travel abroad during retirement so they plan to sell the properties at that time to create a lifetime stream of income from whatever equity they have created from the property investments.

This kind of planning is not hard to understand. What is hard is following through on the plan. If you can follow through with this type of plan, your ability to indefinitely defer capital gains through 1031 exchanges will enable you to continue to build wealth tax-free throughout your life.

Trading Up

Trading up is another common reason for doing a 1031 exchange. There are two types of trading up. The first is to buy a bigger property or to increase the overall amount of your real estate investment. That was adequately described in the preceding section. The second reason is to trade up to a better "quality" of property.

☞ **Example:** Donna owns an eight-unit apartment building in the downtown neighborhood of a medium-sized city. The property is getting a little older and the rental market in the area is becoming increasingly competitive. With the high turnover of tenants and the increasing cost of maintenance, Donna is finding herself spending more time on the property and the bottom line is shrinking. Donna has found another property, a six-unit building, in an outlying area that is newer and is in a better rental area. Both properties have approximately the same market value. Donna does a 1031 exchange, selling the downtown property and "trading up" to the smaller (but better) building.

Lots of exchanges are done for reasons like this. It is not a matter of trading up for quantity or cash flow; it's a matter of trading up for quality and the perceived soundness and suitability of the investment. Even if the projected cash flow on the replacement property is not as good, Donna may be much happier not having to drive into town twice a week to meet repairmen or prospective tenants. Whatever the reason, Donna will see the exchange as a trade-up, and assuming all the other requirements of a 1031 exchange are met, the IRS will let her do it tax-free.

Leveraging

Leverage is king. Well, at least to an aggressive investor. It is also another of the more common reasons for doing a 1031 exchange. Leveraging is simply the concept of putting down as little of your own money as possible on a property and maximizing the amount of financing. The strategy looks brilliant in an up market but can result in a lot of foreclosures in down times.

☛ **Example:** John and Tom both have $150,000 to invest. Tom finds what he considers a suitable investment property priced at $300,000. With his $150,000 down and another $150,000 in financing he buys the property. John is more aggressive in his investing than Tom and is trying to maximize his leverage. The customary loan-to-value lending ratio in his region is 70 percent, meaning that he can buy up to a $500,000 investment property with his $150,000 down. He finds a property he considers suitable, puts down $150,000, and gets a $350,000 mortgage to buy it.

According to John's investment philosophy, with all other things being equal, it is better to have 30 percent equity in a $500,000 property, than to have 50 percent equity in a $300,000 property. After all, if the real estate market is expected to increase in value at a steady 6 percent for the next few years, isn't it better to get a $30,000 ($500,000 × 6 percent) equity growth rather than $18,000 ($300,000 × 6 percent)? Another way to look at this is that with a 6 percent increase in property values, John can boast a 20 percent return on his initial investment ($30,000 ÷ $150,000) whereas Tom received a return of only 12 percent ($18,000 ÷ $150,000). It sounds like John has the better approach, but there is, of course, a down side. If the property is too highly leveraged, the rental income alone will usually not support the debt in a down cycle and all of the sudden Tom's approach may start looking like the wiser of the two. Whatever your personal perspective, leveraging is an important part of real estate investing.

For John in the previous example, a 1031 exchange is the perfect tool. If the $500,000 property he bought increased a total of 50 percent in market value over a ten-year period, its market value would be $750,000 and he would owe just under $350,000. This means he could sell it and use the $400,000 equity as a down payment to leverage into a $1,300,000 property without paying any taxes.

Additional Depreciation

Depreciation in real estate is a wonderful accounting fiction. It allows a certain amount of the income from operating rental property to pass to the owner without taxes. The concept is that buildings and improvements on the property have a life expectancy and will eventually have to be replaced. As such, depreciation is a way to allocate and account for the diminution in value for those buildings and improvements in each successive year. That allocation of depreciation is an "on-paper" expense that offsets an equal amount of *real* dollars coming from rental income. For example, if an investment property generates a predepreciation net cash flow of $10,000 and the scheduled depreciation for the year happens to also be $10,000, there would be no taxes. The on-paper expense would offset the real dollars of income.

Obviously, people view the depreciation write-off as highly desirable. Unfortunately, anyone who has owned a particular investment property 25 years or more has either used up all the available depreciation or soon will. As such, some people use the 1031 exchanges to get to a larger or more valuable property for the additional depreciation. Note, however, that the adjusted basis of the relinquished property will transfer to the replacement property. That means that the replacement property can only provide additional depreciation for that amount of value beyond the market value of the relinquished property.

☞ **Example:** Don has owned a rental property for 25 years and over the years has taken all the scheduled depreciation available on the property. The property has a fair market value of $250,000. He sells it and exchanges into another property with a fair market value of $400,000. His adjusted basis on the relinquished property was $50,000. That adjusted basis would transfer and represent the basis allocated to the first $250,000 of the replacement property. As such, the beginning basis on the replacement property after the exchange will be $200,000 (the $50,000 from the relinquished property and the $150,000 additional paid to get to the $400,000 purchase price).

There would be no depreciation benefit in exchanging properties of equal value, because the adjusted basis from the relinquished property would simply transfer to the replacement property. The only exception would be a trade of vacant land for a property of equal value with buildings and improvements. The basis would transfer, but there would be a reallocation between land and improvements that would allow scheduled depreciation.

Reducing an Investor's Workload

One big difference between investing in real estate and other types of investments is that real estate requires time and effort to maintain. You may have a management company handle the property for you, but a good management company is hard to find and sometimes simply too expensive. For this reason, many investors take a hands-on management approach and eventually get to a point where they are able to run the properties efficiently.

Real estate investments run the spectrum from high maintenance and time-consuming properties to relatively maintenance free ones. For example, at the high-workload end of the spectrum would be a 60-year-old residential apartment building with all singles or one-bedroom apartments. This type of property, while it can be profitable, is considered less desirable because it usually means high tenant turnover along with constant repair and maintenance. At the low-workload end of the spectrum, would be commercial properties with reliable tenants on long-term triple net leases. Setting aside the workload considerations, both the examples above have their own advantages and disadvantages depending on your investment philosophy. Of course, there are many types of properties that would fall somewhere between the two examples given.

With this in mind, many 1031 exchanges are done simply to lighten the investor's workload.

☞ **Example:** Hal owns a small high-maintenance four-unit apartment building that has been having a lot of tenant problems and turnover lately. He feels the property is taking too much of his time and is afraid it will only get worse. He is tired of being a landlord and is considering selling the property to free up his time for other interests. Hal has a son who is getting married in a few months, and while the newlyweds will not be ready to buy their first house for some time, they will be looking for a home to rent. Homes in their desired neighborhood are selling for approximately the same amount as the fair market value of Hal's apartment building. Moreover, the fair rental value of those homes is approximately the same as the net rental income from the apartment building after taking into consideration the vacancy rate and higher cost of maintenance.

The obvious solution for Hal in the above example is to make an arrangement with the soon-to-be newlyweds to rent them a house. Using a 1031 exchange he would sell the apartment and buy a house in their desired neighborhood for them to rent. In that way, Hal has accomplished his goal of reducing his workload without incurring any immediate tax on the capital gain or having to recapture any of the depreciation taken on the apartment building over the years.

Hal's situation is actually very common, but even if he did not have a family looking to rent a house, he could have still accomplished his goal by trading into a rental house. Likewise, a person might be able to lighten his or her workload by trading from eight units to four, or from residential property to commercial.

Whatever the size or property type change may be, a 1031 exchange is the perfect tool when a person wants to lighten the workload but still wants to have some real estate investments.

Relocating Investments

One of the best features of investing in real estate is the investor's ability to supervise directly or indirectly the performance of the property. If you own a property near your own neighborhood, you can drive by it on a regular basis to keep abreast of its condition. This is a significant advantage of real estate investment over other types of investing, like stocks or mutual funds. With the recent burst of the dot-com stock market bubble, corporate accounting improprieties, and major corporate bankruptcies, many property investors find it comforting to be able to drive to their real estate investments and actually "touch and see" where their money is invested.

With this in mind, many people use 1031 exchanges as a way of keeping their property investments geographically nearby. Wanting to relocate or being relocated by your employer to another region of the country can be a problem, especially if you are a hands-on type, property owner. As mentioned before, good property management companies are hard to find and usually expensive. In some cases, having a management company handle the property while you are out-of-area might be a good interim solution, but if your move is going to be permanent, using a 1031 exchange to move the investment closer to your new home is probably a better plan.

Assuming you meet all the other 1031 exchanges requirements, you can relinquish an investment property in Maine and replace it with one in Arizona, Florida, Hawaii, or anywhere else in the United

States for that matter. Any investment property in the United States is considered like-kind and is allowed under the 1031 exchange provisions. However, you *cannot* exchange into a foreign replacement property. So, if you are moving to a foreign country, your investments have to stay here or you have to settle your tax bill before taking your profits out of the country.

Exchanging to a Different Property Type

A 1031 exchange is also referred to as a like-kind exchange because the regulations only allow for exchanges of like-kind property. Like-kind properties are properties of the same nature or character. Keep in mind that the provision of section 1031 of the tax code provides for the tax-deferred exchanges of much more than just real property. You can exchange many business and investment capital assets for like-kind property. You can do a 1031 exchange of aircraft, boats, trucks, and even cattle, but they have to be exchanged for like-kind property. For example, qualifying exchanges would include aircraft for aircraft, trucks for trucks, or cattle for cattle (but strangely enough, not male cattle for female cattle or vice versa).

One of the most common questions from real property investors is about this like-kind requirement. Thankfully, the answer is fairly straightforward. Just about any domestic real estate which you use in business or have held for investment will qualify for a 1031 exchange to any other domestic real estate that you intend to use in business or hold for investment. Arguably, all real estate is held for investment, so the category definition is very broad. However, the rules specifically exclude a primary residence, a vacation home, or second home.

Under the like-kind rule of property used in business or held for investment, all of the following examples would quality for tax deferral under a 1031 exchange:

- Rental house or condominium to an apartment building
- Residential income property to commercial property
- Vacant land to a rental house or apartment building

- Industrial warehouse to vacant land
- Desert or mountain land to urban income property
- Any investment property to a tenant-in-common interest in another investment property

As you can see, just about any real estate you intend to trade for any other real estate will qualify as long as the properties have been and will be used in business or held for investment.

1031 Exchange Requirements

There are many, many requirements, rules, exceptions to rules, time restrictions, and formalities involved in 1031 exchanges. In fact, the authoritative law books on 1031 exchanges run from 800 pages to well over 1,000 pages, so we cannot cover all the possible variables here. What we can cover are the everyday basics and some of the danger areas to let you know that this can be a complex area of law depending on your specific situation. Do not solely rely on the information in this book or the comments of real estate agents without verifying your situation with your own legal and/or tax professional.

The basic considerations and requirements for doing a fully tax-deferred 1031 exchange falls into six general categories:

1. The properties exchanged must be for business use or held for investment.
2. The price of the replacement property must be equal or higher.
3. The mortgage on the replacement property must be equal or higher.
4. The taxpayer must not get actual or constructive receipt of proceeds.
5. The taxpayer must use qualified intermediaries to qualify for safe harbor.
6. The taxpayer must meet the identification and closing time requirements.

We are going to look at each of these categories and discuss some of the ways people have run afoul of the rules by misinterpreting the requirements.

Business Use or Held for Investment

The first basic requirement of a valid exchange is that the property being exchanged and the property being acquired both must be for business use or held for investment. The official code reads in part:

No gain or loss shall be recognized on the exchange of property held for productive use in a trade or business or for investment if such property is exchanged solely for property of like kind which is to be held either for productive use in a trade or business or for investment.

As discussed previously, "for investment" regarding real estate is pretty broad, but primary residences, vacation homes, and second homes are excluded by implication. Additionally, a foreign replacement property is not considered like-kind property even if it meets all the other requirements.

Equal or Higher Price

To completely defer all capital gains tax on the sale of a property by doing a 1031 exchange, the replacement property must have a price equal to or higher than the relinquished property. It does not matter if you sold one larger property and bought multiple smaller properties, sold multiple smaller properties and bought one larger property, or sold multiple properties and bought multiple properties, as long as the replacement property (or properties) has a higher aggregate value. For example, if your relinquished property is sold for $100,000, the value of the replacement property or combination of replacement properties must be over $100,000. That does not mean that you cannot do a 1031 exchange into a lesser-valued property, it simply means you would have to pay taxes on the difference. For example, if your relinquished property had a $100,000 value and the replacement property only had a value of $90,000, you could still do the 1031 exchange, but you would have to pay the capital gains tax on the $10,000 difference. The minor exception to the "higher price" rule is that acquisition expenses are counted toward the total value of the replacement property. Acquisition expenses would include escrow fees, inspection fees, loan fees, points, commissions, and all other fees incidental to the purchase itself.

The higher price requirement is clear cut, but many people and some real estate agents make the mistake of thinking that only the capital gains portion of the investment has to be exchanged/reinvested. After all, you are only deferring the taxes on the gain itself, right? *Wrong.* To qualify under the provision of a 1031 exchange, the whole property value must be exchanged or taxes must be paid on the portion that is not. Another common misconception is that if the replacement property is a lower price, then the taxes due on the portion not reinvested are figured on a capital gains percentage similar to the "payments received" in an installment sale. For example, if the relinquished property is $100,000 (with an adjusted basis of $80,000) and the replacement property is $90,000, the misconception is that the taxes on the $10,000 received will be based on the ratio of gain to total value, meaning that $8,000 of the $10,000 received would be return of invested money and $2,000 would be capital gain. Wrong. The IRS takes the position that the first dollars taken out of an exchange represent capital gain or recapture of depreciation and are fully taxed accordingly. So in the example above, if the replacement property was only $90,000 and $10,000 was received in cash by the taxpayer/exchanger, the full $10,000 would be considered taxable capital gain. If the replacement property was only $80,000 with $20,000 in cash received, there would be no taxable benefit at all for doing an exchange.

If the desire is to "buy down" or buy a lower-priced property, there are ways to structure an exchange in combination with other tax deferral devices to defer the whole gain. However, most people are "buying up" in exchange situations so the higher price requirement is usually not a concern but, rather, just a rule that must be followed.

Remember, you do not *have* to buy a higher-priced property, but if you don't, you will have to pay the taxes on the difference.

Equal or Higher Mortgage

This rule causes a lot of confusion because it doesn't seem to make sense. The rule is that the mortgage on the replacement property must be equal to or higher that the mortgage on the relinquished property or combined mortgages on the combined relinquished properties. If the replacement property has a lower mortgage, the difference is sometimes referred to as mortgage relief or, specifically in 1031 exchanges, "mortgage boot." Remember, the general rule is that the IRS taxes you on recognized increases in wealth and one of the lesser known (and misunderstood) categories is mortgage relief. Thus, if the mortgage on the replacement property will be lower than the existing one on the relinquished property, there will be mortgage boot and taxes will be due on the difference. Another way the IRS looks at this is that if you have a lower mortgage on the replacement property, then you must have somehow, at some time, received the cash difference. Whether you agree with the IRS position is not important to them. What is important is that there will be taxes due if the replacement property's mortgage is not equal to or higher than the relinquished property's. There is, however, an exception.

☛ **Example:** Sheila sells an apartment building for $400,000. Her adjusted basis on the property is $150,000 and the mortgage is $200,000. Setting aside the accounting of expenses for this example, after paying off the mortgage on the relinquished property through the sale, Sheila would have net proceeds from the relinquished property of $200,000 sitting in her accommodator's trust account for a down payment in purchasing her replacement property. Let's say she decides to buy a replacement property for $400,000, and, for whatever reason (usually to have lower monthly payments), she decides to add $20,000 of her own money in buying the replacement property. Sheila completes the purchase and now has a $400,000 replacement property with a mortgage of $180,000.

In the above example, Sheila's mortgage reduction is a result of her adding "cash boot" which dollar for dollar will offset her mortgage boot.

In most cases, the higher mortgage rule is not a significant issue because to fully defer the taxes you need to buy a higher-priced replacement property. So in most cases it naturally follows that the replacement property mortgage will be higher as well.

No Receipt of Funds

The basic concept of an exchange is that one property is "traded" for another. The fact that we can now do exchanges with some time delay between the relinquishing of one property and the purchasing of the replacement property does not mean we can have control of the cash for the time between. The original exchanges had to be simultaneous, meaning that you had to close escrow on the relinquished property and the replacement at the same time. As you can imagine, there are all kinds of problems that arise when trying to do simultaneous exchanges and the end result was a lot of failed exchange attempts. The common sense solution was to allow some closing time flexibility or "delay" between the process of relinquishing one property and the separate process of acquiring the replacement property. In the court battles over this issue, the IRS fought hard not to allow any delay period because that would give the exchanger the use of the proceeds for the delay period. The courts agreed that there needed to be some time flexibility in order to "facilitate" the exchange process, but also agreed with the IRS that the exchanger should not have use or even access to the proceeds from the sale of the relinquished property during the delay period. From this grew delayed exchanges with built-in time allowances to facilitate the exchange, but also the strict requirement that the exchanger not get actual or constructive receipt of funds at any time during the delayed exchange process. The rule is pretty much set in stone; if at any time during the exchange process you get actual or constructive receipt of funds, your exchange will not withstand an audit.

Amazingly, many exchange attempts fail today because the exchanger runs afoul of this no-receipt-of-funds rule. It is a somewhat regular occurrence that an accommodator or real estate attorney will get a phone call from a person who wants to do a 1031 exchange after the property is already sold and closed and they have received the proceeds from the sale. The proper time to arrange the exchange is before the escrow closes on the relinquished property. There is a paperwork process and an exchange agreement that must be in place before closing so that funds go to your exchange accommodator's trust fund account rather than to you. Many times these failed exchange attempts happen because the person was so focused on the time requirements that they did not pay attention to the other required formalities, maybe they got bad information, or simply misunderstood the exchange process. Whatever the reason, by the time that phone call takes place, it's too late. If the escrow has already closed, there has either been actual or constructive receipt of funds and there is no recovery from that. It is a failed exchange attempt and the capital gains tax liability has been triggered.

Using Qualified Intermediaries

Today, the typical 1031 exchange involves the use of an IRS-defined qualified intermediary or accommodator to hold the proceeds of the sale while the exchanger locates and arranges the purchase of the replacement property. The terms *qualified intermediary* and *accommodator* both refer to the same thing; a business entity or person who acts as a facilitator for the exchange process. Generally, a qualified intermediary's function is to document the exchange through what is usually called an "exchange agreement" and to hold the proceeds from the sale of the relinquished property until the purchase of the replacement property is ready to close.

Technically, the use of qualified intermediaries is not required by IRC §1031. There are ways to accomplish a valid exchange without using an intermediary or an accommodator, but none worth discussing because today's accommodators are low cost and easy to use. Additionally, by using a qualified intermediary, you create "safe harbor" or a legal presumption that there was no actual or constructive receipt of funds. Even in a simultaneous closing exchange, where an accommodator is not required, the cost is still worthwhile for the safe harbor presumption and as a safety measure in case anything goes wrong.

There is no government supervision or licensing requirements for exchange accommodators. That fact tends to make attorneys nervous, especially when you consider the large amounts of money entrusted to accommodators on a regular basis. There have been a few cases of accommodators running off with the money or filing for bankruptcy and tying up an exchanger's funds. However, it is very rare. The best way to protect your funds is to use a bonded and well-known intermediary or exchange attorney. Large title companies sometimes offer this service as well.

While there are no set rules for who can act as your accommodator, the IRS has set out who cannot be your accommodator by establishing "disqualified persons." Disqualified persons include your real estate brokers, accountants, spouses, other family-related parties, and any companies or businesses owned or controlled by otherwise disqualified persons. Family attorneys or attorneys with whom you have other attorney-client dealings are also disqualified. However, attorneys are not disqualified if they are retained specifically as an exchange accommodator or to advise you on exchange matters.

The process of using an accommodator has been streamlined over the past ten to 15 years. Basically, once you have selected an accommodator, it's a matter of paperwork. Your escrow or closing agent will supply the necessary property and closing information to the accommodator. The accommodator will in turn draft an exchange agreement that will document your intent to conform to the requirements of IRC §1031 for the tax-deferred exchange. This exchange agreement will probably come to you through your escrow or closing agent for your signature. At the same time, a copy of the agreement will go to the buyer of your property through escrow because his or her signature is also necessary. In essence, the agreement states that both parties are instructing the accommodator to act as intermediary by accepting title to the property on behalf of the seller and then deeding it to the buyer under the terms of the purchase contract. The accommodator is then authorized to accept and hold the proceeds from the sale in trust for the seller while he or she is looking for the replacement property.

Originally, on the sale of the relinquished property, the seller/exchanger would deed the property to the accommodator and the accommodator would deed the property to the buyer in exchange for the contract price. Likewise, on the purchase of the replacement property, the seller of the replacement property would agree to deed the property to the accommodator in exchange for the purchase price and then deed the property to the exchanger thereby completing the exchange process. However, with the rise of liability for property conditions (toxics), most accommodators are less willing to have any ownership (vesting) in the exchanged properties at all. Most now do what is called direct deeding, meaning that buyer and seller in both stages of the exchange will deed directly to each other. This approach is common now and the IRS will not audit or disallow your exchange for that reason alone. Whichever deeding method your accommodator chooses to use should make no difference to you. What's important is that the proper qualified intermediary paper trail is created.

Time Requirements of Selecting the Replacement Property

Prior to the landmark *Starker v. U.S.* case, 1031 exchange provisions were thought to require a simultaneous exchange, meaning that both the relinquished property and the replacement property had to close escrow at the same time. That requirement limited the use of like-kind exchanges because it was overly cumbersome trying to sell one property, locate a suitable replacement, and negotiate the simultaneous closing of both. The alternative of finding two property owners who actually wanted each other's property to do a true property-for-property exchange was simply not practical. *Starker v. U.S.* challenged and defeated the IRS's position that 1031 exchanges had to be simultaneous. This case gave rise to terms *Starker exchange* and *delayed exchange.* Five years after *Starker v. U.S.,* Congress enacted changes to IRC §1031 that specifically allowed delayed exchanges and set the time requirements that are still in effect today.

The 45-Day and 180-Day Requirements

According to Congress's revision of IRC §1031, for a delayed exchange to be valid it must meet two requirements (see Figure 7.3):

1. The replacement property must be identified within 45 days of the closing/transfer of the relinquished property.
2. The replacement property must be received (title acquired) within 180 days of the closing/transfer of the relinquished property, or the due date with extensions, for the transferor's tax returns for the taxable year in which the transfer of the relinquished property occurs.

The IRS takes both of these requirements very seriously. If you are a day late, your exchange will be disallowed. Count on it. With this in mind, we are going to look closer at what both of these time requirements mean in practice.

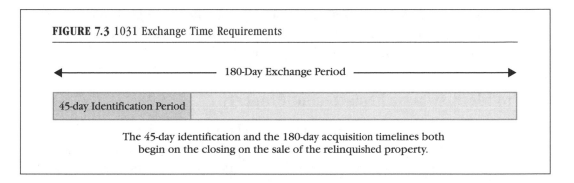

FIGURE 7.3 1031 Exchange Time Requirements

The 45-day identification and the 180-day acquisition timelines both begin on the closing on the sale of the relinquished property.

The 45-day identification period seems more like a requirement designed to annoy than to actually accomplish any useful purpose. Nevertheless, the rule as enacted is strictly followed today. Many people are hesitant to do 1031 exchanges knowing they only have 45 days to locate and identify the replacement. However, in practice, it usually takes some time to sell the relinquished property and more time still to complete the escrow process. Presuming you are diligent in trying to locate your replacement property, it works out that there is much more than just 45 days available. For example, if it takes 30 days to sell your relinquished property and another 45 days to close the escrow, you really have 120 days to identify the replacement property (30 days to sell, plus 45 days of escrow, plus 45 days allowed by code). Of course, that presumes you are out there searching for a replacement property as soon as you decide to sell and do an exchange. It is also common to negotiate a longer escrow period (60, 90, or 120 days) to allow you extra time to locate your replacement property. It is even possible to negotiate a contingency in the sale agreement that makes the closing contingent upon your ability to locate a suitable replacement property. While these types of contingencies are possible, they will not be warmly received by real estate agents and buyers because they introduce a sometimes-unacceptable degree of uncertainty into the transaction.

The best way to increase your available time to locate and identify your replacement property is to start looking for it as soon as you have made the decision to sell and do the exchange. Unfortunately, many people do not even consider what they will be buying or start looking for the replacement property before they actually close on the sale of their relinquished property.

How to Identify Your Replacement Property

The 45-day identification period is one area that is ripe for abuse for two reasons: the severe consequences of being late, and the ambiguity in the required method of notification and the person(s) who must be notified. The official rule states:

A replacement property is properly identified only if it is designated as replacement property in a written document signed by the taxpayer and hand delivered, mailed, telecopied, or otherwise sent to either:

1. The person obligated to transfer the replacement property to the taxpayer, even if that person is a disqualified person, or
2. To any other person involved in the exchange other than the taxpayer or a disqualified person before the end of the 45-day identification period.

Crystal clear, right? It seems fairly straightforward if the identification is made to the person who is obligated to transfer the replacement property to the exchanger. That person is usually your intermediary or accommodator. But there is also the alternative category of providing the identification to "any other person *involved* in the exchange" except a disqualified person. Examples of disqualified persons would include your real estate agent, family members, and your accountant. Examples of involved persons not "disqualified" would include your escrow company, title company, or an attorney hired specifically to oversee or advise you on the exchange.

Properties actually acquired prior to the 45-day identification are considered to satisfy the code requirements, so you will not need to notify anyone if the escrow on the replacement property actually closes within the identification period. Otherwise, identification of the replacement property must be sent or delivered before the end of the 45-day identification period, *without* extensions for Saturdays, Sundays, or holidays.

Identifying Alternative and Multiple Properties

Generally, the rules allow you to identify three potential replacement properties. This is important because if something happens to make your first replacement property choice undesirable or unavailable after the expiration of your 45-day identification period, you are out of luck. If you identified only one property and this situation arises, your exchange will be disallowed and a tax will be triggered on your capital gain. So make sure you allow yourself a back-up position by identifying at least three potential replacement properties. There are also some obscure exceptions to the three-property-identification rule which allow you to identify as many properties as you want as long as the aggregate value does not exceed 200 percent of the value of the relinquished property (the 200 percent rule), or if the exchanger actually acquires 95 percent of the aggregate value of all properties identified (the 95 percent rule). If you find yourself wanting or needing to use either the 200 percent rule or 95 percent rule, get an attorney experienced in 1031 exchanges to actively oversee your exchange.

The properties you identify must be unambiguously described in the notification. For real estate, an adequate description is the street address, legal description, or a county assessor's parcel number. A sample of a 45-day identification has been included in Appendix A.

Avoiding Potential Problems

Exchanges are fairly commonplace today and in most cases will go smoothly without much risk of running into problems. However, when there are problems, the consequences can be harsh. The IRS does not commonly audit exchanges, but when they do, it will usually be a few years after the exchange was completed. Finding a problem or a failed requirement at that point can be devastating. For example, if you deferred $200,000 in capital gain and your exchange was disallowed three years later in an IRS audit, you would immediately owe the original taxes due on the gain plus interest and in cases of willful neglect, a 25 percent penalty. So, while it is not all that common that the IRS disallows an exchange, the severity involved justifies due care.

Getting Professional Advice and Guidance

There are a tremendous number of exchange accommodators and qualified intermediaries in the industry today. Just searching for "1031 exchange" on the Internet will yield hundreds of accommodators, qualified intermediaries, exchange advisors, real estate agents, attorneys, accountants, and so on.

Given the modern world of e-mail, faxes, and overnight express, there probably isn't a compelling reason that a qualified intermediary physically located in Oregon could not handle the exchange agreement paperwork for exchange of property taking place in Florida. On the other hand, if there are qualified advisors and accommodators in your area, why not pick someone local?

Real estate agents are usually the first professionals people turn to get advice on exchanges. Some real estate agents really do know exchanges well enough to advise you and some don't. Advice is only as good as the experience and qualifications of the advisor. It is in your own best interest to make sure you are comfortable with the level of expertise of your advisor.

The two best sources of information on exchanges will be from real estate attorneys and experienced accommodators. The problem is, of course, that advice from attorneys is not free and the "words of wisdom" from the local real estate agent are. So, many people have a tendency to settle for the free advice, good or bad. There is, however, a way to get a good advisor without running up attorney fees. If you are contemplating doing an exchange, you *will* want to use a qualified intermediary. Most qualified intermediaries have attorneys either on staff or on retainer. There are even real estate attorneys who are also qualified intermediaries. It is a competitive business, so most qualified intermediaries are big on customer service. If you call one with questions, you will probably get a return call by someone who can actually answer your questions. Your real estate agent is going to know the names of a few qualified intermediaries in your area or can get the names for you. It is a good resource, and usually free, so take advantage of it.

If you find your situation more complicated than the garden-variety exchange, make sure you are clear on the legal process and tax outcome before you commit. In more complicated exchanges, having your own real estate attorney to at least oversee the process is probably well worth the cost.

Follow the Timing Rules and Don't Cut Your Time Short

Earlier in this chapter, I told you that for an exchange to be valid, the IRS requires that you meet two time requirements:

1. The replacement property must be identified within 45 days of the closing/transfer of the relinquished property.
2. The replacement property must be received within 180 days of the closing/transfer of the relinquished property, or the due date with extensions, for the transferor's tax returns for the taxable year in which the transfer of the relinquished property occurs.

The IRS takes the 45-day identification and 180-day acquisition time requirements very seriously. If you are a day late and your exchange is audited, it will be disallowed. As far as the IRS is concerned, these time requirements are set in stone. In addition to the strictness of the 45-day and 180-day timelines, there are two little lesser-known rules that tend to trip people up.

The first potential problem is that if the 45th day of the identification period or the 180th day of the acquisition period falls on a holiday or a weekend, the time requirements are *not* extended to the following business day. That means that if the 45th day of your identification period falls on a Sunday, you must identify your replacement property by the Friday before.

The second lesser-known rule that tends to cause problems is the way the 180-day replacement property time requirement is written. The rule states that the property must be received within 180 days, but then goes on to add "or [by] the due date (with extensions) for the transferor's tax returns for the taxable year in which the transfer of the relinquished property occurs." The problem is that everyone focuses on the 180-day requirement and fails to pay attention to this secondary language.

☛ **Example:** Hal is doing a 1031 exchange. His relinquished property was a rental house, which has already sold. The escrow for the relinquished property closed a little over three months (approximately 105 days) ago on December 31. It is now the second week of April and Hal has properly identified three potential replacement properties. He has decided on one of the three properties and is on schedule to close the escrow at the end of April well within the 180-day requirement. Hal has always been diligent about filing his taxes on time and being true to form he files them on April 15. At the end of April, on the 115th day of the exchange period, Hal closes escrow on his replacement property. Two years later, Hal receives a letter from the IRS disallowing his exchange for not receiving the replacement property within the statutory exchange period.

In the example above, Hal was his own worse enemy. He focused on the "within 180 days" language of the requirements and failed to follow the secondary language saying " . . . or [by] the due date (with extensions) for the transferor's tax returns . . . ." Hal cut his own exchange period short by filing his income tax return on time.

This is a potential problem faced by every exchanger who closes the sale of a relinquished property during the late months of the calendar year. If Hal in the above example had been aware of the situation, he could have sidestepped the problem by simply filing an extension for his income tax returns and waiting to file until after the replacement property had been received. The code specifically allows you to file an extension of your tax return so the 180-day requirement will not be cut short, but once again, you have to be aware of the potential problem to know to fix it. Almost all qualified intermediaries will have you sign something that is intended to alert you to this situation. Unfortunately, it is sometimes buried in the stack of paperwork that comes to you in the sale/exchange process and may go unnoticed.

Holding Period Requirements

Here's another of those areas of tax law that defies any easily understandable explanation and can cause a lot of frustration if you find yourself in a position where you need a clearly defined answer. Almost everyone agrees that there is some holding period required for investment properties before they will qualify for tax deferral under the provisions of 1031 exchanges. The problem, however, is trying to pin down exactly how long you have to hold before you can do an exchange, or, conversely, how long you have to hold a property after you do an exchange.

Part of this problem stems back to the ambiguous rules of "dealer" property, which was covered in Chapter 3. If you have not read that chapter, go back and read it now because anything labeled dealer property will not qualify for 1031 exchange tax treatment. With that said and presuming the property gets past being labeled as dealer property, the question still remains: What is the required holding period? Actually, that's not one question, it's two because the IRS can look at both how long a relinquished property is held before an exchange is done *and* how long a replacement property is held after an exchange. Both periods are equally important because of the wording of IRC §1031(a):

> No gain or loss shall be recognized on the exchange of property held for productive use in a trade or business or for investment *if such property is exchanged solely for* property of like kind which is to be held either for productive use in a trade or business or for investment. [Emphasis mine.]

The IRS takes the position that any property acquired "immediately" before an exchange or disposed-of immediately after an exchange was not primarily "held for productive use in a trade or business or for investment." This means that if property on either side of the exchange was not held long enough, the IRS will disallow the exchange as not being of like-kind property. The question then becomes what does "immediately" mean? Unfortunately, there is no clear answer. The IRS has challenged exchanges based on holding periods ranging from a few days to extreme cases where the IRS claims a few years is too short a holding period.

Luckily, the courts do differ with the IRS on the issue of required holding periods. The courts have consistently held that the length of time an investment is held is only one factor in determining whether it qualifies for tax deferral under the provisions of IRC §1031. The courts, on rare occasions, have sided with taxpayers where the holding period was as short as five days and court decisions favoring the taxpayer are much more common where the holding period was more that a few months. But in every short holding period case that went in favor of the taxpayer, the taxpayer was able to show some unforeseen change in circumstances that supported a need for the quick disposition.

It's nice that the courts commonly side with the taxpayer in cases where there are circumstances justifying a short holding period. However, a taxpayer doesn't get to argue the justifying merits of his or her circumstances until after being audited. Given the fact that most investors prefer not to draw the attention of the IRS in the first place, the you-will-probably-win-in-tax-court answer is not very satisfying. So now the question becomes, how long is long enough so that the exchange does not draw IRS scrutiny? The conventional wisdom from legal and accounting professionals is that there are two answers: to be *reasonably* sure you are safe, the holding period needs to be one year plus; to be "*darn-sure*" you have to wait two years or more.

Now with all of that said, let me add that I know there are a lot of investors out there who do exchanges without regard to the amount of time the investment has been held. Frankly, I think the IRS has more important things to do than to scrutinize holding periods in exchanges. But you never know when the IRS's priorities will change, so prudence would dictate you stay within the rules as best you can. If you do find yourself in a situation that necessitates a quicker than anticipated sale of an investment, be sure you well document the justifying unforeseen circumstances.

Splitting Up Partnerships and Joint Ventures

Another common use for 1031 exchanges is to split up partnerships, joint ventures, and other types of co-ownership of property without triggering unwanted taxes. It is common to find properties where there is more than one owner. Usually this comes from a loosely formed partnership like a couple of people who joined together for the sole purpose of investing in a specific property. It is also common to find a situation where a property was inherited from parents years ago and all the names of the children were placed on the title. However the joint ownership came to exist, there will come a time when at least one of the joint owners wants his or her money out. When this happens there are a number of options available to the departing owner: the remaining owner(s) can buy out the interest of the person wanting out, or the departing owner can sometimes attempt to sell his or her share, or if everyone agrees, the property can be sold. If the property is sold and there is a capital gain involved, the remaining owners are usually not happy about having their taxes triggered because one owner wants out. Luckily, each person has the ability to do an exchange on his or her portion of the investment property.

☞ **Example:** John and Jane were married to each other, as were Ed and Betty. In 1980, the two couples decided to pool funds and invest in an apartment building. They owned the property in equal shares of 50 percent to each couple. They jointly managed the apartment building for six years and everything went smoothly. In 1986, Ed and Betty moved out of state when Ed was transferred by his employer. At the time, the apartment building was pretty much trouble free, so John and Jane agreed to continue managing it until Ed and Betty returned. In 1992, John and Jane divorced with an agreed marital settlement that called for an equal split of their ownership in the apartment building. At the time, the real estate market was very bad so everyone agreed to hang on to the investment until the market recovered. Jane continued to manage the property. In 2000, the fair market value of the apartment building was $1,000,000. The adjusted basis on the property stood at $200,000. The ownership of the property had evolved into Ed and Betty owning 50 percent as joint tenants to each other and as tenants in common with both John and Jane separately owning 25 percent each.

What usually happens in a case like this is that the person who still lives near the property is continuing to manage it and will want out. After all, Ed and Betty in the example have been out of state for 14 years and the management of the property fell to John and Jane for a number of years and to Jane alone for a number of years thereafter. At some time, (usually much sooner than in this example) the inequity of the situation forces the sale of the property.

In the above situation, each person has the ability to use a 1031 exchange for his or her portion of the property and will be able to go his or her own way. However, in most cases, married couples jointly exchange. So, Betty and Ed will be jointly exchanging out of their one-half ownership or the equivalent of a $500,000 property investment with an adjusted basis of $100,000. Both John and Jane will be exchanging out of their respective one-quarter ownership or the equivalent of a $250,000 property investment with an adjusted basis of $50,000 each. While all parties can do a 1031 exchange, any of them individually could also choose *not* to do an exchange and would simply receive their portion of the sale proceeds and be responsible for their own taxes attributable to their ownership share.

The division and sale of property in this way is fairly common and uncomplicated. If instead, the two couples had created a formal general partnership, limited partnership, LLC, or corporation to own the property, the complexity increases significantly. The tax consequences on the dissolution of any of the more formal business entities are beyond the scope of this book and you will need expert tax advice. It's not smart to begin the process of buying out a partner or doing a 1031 exchange upon the dissolution of the business entity without knowing the specific tax consequences of your actions. Get expert advice before you act.

Recharacterizing Property to Qualify for Exchanges

The way the IRS determines whether a property has been used in business or held for investment will usually hinge on your treatment of the property. One of the best indicators is how you have characterized the property on your tax returns. If you have historically taken depreciation and showed rental income, there usually isn't any question that the property will qualify. However, what about a vacation home that you occasionally rent to others, but usually just leave vacant for your own or family use? The answer will depend on how you have characterized the property. If you have previously declared the home a "second home" and have been taking a second home mortgage deduction on your taxes, the property will not *immediately* qualify. However, you can always *recharacterize* a property by simply using it differently. In the case of a vacation property, if you were to change its use to a rental property instead of the family vacation home, it would qualify under the 1031 exchange rules. For example, you could list your vacation home with the local vacation home rental agents and rent it for a couple of years. You would show rental income and expenses (including depreciation) from the property on your tax returns. If you did so, the property would qualify under the rules for a 1031 exchange. The question always becomes, how long do you have to rent it? Conventional wisdom says that two years is a safe number, but many people only wait one year. Some people even back up and amend previous tax returns to recharacterize a property. The amendments would show income and expenses attributable to the property and take any depreciation available. Of course, if any tax deficit exists because of the changes made, the back taxes would be immediately due along with any applicable interest, but sometimes it is well worth the back taxes if the property will qualify sooner. Still, the question is, how long should you wait? The answer is not entirely clear, so if you are thinking about recharacterizing a property to qualify for an exchange, see your accountant or a tax attorney for advice and guidance.

Exchanges between Related Parties

There are special rules that apply and issues that arise when a 1031 exchange is done between related parties. The IRS defines related parties as "you and a member of your family (spouse, brother, sister, parent, child, etc.), you and a corporation in which you have more than 50 percent ownership, you and a partnership in which you directly or indirectly own more than a 50 percent interest of the capital or profits and, two partnerships in which you directly or indirectly own more than 50 percent of the capital interests or profits."

Basically, the rule is that if either person resells or otherwise disposes of the exchanged property within two years, the exchange will be disallowed and the tax on the original exchange must be recognized as of the date of the *later* disposition.

If you are contemplating doing an exchange with a related party, be sure to consult your tax advisor and keep in mind the general rule requiring a two-year *after-exchange* holding period.

Primary Residence Issues in Exchanges

There are two 1031 exchange issues that seem to come up all the time. The first issue is whether an existing investment property can be converted to, or recharacterized as, a primary residence in order to qualify it under the primary residence tax exemption.

The second issue is whether a taxpayer can do an exchange from an investment property and purchase a replacement property that will be used, immediately or in the future, as a primary residence.

Both issues are closely related because they both require a recharacterization of investments. In the first case, the taxpayer is *directly* attempting to qualify investment profits for exempt treatment. In the second case, the taxpayer is *indirectly* attempting to exempt investment profits by banking the proceeds from selling a primary residence *while* using a 1031 exchange of an investment property to purchase a replacement primary residence. In either case, the taxpayer is looking for a tax "loophole" and in some situations will find one.

Converting an Investment Property to a Primary Residence

The Taxpayer Reform Act of 1997 changed the way we are taxed on our primary residences. Prior to 1997, there was a primary residence 18-month capital gains rollover provision and a one-time $125,000 exemption for persons over 55 years of age. In 1997, both of those provisions were basically discarded and a new exemption created. The new exemption allows everyone, regardless of age, a capital gains tax exemption of up to $250,000 for an individual and $500,000 for a married couple on the sale of their primary residence. For the property to qualify for the exemption, the taxpayer needs to show that the property was used as his/her/their primary residence for two of the last five years. If the property qualifies, the first $250,000 in capital gain for individuals or $500,000 in capital gain for couples is absolutely tax-free.

Understandably, this primary residence exemption is looked at longingly by real estate investors because it eliminates, not just defers, taxes on the profit from a sale of property up to the $250,000/$500,000 exclusion. As such, many investors owning rental homes or condominiums look for any possible way to convert or recharacterize rental property so that it qualifies for primary residence tax treatment.

☞ **Example:** Sally and Sam own two single-family homes in the same neighborhood. They live in one of the homes, their primary residence, and rent the other. Both their rental house and their primary residence have been in their family for a long time. The rental house has been rented for over 20 years and has been fully depreciated. The adjusted basis on both properties is very low at about $20,000 and their current market values are about $350,000 for the rental house and

$400,000 for their primary residence. Sally and Sam have decided to move out of state but are not in any real hurry. They have decided to sell both properties because they don't want to be long-distance landlords. After looking at the tax situation, Sally and Sam realize that if they sell the rental property outright, they will have to pay capital gains taxes on approximately $330,000 ($350,000 sales price less a $20,000 adjusted basis). Their accountant has estimated the capital gains and recapture of depreciation taxes due on the sale of the rental property to be about $95,000. Sam and Sally decide to sell their primary residence first and move into their rental property for two years. By doing this, Sally and Sam intend to use their primary home exemption to shield them from taxes on the sale of their first home and then again two years later when they sell their newly qualified primary residence.

Presuming Sam and Sally have no objection to actually moving into and residing in the rental house for two years, they will be able to use the primary home exemption twice to shield themselves from all capital gains taxes in the example above.

The ability to convert a rental house into a primary residence can be well worth the two-year relocation, but there is a potential down side that must be considered. While a rental home converted to a primary residence will escape capital gains taxes to the extent of the primary residence exemption, it will not escape taxes due as a result of recapturing any depreciation taken on the property after May 6, 1997.

Exchanging into a Future Primary Residence

A common question that arises in 1031 exchange discussions is whether a taxpayer may exchange an investment property into a replacement property he or she intends to occupy as a primary residence in the future. If the question is stated exactly as it is above, the answer is clearly no. Remember, Internal Revenue Code for like-kind exchanges states that:

> No gain or loss shall be recognized on the exchange of property held for *productive use in a trade or business or for investment* if such property is exchanged solely for property of like kind which is to be held either for *productive use in a trade or business or for investment.* [Emphasis added.]

Obviously, if the replacement property is intended as a primary residence, it will not fit the "productive use in a trade or business or for investment" requirement. Seemingly at odds with this is the fact that you are allowed to change the characterization of a property from investment property to primary residence and vice versa. So, if you owned a rental house or condominium, it would fit the "productive use in a trade or business or for investment" requirement. If you decided to move into that rental house or condominium as your primary residence, you could and no capital gains tax would be triggered. So, logically it follows that you should be able to do a 1031 exchange into a house or a condominium, rent it for some period and, then move in and make it your primary residence right? The answer is, maybe. Whether the 1031 exchange will be disallowed in an audit will be based on your *intention* at the time of the exchange.

☛ **Example:** Pete has a triplex he has owned and managed for about 20 years. He has been showing the income and expenses as well as taking the depreciation each year on his tax returns. Pete also has a home he has lived in for about 20 years. Both properties have appreciated significantly since they were originally purchased. Pete is planning to retire in about a year and wants to move to the small beach community of Seaside, where he has friends and family. Both Pete's house and his triplex have a fair market value of approximately $300,000. The adjusted basis on the triplex is approximately $50,000 and there is a mortgage on the property.

Pete has calculated his taxes and knows that if he sells the triplex outright, he faces about $70,000 (state and federal) in capital gains tax and recapture of depreciation. Prices of homes in Seaside are running around $320,000. Pete plans to avoid taxes by selling his triplex immediately and doing a 1031 exchange into a home in Seaside that he intends to rent for the one year until his retirement. Upon retirement, Pete plans on selling his current home (avoiding taxes on that sale by using his $250,000 primary residence exemption) and then moving into the Seaside house.

In the example above, Pete's exchange will be disallowed if audited and the IRS feels that Pete's "intent" at the time of the exchange was to use the replacement property as a future primary residence. Even though the replacement property was rented for one year, Pete's "intent" at the time of the exchange will be the deciding factor on whether the exchange will be disallowed. How would the IRS know what Pete was intending? After all, it is unlikely that Pete is going to volunteer any information about his planning or intentions. However, in Pete's case, his intention was fairly easy to see. The biggest red flag was the relatively short time the property was rented and the timing of the exchange in relation to Pete's scheduled retirement. If the Seaside house were rented for a few years instead of just one, the exchange would probably have never been scrutinized at all. But once an audit is started, the IRS will probably look at all of Pete's actions and conduct. If the IRS disallows the exchange, Pete will have the burden of proving his intent was to hold the property for investment.

On the other hand, Pete could have done the 1031 exchange with the primary intention of simply moving the investment closer to the area where he planned to retire. As such, there would be no question that the exchange would be valid. Then, after the exchange was completed, there were some unforeseeable change in circumstances and Pete *then* decided to move into the rental house and recharacterize it as his primary residence, he could legally do so.

The Future of 1031 Exchanges

There has been a lot of political rhetoric about eliminating capital gains taxes. That possibility seems very remote when you consider the IRS's appointed task of taxing increases in wealth. A capital gain is, of course, an increase in wealth. Nevertheless, if capital gains taxes were abolished the entire qualified intermediary industry would probably collapse. Arguably, 1031 exchanges would still be used even if there were no capital gains taxes because recapture of depreciation on the sale of a property would still be taxed. Realistically, though, capital gains taxes are probably going to exist in one form or another into the foreseeable future and, for that reason, so are 1031 exchanges.

CHAPTER 8

Reverse Exchanges

"Why does a slight tax increase cost you two hundred dollars and a substantial tax cut save you thirty cents?"

Peg Bracken

In a typical deferred exchange, the taxpayer, conforming to the requirements of the code, sells/transfers the relinquished property first and then goes about the process of identifying and acquiring the replacement property. In a reverse exchange, the replacement property is acquired *before* the relinquished property is sold. At first, this sounds simple enough, but in practice reverse exchanges are considerably more sophisticated and complex. Nevertheless, in the right situation, a reverse exchange is a viable exchange method and offers some unique opportunities.

☞ **Example:** Byron owns a 12-unit apartment building and two rental houses. He has a long-time, dependable, on-site manager for the apartment building and things seem to pretty much take care of themselves. Both rental houses, however, seem to always have problems and take up a disproportionate amount of Byron's time. Byron has just learned that the apartment building owner adjacent to his property intends to sell in the next couple of months and has offered Byron first shot at buying it. The price is agreeable and Byron feels it's a great opportunity because he could use the same on-site manager for both buildings. The problem is that Byron has a lot of equity tied up in the two rental houses and would need that money to arrange the purchase. He could borrow on the houses for the down payment on the new apartment building, but he really doesn't want more rental property unless he can free up some of the time he now spends on the rental houses. He knows he could borrow against the equity of the rental houses, buy the new apartment building, and then sell the houses. However, in doing that, he would have to pay taxes on the sale of the rental houses.

The situation above is perfect for a reverse exchange. Presuming Byron can, in fact, arrange the financing and be able to close on the new apartment building, he can structure the purchase so that it qualifies as the replacement property in an exchange even though he will have to close on it prior to selling the two rental houses.

Reverse Exchange Opportunities

The preceding section was only one example of where a reverse exchange is appropriate. Some of the other common reasons for doing a reverse exchange include:

- *Finding the right property.* Many times a property owner will be interested in doing an exchange, but is not confident a desirable property can be found within the 45-day and 180-day time requirements. A reverse exchange will allow that person to find the "perfect" property and arrange for its purchase before placing the relinquished property on the market.

- *Picking up a "great deal" or distressed property.* Sometimes a taxpayer has no intention of selling a property he or she already has, but like Byron in the example above, an irresistible opportunity presents itself. Maybe it's a great price on a foreclosure property, a divorce situation, bankruptcy liquidation, or whatever. Good deals never last long and the successful buyer will usually have to close very quickly. The reverse exchange can be the perfect tool when trading into an unforeseeable opportunity.

- *The sale on the relinquished property falls apart.* Any real estate agent can tell you, not all property sales close. So if you have already found your perfect replacement property and the escrow on your relinquished property falls apart, you can use a reverse exchange to complete your acquisition while seeking another buyer for your relinquished property.

- *Construction of a build-to-suit property.* In some cases, reverse exchanges can be the best approach when a taxpayer wants to exchange into a different property, but the proposed replacement property has not yet been built. Build-to-suit exchanges, whether normal or reverse, can be risky because of the potential for construction delays. If a build-to-suit situation is done using a reverse exchange and the project exceeds the time requirements, the reverse exchange may no longer work, but the yet-unsold relinquished property can be retained and the capital gains tax liability never triggered. Build-to-suit exchanges are tricky; see your tax attorney or accountant (see Chapter 9 for more information about build-to-suit exchanges).

Legal Status and Costs Involved

Historically, reverse exchanges met significant resistance from the IRS. Reverse exchanges have never been expressly authorized under the regulations for 1031 exchanges. Prior to 2000, the most common way to do a reverse exchange was to arrange a "friendly" party to buy and hold (warehouse) the desired replacement property. A taxpayer would then sell the relinquished property and complete the exchange by acquiring the replacement property from the "friendly" party. This type of arrangement was called "parking" the property and caused a great deal of anxiety for accountants and attorneys.

Prior to 2000, there was no real authority that supported the concept of reverse exchanges and most attorneys and qualified intermediaries avoided them. Without clear authority, advisors feared that the IRS would audit and attack the parking arrangements by disputing the acquired property as a valid replacement property, disputing the relinquished property as qualified, or attacking the "friendly" party titleholder as a sham or straw-man owner that had no true beneficial ownership of the property. The reverse exchange itself was thought to be a red flag that could potentially draw an audit or at least some extra scrutiny of the taxpayer's tax returns. In an actual audit, if any of the three attacks above succeeded, the exchange would be disallowed triggering harsh tax consequences.

In September of 2000, Revenue Procedure 2000-37 was published to address these parking arrangements and specifically allowed reverse exchanges under certain circumstances. It laid out a set of conditions that, if followed, created a safe harbor allowing taxpayers to arrange the acquisition of a replacement property prior to selling the relinquished property. Specifically, Revenue Procedure 2000-37 contained the stated purpose:

> This revenue procedure provides a safe harbor under which the Internal Revenue Service will not challenge (a) the qualification of property as either "replacement property" or "relinquished property" (as defined in section 1.1031(k)-1(a) of the Income Tax Regulations) for purposes of section 1031 of the Internal Revenue Code and the regulations thereunder or (b) the treatment of the "exchange accommodation titleholder" as the beneficial owner of such property for federal income tax purposes, if the property is held in a "qualified exchange accommodation arrangement."

Revenue Procedure 2000-37 put most reverse exchange advisors at ease and created the new terminology *exchange accommodation titleholder* (usually referred to as an EAT or an AT) and *qualified exchange accommodation arrangement* (usually referred to as a QEAA). Both these terms and their acronyms are in common use today. An exchange accommodation titleholder is usually just the qualified intermediary you select and a qualified exchange accommodation arrangement is simply the written agreement between the taxpayer and the EAT setting out the requirements specified in Revenue Ruling 2000-37 (a copy of the relevant sections of Revenue Ruling 2000-37 has been provided in Appendix B). In summary, a QEAA must be in writing and specify that the accommodation titleholder is holding the parked property for the benefit of the taxpayer in order to facilitate an exchange and that the AT will be "beneficial owner" of the parked property for income tax purposes.

Interestingly, the revenue ruling allows the taxpayer five business days to enter into a QEAA *after* the accommodation titleholder (AT) acquires "qualified indicia of ownership" (which usually just means legal title) of the parked property. The QEAA relationship is allowed to exist for up to 180 days. Arguably, this extends the total time an accommodation titleholder can park a property from the 180 days of the QEAA to the 180 days plus the five business days provided for in the revenue ruling. It is unclear if the IRS actually intended this result.

Revenue Ruling 2000-37 also attempted to clear up some of the other issues that can arise in a QEAA by specifically listing "permissible agreements" between the accommodation titleholder and the taxpayer. The revenue ruling allows the QEAA to include provisions that allow:

- An accommodation titleholder to act concurrently as the qualified intermediary in the 1031 exchange
- The taxpayer to guarantee the obligations of the accommodation titleholder
- The taxpayer to loan or advance funds to the accommodation titleholder

- The taxpayer to rent or lease the property from the accommodation titleholder
- The taxpayer to manage the property or otherwise provide services on or related to the property

With the guidance and relative certainty of Revenue Ruling 2000-37, reverse exchanges, previously shunned by most professional qualified intermediaries, are now being embraced. The expenses associated with doing a reverse exchange are still much higher than the traditional exchange but the growing competition among professional intermediaries performing the services has significantly reduced the fees. At the time of the this writing, in the Los Angeles area, where the cost of doing a traditional exchange is $500 to $700, the cost of doing a reverse exchange with a professional qualified intermediary will run you around $5,000 or more. That cost may seem high, but in the right situation it can be well worthwhile.

In general terms, here's how a reverse exchange works:

1. The taxpayer signs a qualified exchange accommodation agreement with the parking intermediary. This is the blanket document that the IRS announcement requires.
2. The parking intermediary takes title to the new property, taking a loan from a bank and/or the taxpayer. If the loan is from a bank, the taxpayer generally will be asked to (and may) give a guaranty.
3. The new property (now owned by the parking intermediary) is leased to the taxpayer on a triple-net basis. Rent under the lease generally is equal to the carrying costs of the new property, including any debt service.
4. On the day that the parking intermediary acquires the new property, the parking intermediary and the taxpayer sign a contract by which taxpayer agrees to acquire the new property from the parking intermediary within the next 180 days.

5. The taxpayer begins to market the old property. Prior to selling the old property, the taxpayer signs a forward exchange agreement with a qualified intermediary.

6. When a contract to sell the old property has been executed, the taxpayer's rights under that contract are assigned to the qualified intermediary pursuant to the ordinary forward exchange rules. The buyer of the old property is given notice of this assignment. Most forward qualified intermediaries have forms for this.

7. When the sale of the old property closes, proceeds of sale are deposited with the forward qualified intermediary.

8. The taxpayer contacts the parking intermediary and advises that he or she is ready to acquire the new property from the parking intermediary to close out the taxpayer's exchange.

9. The taxpayer assigns his or her rights under contract with the parking intermediary (see number 4), to the forward intermediary. Because most reverse exchanges are closed out within 45 days of sale of the old property, a separate notice of identification need not be filed with the forward qualified intermediary, but the taxpayer must keep this 45-day identification requirement in mind.

10. The new property is conveyed to the taxpayer in exchange for the funds in the taxpayer's forward exchange account. The parking intermediary uses these funds to repay all or part of the loan that the parking intermediary received from the taxpayer or the bank to finance the acquisition.

11. The lease from the parking intermediary to the taxpayer is cancelled (because the taxpayer is now both the owner and the tenant of the property).

As you can see, a reverse exchange is significantly more complicated than a traditional 1031 exchange. Don't let that deter you from considering this type of exchange, however, because a good advisor or experienced qualified intermediary can guide you through the process. After all, that's what you pay them to do, and as mentioned earlier, the fees for a reverse exchange are higher because of its complexity.

The last reverse exchange in which I was involved went pretty smoothly. The client found a property in North Carolina that he wanted to buy, but needed (and wanted) to sell his California property as part of an exchange into the North Carolina property. I was asked to coordinate the reverse exchange process as well as to supervise the sale of the California property. We selected a North Carolina–based intermediary to establish a North Carolina limited liability company to act as the accommodation titleholder, and then completed the purchase of the North Carolina property within the newly formed LLC. The California property was then sold with the sale proceeds flowing to the LLC which then repaid the funds originally used for the North Carolina purchase and deeded the North Carolina property to the client.

This may sound too complicated, but it really is not. Just remember to hire good advisors and let them work out the details.

CHAPTER 9

Build-to-Suit Exchanges

"What is the difference between a taxidermist and a tax collector? The taxidermist takes only your skin."

Mark Twain

One of the more valuable techniques to use when doing an exchange is the build-to-suit exchange, also sometimes referred to as a construction or improvement exchange. In some cases, taxpayers want to do an exchange of their investment property, but anticipate having a tough time finding replacement property that fits their needs. The difficulty may be a tight market or a special need for a particular type of property or one located in a specific location. In such a case, a build-to-suit exchange gives you the ability to use all or part of your exchange funds for construction of the replacement property and still accomplish a tax-deferred exchange. The rules and tax treatment that apply to more traditional exchanges will generally apply to build-to-suit exchanges. In addition, build-to-suit exchanges present their own set of unique problems that can significantly complicate planning an exchange.

There are three basic types of build-to-suit exchanges: the traditional delayed (forward) exchange, the reverse exchange, and the structured leasehold build-to-suit exchange. The most common of these are the forward and reverse build-to-suit exchanges. The majority of this chapter will focus on these two types. The third, more cutting-edge variation is the leasehold build-to-suit exchange that is designed to allow you to build or make improvements to land you already own or control. This is cutting edge because in 1951 a landmark case, *Bloomington Coca-Cola v. Commissioner,* solidly disallowed an exchange scheme where the taxpayer was trying to use exchange funds for improvements on land it already owned. Nevertheless, there are two recent IRS private letter rulings (PLR 2002-51008 and PLR 2003-29021) that have been published in which the IRS has allowed the use of exchange funds from the sale of one property to build improvements on a piece of land the taxpayer already owned. Many in the 1031 exchange industry were surprised by these private letter rulings because they represent a significant change in the IRS's position on this issue. This variation of build-to-suit exchanges is very sophisticated and considered fairly aggressive. If this type of build-to-suit exchange fits your needs, be sure to get ample guidance from well-qualified legal counsel.

The two more common build-to-suit exchange types are basically variations of the delayed or reverse exchange allowing the taxpayer the ability to renovate an existing improved property or construct new improvements on raw land. The improvements made in a build-to-suit exchange can range from simple repairs or remodeling to the construction of a whole new facility from the ground up.

How a Built-to-Suit Exchange Works

Most traditional (forward) build-to-suit exchange situations would go something like this:

1. You sell the relinquished property in a delayed exchange.
2. The sale proceeds from the relinquished property go to a qualified intermediary.

3. You identify the replacement property and the improvements to be made within the required 45-day period.
4. You enter into a contract to purchase the replacement property.
5. You assign the contract to your qualified intermediary.
6. Your qualified intermediary forms a holding entity (usually an LLC) to act as the exchange accommodation titleholder.
7. You, your qualified intermediary, and the newly formed EAT execute a qualified exchange accommodation agreement allowing the EAT to take title to the replacement property and to contract for the improvements.
8. If there is financing, the EAT signs the note or mortgage.
9. At closing of the replacement property, the qualified intermediary disburses the necessary funds to the closing agent and the EAT takes title to the property.
10. Your previously arranged construction contract is assigned to the EAT with the EAT executing a project management agreement (PMA) allowing you to coordinate and supervise the construction effort.
11. When construction is complete or at the 180-day mark (whichever is first), the EAT transfers the improved replacement property to you thereby completing the exchange.

It is important that any improvements be made prior to you taking title of the replacement property. Any improvements made after title has passed to you from the EAT are considered to be "goods and services" and are not like-kind property for exchange purposes. That does not mean the construction has to be completed by the 180th day. But only that portion of the construction completed and paid for during the 180-day period will qualify for 1031 exchange treatment. Money paid to a contractor during the 180-day period to perform future work after the 180-day period does not qualify under the rules. However, payments made after the 180-day period for work done within that time may qualify. The basic rule is that you can take title to the replacement property at the 180-day point and continue the construction improvement process, but you will only be able to defer taxes on that portion accomplished during the exchange period. This may not create any real problem depending on the amount the exchanger is trying to defer in relation to the whole project.

☛ **Example:** Paul sold an apartment building for $800,000 and did a traditional exchange. His adjusted basis on the relinquished property was $200,000. He properly identified and bought a piece of commercially zoned land following the build-to-suit process previously listed. The purchase price of the raw land was $500,000. Paul is building a small shopping center and the total cost of construction is projected to be $600,000. The construction has been progressing and is about half completed. The 180-day period has arrived and Paul intends to take title to the property now.

In the above example, there would be no problem because Paul's build-to-suit exchange has progressed far enough to defer taxes on the amount of exchange funds received from the sale of the relinquished property. Paul will need to document (and preferably pay for) the $300,000 of work completed. Those improvements, along with the $500,000 purchase price of the land, will be sufficient to fully defer the sale of the $800,000 apartment building as long as all the other qualifying exchange guidelines have been followed. Paul would take title to the replacement property at the 180-day mark and go on to finish the construction. Improvements made after Paul takes title will be treated like any other capital improvements to an investment property; they will be added to the adjusted basis of the investment.

Built-to-suit exchanges are not without their fair share of potential problems and issues. The first and most obvious potential problem is the strict timelines.

Strict Timelines

As said in the beginning of this chapter, all the rules and tax treatments that apply to more traditional exchanges will generally apply to build-to-suit exchanges. So, the replacement property must be properly identified within 45 days. This is usually not a problem in build-to-suit exchanges because the exchanger usually knows which property will be the replacement property before starting the process. The 180-day rule, however, causes a lot of anxiety. Even a well-planned construction project can have problems that cause unforeseen delays—anything from inclement weather to material shortages and last minute design changes. Also, if building plans have not been submitted and approved prior to the closing on the relinquished property, there is a whole additional set of zoning and city planning issues that can easily absorb 180 days.

In the case of a reverse build-to-suit exchange, the requirements are reversed. The exchanger must identify the *relinquished* property within 45 days of the EAT acquiring title to the replacement property. This seems odd even by IRS standards. However, perhaps the reasoning here is to get the exchanger to commit to which property(s) will be relinquished.

Financing Issues

The structure of this type of exchange requires the EAT to hold title of the property during the construction or improvement process. With this in mind, traditional financing becomes difficult. As said earlier, title is usually vested in a newly formed LLC specifically created to temporarily hold title and then to be dissolved. This concept is not easy for many lenders to grasp. As such, financing should be worked out ahead of time. There are specialized lenders who handle these types of arrangements, but, as would be expected, there is usually a higher cost and interest rate.

Insurance Issues

One of the general rules of insurance is that a person cannot insure the property of another. If you think about it for a moment, the rule makes good sense. Now, applying that rule to a situation where you are trying to insure a property titled to an EAT holding entity, and you may start to see the possible difficulties here. Hazard and commercial general liability insurance is going to be required, but may not be easily purchased from your local insurance agent. On this issue, you may want to ask for advice from your qualified intermediary who has handled the insurance needs on built-to-suit exchanges he or she has done in the past.

Summary

Build-to-suit exchanges are fairly complicated, come with some unique risks, and have some downside aspects. Nevertheless, in the right situation, this type of exchange can be the perfect tool for deferring taxes while acquiring a hard-to-find or special-needs-type property. As I write this today, my area of Southern California is experiencing the highest investment property market ever. As strange as it sounds, right now in this area of the country, it might actually be less expensive to build a new small apartment building than it is to purchase an existing one.

Given the right circumstances, the build-to-suit exchange is a perfect solution for some real estate investors. Even if you think you have no use for build-to-suit exchanges now, understanding how they work will open up more potential opportunities when contemplating 1031 exchanges in the future.

CHAPTER 10

Tenant-in-Common Exchanges

"The reward of energy, enterprise, and thrift is taxes."

William Feather

Introduction to Triple Net or TIC Offerings

Since the beginning of like-kind exchanges, some investors have looked for a way to exchange into properties that involve little or no management activity on their part. The perfect solution was to buy a replacement property that was occupied by a long-term "triple net" tenant. The term *triple net* basically means that the tenants are responsible for all the expenses (including insurance and taxes), as well as doing all the repairs on the property. This may seem strange to you if you own residential property, but it is common in commercial landlord-tenant situations (large retail or restaurant tenants in a mall would be a good example). Obviously, whenever possible, triple net leases would be the preferred landlord-tenant arrangement. Unfortunately, triple net situations are generally only workable in fairly large proper-

109

ties that are usually too expensive for most individual investors. Enter the concept of fractional ownership.

At one time, there were a lot of promoters suggesting that a taxpayer could sell a relinquished property and exchange into an interest in a real estate investment trust (REIT) or a partnership specifically designed to own and operate real estate. At the time, these promoters argued that, regardless of the entity type, the taxpayer was exchanging from one real estate investment to another real estate investment and therefore it was an exchange of like-kind property. The IRS did not agree. At this case, it is clear that the IRS's position is that an exchange of real estate for an interest in a REIT or a real estate partnership does *not* qualify as an exchange of like-kind property. However, that is not the end of the line.

As alternatives to the REIT or real estate partnership structure, some promoters started packaging their triple net properties into smaller "undivided fractional interests" and selling those interests as replacement property in 1031 exchanges. These undivided fractional interests are commonly marketed as tenant-in-common (TIC) or triple net (NNN) interests. Generally, the tenant-in-common offerings are made on properties that are already occupied by long-term triple net corporate or government tenants. Occasionally, however, there are offerings on newly built or planned developments.

☛ **Example:** Carla has owned an eight-unit apartment building for about 25 years. She has managed the property herself during that time and does not like the idea of having a management company manage it for her. She does however want to retire and spend more time traveling. The building has a small mortgage and is almost fully depreciated. Carla knows if she sells the building outright she will have to pay capital gains tax as well as tax on the recapture of the depreciation she has taken over the years. Carla's main goal is to have a dependable stream of income without any management headaches to keep her from traveling. Carla has done her homework and has decided to do a 1031 exchange into a fractional ownership of large tenant-in-common commercial property. By doing so, she is able to defer her taxes and create steady stream of income for her retirement.

As indicated in the example above, the way these tenant-in-common offerings work is that the exchanger buys into a fractional portion of the property and becomes one of a group of owners. The appeal is that the real estate investor can achieve the desired workload reduction and eliminate management headaches by becoming a co-owner of a large property, which is then professionally operated by a management firm (usually owned by the promoter). By doing this type of exchange, the taxpayer ends up with a more equity-like stream of income based on the scheduled performance of the rental activities of the larger investment property.

Many landlords approaching retirement find this concept very appealing and there is no shortage of companies offering these arrangements. Traditionally, however, the problem has been that these offerings sound a lot like prohibited REIT or real estate partnership interests so they tend to make advisors leery. Adding to the problem, the IRS had resisted providing any supporting documentation or guidance as to whether these undivided fractional interests will qualify as like-kind property under the provisions of IRC §1031.

Revenue Procedure 2002-22

Some of the anxiety surrounding tenant-in-common offerings was relieved in October of 2002 when the IRS released Revenue Procedure 2002-22 which contained information related to tenant-in-common interests. A text of Revenue Procedure 2002-22 has been provided in Appendix C. This revenue procedure does not provide a simple yes or no answer on whether tenant-in-common arrangements qualify as like-kind property. Instead, it contains guidelines that must be met before the IRS will provide an advance ruling on particular tenant-in-common structure. Nevertheless, Revenue Procedure 2002-22 has been quietly celebrated as an implicit approval of the prepackaged tenant-in-common programs.

Here is a summary if the 15 conditions set out in Revenue Procedure 2002-22 that must be satisfied before the IRS will provide an advance ruling:

1. *Tenancy in common ownership.* Each of the co-owners must hold title to the property (either directly or through a disregarded entity) as a tenant in common under local law.
2. *Number of co-owners.* The number of co-owners must be limited to no more than 35 persons.
3. *No treatment of co-ownership as an entity.* The co-ownership may not file a partnership or corporate tax return nor hold itself out as a form of business entity.
4. *Co-ownership agreement.* The co-owners may enter into a limited co-ownership agreement that may run with the land.
5. *Voting.* The co-owners must retain the right to approve the hiring of any manager, the sale or other disposition of the property, any leases of a portion or all of the property, or the creation or modification of a blanket lien.
6. *Restrictions on alienation.* In general, each co-owner must have the rights to transfer, partition, and encumber the co-owner's undivided interest in the property without the agreement or approval of any person.
7. *Sharing proceeds and liabilities upon sale of property.* If the property is sold, any debt secured by a blanket lien must be satisfied and the remaining sales proceeds must be distributed to the co-owners.
8. *Proportionate sharing of profits and losses.* Each co-owner must share in all revenues generated by the property and all costs associated with the property in proportion to the co-owner's undivided interest in the property.

9. *Proportionate sharing of debt.* The co-owners must share in any indebtedness secured by a blanket lien in proportion to their undivided interests.

10. *Options.* A co-owner may issue an option to purchase the co-owner's undivided interest.

11. *No business activities.* The co-owners' activities must be limited to those customarily performed in connection with the maintenance and repair of rental real property (customary activities).

12. *Management and brokerage agreements.* The co-owners may enter into management agreements.

13. *Leasing agreements.* All leasing arrangements must be bona fide leases for federal tax purposes. Rents paid by a lessee must reflect the fair market value for the use of the property.

14. *Loan agreements.* The lender on the property may not be a related person to any co-owner, the sponsor, the manager, or any lessee of the property.

15. *Payments to sponsor.* Payment to the sponsor for the acquisition costs must be those ordinary and customary for an acquired co-ownership interest.

The IRS has been very clear that meeting the 15 conditions above does not approve the tenant-in-common structure, but rather qualifies it for an advance ruling on whether the structure will be approved. Nevertheless, the obvious *implication* is that structures meeting these guidelines will be okay.

This revenue procedure is expected to give rise to a whole new approach to marketing tenant-in-common structures as having a "favorable advance ruling" or being "Revenue Procedure 2002-22 compliant." Although the new revenue procedure doesn't go as far as creating a true safe harbor, it does reduce the anxiety that existed from the complete lack of guidance that existed before it. The new guidelines are considered strong support that tenant-in-common arrangements are a valid approach for clients seeking to exchange their current property into a more management-free position that provides a steady stream of income.

How TIC Property Investments Are Structured

Conceptually, the way TIC property offerings work is fairly easy to understand. The sponsor acquires a large property, puts together the best possible long-term triple net lease arrangement, divides the property into smaller fractional interests (undivided fractional interests or UFIs), and then sells the UFIs. The exact structure, risk, and return on each of the TIC offerings vary depending on how well the sponsor does his or her job. Ideally, the sponsor is able to put together a package that contains a long-term lease with built-in rate increases which will cover the expenses of operating the property, service the mortgage debt, and pay the investors a more predictable return.

Most TIC offerings provide the investor an increasing stream of income based on projected or scheduled tenant lease payment increases.

How a 1031-to-TIC Exchange Works

The process is basically the same as the traditional 1031 exchange:

1. You list your property for sale with your chosen real estate agent making sure he or she understands that you intend to do a 1031 exchange for another property.
2. When you get an offer, your agent will include a counteroffer provision that states the "buyer agrees to cooperate with seller's 1031 exchange."

3. You open escrow, and then choose your accommodator (your real estate agent or escrow/title agent can give you names of companies in your area).

4. You sign an exchange agreement with your accommodator through escrow along with the other customary escrow paperwork.

5. On the close of escrow, your proceeds will be transferred to your accommodator's trust fund on your behalf and held there until you begin the process of buying your replacement property.

After selling your relinquished property and documenting the exchange process with your chosen accommodator you would complete the following steps:

1. You identify three potential tenant-in-common replacement properties within the 45-day identification period. You choose three in case the first one you have in mind doesn't work out for whatever reason. (More on this in the next section.)

2. You execute the TIC intent to purchase agreement and do your due diligence investigation of the offering.

3. Once you are satisfied with your investigation of the sponsor and the offering, you instruct your accommodator to complete the transaction.

4. Your accommodator transfers your exchange funds to the sponsor in exchange for the deed to your TIC replacement property.

Selecting the Right Tenant-in-Common Property

There is no shortage of sponsors or TIC offerings across the country. Remember, you won't be a *managing* owner any more, so as long as it is a solid property, it shouldn't matter where it is located.

In fact, you will find that properties offered will be located all over the country.

The standard operating procedure is that sponsors will have their own in-house sales representatives with whom they would prefer you work. That's both good and bad. The good part is that in-house sales reps are usually (but not always) very knowledgeable about the properties being offered by that particular sponsor. The bad part is you will only have that one sponsor's packaged properties from which to choose. You do, however, have another choice.

In the TIC exchange industry, there are TIC sponsors and then there are TIC advisors/brokers. Sponsors put together properties and then must sell their offerings to the public. The advisors/brokers, on the other hand, make it their job to compare and know which sponsors are the most reputable and which property offerings represent the best investment choices. Obviously, common sense should tell you to work with an advisor/broker rather than being locked in with any one specific TIC sponsor. The best part is you pay nothing for the services of your advisor/broker. All the reputable TIC sponsors offer compensation to outside advisors/brokers. No, it doesn't raise your cost of buying into the property. The cost of compensating outside advisor/ brokers is built into the overall project at the planning stage. Now, with that said, you are going to hear arguments from sponsors or in-house salespeople about them not cooperating with outside advisors/ brokers because they want to "keep the costs down," or because it's a "private" offering, or some other nonsense. Presumably, the sponsor's salespeople get paid a commission, so it's not going to change the costs involved. Likewise, a reputable sponsor is always looking for more investors so why would they keep the offerings "private." Besides, how "private" can the offering be if they are trying to sell it to you or me? The bottom line usually is that sponsors who won't cooperate with outside advisors/brokers know that their offering won't measure up when compared to other offerings in the market. My suggestion is, if a particular TIC sponsor discourages you from having your own advisor, walk away from that sponsor.

You can find TIC advisors/brokers on the Internet by simply doing a search for "tenant-in-common advisor." However, the TIC advisor/broker I recommend to clients is Ed Dowd. Ed Dowd is not the "Wall Street suspenders and Gucci shoes" type. He's the "25 years in the business and usually knows what he's talking about" type. Ed's contact information is listed in the Recommended Advisors section at the back of this book.

CHAPTER 11

Using Installment Sales

"The taxpayer is someone who works for the federal government but doesn't have to take a civil service examination."

Ronald Reagan

Introduction to Installment Sales

In its simplest definition, an installment sale is merely a situation where the seller of a property agrees to accept payments on the purchase of the property. Installment sales are sometimes the perfect way to sell real estate when the seller's goal is to defer the capital gains taxes and create a stream of income. Installment sales on real estate are a well recognized and commonly used tax deferral technique. The IRS allows the seller of an appreciated property to provide financing for the buyer and defer the payment of capital gains and recapture of depreciation until the future payments are actually received. The IRS defines an installment sale very broadly as the "sale of property where the seller receives at least one payment after the tax year of the sale." The buyer's obligation to make future payments is usually documented in a separate financing agreement. These financing agreements are commonly (and sometimes incorrectly) referred to as a mortgage, a debt contract, or simply a note. There are different types of financing agreements and different legal requirements on debts secured by property depending on where the property is located. For example, in California, "mortgages" are not commonly used; instead property financing is done through a note and deed of trust. Nevertheless, the common terminology in California is to call property financing a mortgage. Throughout the rest of the chapter we will be using the terms *mortgage* and *note* interchangeably.

How Installment Sales Work

The concept of an installment sale is fairly simple. The seller of a property offers to provide the financing for the buyer by agreeing to accept a series of scheduled payments. This is sometimes referred to as a *seller carry-back,* an *owner will carry* situation, or just plain *seller financing.* In most situations, the market will react favorably to seller financing because many of the traditional buyer costs of getting a commercial loan (appraisal fees, processing fees, points, etc.) are avoided. There is little difference in the sale process except in the negotiating. In addition to negotiating the ultimate sales price, the buyer and seller have to also agree to terms and conditions of the financing. Once the price and financing terms are agreed, the transaction proceeds like any other. Depending on your area of the country, you will have either an escrow company or closing agent facilitate the transaction and draft the note for you according to the purchase agreement. Some people prefer to have an experienced attorney draft the financing agreement (the note) to make sure it is drafted correctly and that it provides the seller any advantages available under lending laws. Even if the note is simple and is drafted by the escrow or closing agent, it is probably a good idea to have a real estate attorney review it before the transaction closes.

Advantages of Installment Sales

Like every other method of deferring capital gains, installment sales have their advantages and disadvantages. One of the big advantages of installment sales and perhaps the main reason they are so widely used is because they are easily understood. You don't have to be an attorney or an accountant to understand the pros and cons of an installment sale. You should have a discussion with your tax advisor about exactly how a proposed installment sale will impact you on an accounting level, but the concept itself is not a difficult one. Let's take a look at some of the main advantages and then explore the disadvantages.

Tax Deferral

The main advantage, of course, is the ability to defer capital gains and recapture of depreciation (straight line) for a period of time. How long you can defer the capital gains tax is basically up to your own creativity. The capital gains tax will only be due on that portion of the payments received that represent repayment of principal on the note. An "interest only" note for ten years could effectively defer all capital gains taxes (on the note portion of the sale) for a full ten years. Taken to an extreme, a 30-year carry back that is set for interest-only payments would mean 30 years of tax deferral.

Stream of Income

Many times the monthly payments from a note on the sale of a property will actually be higher than the net profit of operating the property. Obviously, the less productive the property (vacant land for example) the more attractive the idea of trading it for a stream of income from a mortgage note becomes. Installment sales on real estate have become widely used as a hedge against the ups and downs of

1.1 Differed Investment versus After-Tax Investment

	After Tax	Installment Sale
Sale Amount	$1,000,000	$1,000,000
Adjusted Basis	200,000	200,000
Capital Gain	800,000	800,000
Net Proceeds	1,000,000	1,000,000
Taxes (state and federal, plus recapture)	250,000	0
Amount Invested	750,000	1,000,000
Yearly Income at 7%	52,500	70,000
Net Yearly Advantage	0	$17,500

other investments, like stocks and mutual funds. The ability to control the interest and, to some extent, the amount of risk is appealing to persons looking for a long-term stream of income.

Investment Leverage

The rate of return on an installment sale note is hard to beat when you consider the leverage provided by the capital gains portion of the note. In the simplest terms, a capital gains tax-deferred dollar earns approximately 20 to 30 percent more interest than the after-tax dollar. Why? On tax-deferred dollars you earn interest on both your dollars and the dollars that would have gone to the government for taxes. The following table in Figure 11.1 shows the difference in deferred proceeds invested at 7 percent return and an after-tax investment at the same rate.

The above example is overly simple and excludes sale expenses, down payment considerations, and generalizes the tax impact. Nevertheless, it makes the point that installment sales include a deferred capital gain component and will, therefore, always offer an enhanced return on investment.

Marketability and Desirability of the Property

In the open real estate market, seller financing is almost always preferred by buyers. Lower costs and less administrative hassle are among the main reasons. The fact is that most commercial mortgages have a processing time of 45 to 90 days and the costs include things like appraisal fees, processing fees, and, most important, discount points. A discount point is 1 percent of the loan amount. On a $200,000 loan with 1.5 points, the fee to the buyer for points alone is $3,000. When you add together all the lender fees, loan related title insurance fees, and processing fees, the cost of borrowing $200,000 can easily reach $4,000 to $8,000. In most cases, seller financing eliminates all of these buyer fees and expenses so it's no wonder buyers prefer properties where the seller will carry.

Another situation that favors seller financing is properties that have limited commercial financing available. For example, commercial financing is hard to find on mixed-use and nonconforming properties. Vacant land can also sometimes pose a problem because many banks will not make loans of more than 50 percent of the value of the land. In both of these cases, seller financing greatly enhances the marketability of the property and may offer the only realistic way of getting the property sold.

Disadvantages of Installment Sales

Installment sales are not for everyone. Likewise, some property types and/or proposed property uses are not appropriate because the financing risks are simply too high. Taking the time to thoroughly think through the risks and how they would affect you in a worst-case scenario is always important.

Installment sales have one very large advantage over other types of investing; the note is secured by the underlying real estate. With that in mind, it is easy for some to shrug off the potential risks by thinking, "I'll just take the property back if they don't make the payments, right?" Yes . . . and no. The idea of being able to take the property back if the borrower defaults is correct. That is why the note is secured by the property. However, along with the risk of default there are other concerns. In the following sections we are going to look at some of the more common risk considerations associated with seller carry-back and retaking the property in the case of a default.

Risk of Foreclosure

The mortgage lender on a property has the right to the underlying property in case of a default. Unfortunately, it is not as easy as it sounds. There are laws that specifically control lending practices and especially foreclosure practices. If a borrower stops making payment, the lender must follow the state-required legal formalities of filing notice, service of process, and publication. The rules themselves vary greatly by state and are beyond the scope of this book. Most banks and commercial lending institutions have full departments that deal with the day-to-day issues of handling their foreclosures. Even the smaller lending institutions will have legal counsel on staff or on retainer to foreclose on properties if borrowers default. Unfortunately, the concept of foreclosing on a property or even getting involved in this type of legal process intimidates many property sellers and causes many to shy away from offering seller financing no matter how attractive the tax benefits. However, the reality is that the foreclosure process is streamlined in most states and there are mortgage and trust deed service companies that specialize in providing this service. Today, the process of foreclosing on a property is relatively quick and inexpensive. Of course, there are the "nightmare" situations where a borrower mounts an extensive legal battle, but those are rare. In the vast majority of cases, the property is back in the hands of the seller/lender in four to five months.

Risk of Early Pay-off

Some people might consider a borrower paying off a debt early a benefit not a risk. However, the motivation for a seller to offer seller financing is usually to defer taxes and to establish a fixed return on the invested funds. So, for the installment sale noteholder, early pay-off is undesirable. There is virtually no legal way to stop a person from paying off a mortgage early, but there are ways to strongly discourage them. The most common way to discourage an early pay-off is to include a prepayment penalty in the note itself. Prepayment penalties are discussed in more detail below, but it is important to note that on certain types of residential properties there are restrictions on the amount of prepayment penalty that can be negotiated. On residential property, the legally allowable prepayment penalties are controlled by state law and in most states cannot exceed five years for the prepayment period and cannot exceed six months of interest as the penalty (check with your state's rules). While a prepayment penalty will discourage early pay-off it will not stop it in some situations. In some cases, the profit opportunity for the new owner to resell the property simply outweighs the penalty. Alternatively, in some cases, the need to refinance the property is more attractive than avoiding the penalty. In situations where an equity line or second mortgage is needed on the property, there may not be any alternative but to refinance and pay off the seller's carry-back. Commercial lending equity lines and/or second mortgages are generally not available "in back of" private mortgages. The term *in back of* refers to situations where the private note would have a creditor priority over the commercial lender's note. In situations where a property improvement loan is desired, the borrower may be forced to refinance the whole property. There is usually the option of the installment sale noteholder subordinating to the (presumably) smaller equity line or property improvement loan, but the risk factor of holding the note changes and needs to be reevaluated.

☞ **Example:** Mr. Jones sells a rental house to a young couple and carries back the whole mortgage to defer his capital gains tax on the sale. One year later, the couple goes to get a home equity loan and although they qualify for the equity line the bank will not make the loan because the existing first mortgage is private seller financing. The couple did not want to refinance the whole property and the seller did not want the note paid off early. In this situation, the seller/note holder was comfortable with the couple's ability to repay both notes so he agreed to subordinate to the equity loan. The money from the equity loan was specifically intended for improvements to the property and when the improvements were completed, both loans combined were less than 80 percent of the new (improved) market value of the property.

In the example above (an actual case), everyone came out happy—the couple was able to get the equity loan funds they wanted to remodel the house and there was no real loss of security for the private note holder because the funds were used to enhance the value of the private note holder's security. If the private note holder had not agreed to subordinate to the equity loan, the couple would have had no choice but to refinance the property and pay off the private note. By doing so, they would have triggered the capital gains tax for the note holder.

The best way to discourage an early pay-off of the note is to simply make sure the terms on the seller carry-back note are more attractive than other financing options available. Common sense should tell you that if the private note is at 8 percent interest and the current market rate is 6.5 percent, the private note holder should probably expect an early pay-off. If you don't want to be paid off, stay flexible and competitive with your interest rate.

Risk of Property Deterioration

Perhaps the highest risk in doing an installment sale is the possibility that the new owner will let the property fall into serious disrepair. In a situation where that happens, the risk of having to foreclose on the property increases *and* at the same time the value of the security itself declines. The thought of foreclosing on a property that needs tens of thousands of dollars in repairs is not very comforting. To try to avoid this situation, it is sometimes smart to make sure the person buying the property is capable of managing it. Sometimes it is smart to find out if the proposed borrower has other similar properties and take a drive by those other properties to see how well they are maintained. How a person maintains a property they already own is probably a really strong indication of how well they will maintain your property.

Some of the more sophisticated commercial lenders go as far as to contractually give themselves the right to inspect the property. They periodically do inspect and require repairs if there is any unreasonable deferred maintenance. If the borrower then fails to make the required repairs the acceleration clause of the note is triggered and the whole principal is due immediately. If the borrower then fails to pay off the note, it goes into default and the lender can foreclose immediately. In the alternative, the lender could bring legal action to compel the borrower to make repairs and to hold the borrower responsible for the legal fees.

Mortgage over Adjusted Basis Issues

When a potential installment sale seller has an existing mortgage on the property that is higher than the adjusted basis, a special IRS rule comes into play. The IRS will generally treat the excess of the mortgage over adjusted basis as 100 percent taxable when the seller is relieved of this debt in the year of sale. Under the IRS rules, the seller is usually relieved of this debt when the debt is repaid or when the debt is assumed or the property is taken "subject to" that existing mortgage. As a result, you can actually have capital gains tax liability in the year of sale even though you may not have received any cash. For example, assume that a taxpayer's basis is $175,000 and there is a loan against the property of $200,000 that the buyer is going to assume. The difference of $25,000 is going to be taxable to the seller in the year of sale.

Lack of Liquidity

Another consideration that is usually overlooked in agreeing to an installment sale is the lack of liquidity on the note. This is the flip side of the early-pay-off concern. In most situations, investors are usually trying to pin down the borrower to prevent an early pay-off of the note because it triggers liability for the deferred taxes. However, what if the seller-turned-note-holder encounters a situation where he or she needs to cash out? The note itself will, of course, lock the note holder into the time periods agreed to in the terms of the note. As such, if the note holder really does need to cash out, there are not a whole lot of attractive options.

There is a resale market for mortgage notes. The market itself has little or no formal structure; rather it is simply private parties who purchase private notes. Mortgage brokers in your area would likely be able to point you in the right direction, but you will probably not like what you find. The buying of private mortgage notes is usually considered a high-risk investment. The people who are willing to take that risk are going to want a significant discount from the face value of the note. There are a lot of variables taken into consideration when valuing a note for resale. However, a reasonably well-drafted and secured (second mortgage) note with a face value of $10,000, will usually only have a resale value of $5,000 to $8,000. Even a strong first mortgage with a good loan-to-value ratio and an excellent borrower is going to have to be discounted if sold.

In most cases, however, the lack of liquidity is not a significant factor because the long-term, locked-in investment is exactly what the investor wants.

Balancing the Risk

There are three things you should consider when trying to balance the risks with the benefits of installment sales:

1. Decide upon an acceptable loan-to-value ratio.
2. Determine how long you are willing to carry the note.
3. Structure the terms and conditions of the note so that the foreseeable risks will be addressed.

Deciding on an Acceptable Loan-to-Value Ratio

As mentioned earlier, a loan-to-value ratio is the amount of financing in relation to the market value of the property. An $80,000 note on a $100,000 property is an 80 percent loan-to-value ratio. If you were going to carry back $10,000 and the buyer was going to get an $80,000 bank loan, the *total* loan-to-value ratio would be 90 percent. The loan-to-value ratio is important because it is traditionally the first risk criterion considered by commercial lending institutions. From a lender's perspective, with all other things being equal, an 80 percent loan-to-value ratio mortgage is less risky than one with a 90 percent loan-to-value. Likewise, a 70 percent loan-to-value is better than 80 percent, and so on. Lenders traditionally have what they consider a "preferred" loan-to-value ratio. The next loan-to-value consideration is that of property type. Risks of mortgage default differ by property type, so the customary practice in commercial lending is to assign varying loan-to-value requirements for each property type. A commercial strip center would have a significantly different preferred loan-to-value ratio than a residential duplex and different still from a 20-unit apartment building. Finding out the preferred loan-to-value ratio for your property type in your particular area is pretty simple; just ask a local lender or perhaps your real estate agent.

The lending industry's preferred loan-to-value ratio on your property might be a good indicator of the acceptable risk to a commercial lender, but you are not a commercial lender. Commercial lenders are traditionally much more conservative than sellers offering financing. After all, banks really don't know much about a given property before they make a loan. Sure, they do an appraisal, but they are not in the property business, they are in the money business. The last thing a bank wants is to have to foreclose on a property. On the other hand, a seller who is offering financing on their property does know the property and whether it is a solid basis for security on the note. Sellers carrying notes on their properties generally do not want to foreclose on them either, but are usually not as afraid of that risk as a bank. The other main difference between a commercial lender and a seller offering financing is that a seller is motivated by tax deferral. The interest earned on the tax-deferred portion of the principal greatly enhances the overall return on the mortgage investment. Many banks do offer loans in higher-than-customary loan-to-value ratios if they are able to get better-than-usual return on the investment.

How much down payment you should require is up to your own personal comfort level with the security and the person buying the property. Simply put, a higher down payment (lower loan-to-value ratio) is better for security, but a lower down payment (higher loan-to-value ratio) is better for tax deferment and investment return.

Determining How Long to Carry the Note

How long to carry a note is also a matter of comfort level. Many of the sellers offering seller financing are older so they tend to think they may not be around to continue collecting on a note 20 or 30 years into the future. Even if that were the case, the note would pass to their heirs just as any other asset would. Nevertheless, most seller financing is set for less than the commercial lending standard of 30 years. Common terms are "30-due-in-5," "30-due-in-7," or "30-due-in-10." The "30" represents the amortization schedule followed and the "due-in- . . . " represents the number of years until the loan becomes due and payable. The example previously given, a 30-due-in-5, means that the borrower's monthly payment amount is based on the 30-year amortization schedule with a balloon payment due to pay off the loan in five years.

Why use a 30-year amortization schedule? First, from the buyer's perspective, business and profit planning on income property is usually based on 30-year amortized monthly mortgage payments. Using a shorter amortization period will usually make a property less profitable from an operating perspective and therefore less appealing. Second, from the seller's perspective, the monthly payment (in the beginning years) using 30-year amortization schedule is almost all interest. As such, the seller/noteholder gets to maximize the capital gains tax deferral and the interest earned on the deferred portion.

The real question is how long should the note run before full payment is due. I have seen seller notes as short as 90 days and notes set for a full 30-year payment period with interest-only payments. In the case of the interest-only note, there are no capital gains taxes until the principal is paid. The payment period is up to you but remember, as long as you are comfortable with the property as security for your note, there are very few investments that will perform as well as a mortgage note made from tax-deferred capital gains.

Drafting the Note to Protect You

How the note is drafted is very important in the overall security and performance of the mortgage note. It is crucial that the seller has control over the note drafting and uses that control to incorporate well-thought-through terms and provisions. In this area, it may be smart to hire an attorney specifically experienced in real estate note drafting. Real estate agents and escrow personnel can draft a note for you, but it will be a neutral third-party generic document with basic provisions only. If you are going to offer the financing, you are in the driver's seat; why not have your note drafted to afford you a favorable position if things get difficult in the future. The following are some of the less obvious drafting provisions that should be considered:

- *Late fees.* State when a payment is late and what the penalty will be.
- *Attorney's fees.* If a dispute arises, the prevailing party should be entitled to reimbursement of attorney's fee.

- *Due-on-sale clause.* There should almost always be a provision that the note becomes due if the property is resold.
- *Due-on-transfer clause.* Some people have gotten around a due-on-sale clause in notes by simply not "selling" the property, but rather simply transferring it. A due-on-transfer clause acts to prohibit potentially undesirable transfers.
- *Due-on-(further)-encumbrance clause.* This provision would require the repayment of your note should the borrower further encumber the property lessening your security. An alternative that accomplishes a similar objective would be a maximum loan-to-value ratio clause.
- *Tax service.* This is a service paid for by the borrower that notifies the lender if the borrower fails to keep the property taxes current.
- *Insurance requirements.* You should require a borrower to maintain a minimum amount of property insurance and name you as a payee under the policy.
- *Assignment of rent provisions.* If the property is a rental property, an assignment of rents allows the lender to collect rents if the note goes into default.
- *Inspection and maintenance provisions.* This provision allows you to require reasonable maintenance of the property and gives you the right to inspect.
- *Prepayment penalties.* In most states, law sets the maximum allowable prepayment penalties on certain types of properties. If you want to include a prepayment penalty, you need to make sure you conform to what is allowed.
- *Assumption clause.* Are you willing to allow the note to be assumed by a subsequent buyer? If so, under what conditions and terms?

This list is not by any means complete, but it does show that there are potentially many provisions that should be considered beyond the basic interest rate and time period. Not all of the provisions listed above need to be in every note, but the better you protect yourself up front, the more likely your seller-financing experience will go smoothly.

Structuring the Deal

The transactional mechanics are pretty straightforward. The more important area of focus should be deciding on the rate and terms.

Higher Down Payment or Lower Taxes

Common sense says that a seller or any other lender offering financing would want the best security for the loan. From a commercial lender's perspective, "best security" means getting the highest down payment possible and providing financing at a low loan-to-value ratio. However, in seller financing, as mentioned earlier, there is the competing goal of deferring the taxes. A high down payment does provide a better security position but the down payment is taxed immediately because it is a payment received. The other extreme would be for the seller to offer 100 percent financing and thereby defer 100 percent of the taxes until the payments are received. However, in most situations there will be expenses of selling the property like real estate commissions, title insurance, repairs, property tax proration, and escrow fees that must be paid.

If you are more interested in security than you are in deferring the taxes then you may want to require the same amount of down payments that banks find commercially acceptable: 10 to 20 percent down on one to four residential units where the buyer will be occupying the property, 25 to 30 percent down on residential apartment buildings, and 30 to 40 percent down on business commercial property.

On the other hand, if you are more interested in deferring the taxes and are reasonably comfortable with the buyer and property, then you would want to minimize the down payment. In a normal and customary sale of a property, you can expect the selling expenses to be approximately 7 percent to 7.5 percent (based on 6 percent sales commission, title, and escrow fees). So you would need to get at least that amount as a down payment just to cover the expenses of the sale. However, keep in mind that there will be taxes due on the payment received for the down payment just like there will be on all the other payments received over time. That means you will need to require a down payment of sufficient size to cover the costs of selling the property as well as the taxes that will become due on the down payment itself.

Interest Rate Considerations

Obviously, everyone wants to maximize their own investment returns, but this is one area where more (interest) may actually cost you money. If you are doing an installment sale to defer taxes and create a stream of income, then you want to create a situation where the buyer will not want to refinance or prepay the loan. This comes down to simple economics; if the interest rate you charge is higher than what is available from commercial lenders, the buyer will eventually refinance. There is a direct relationship here; the higher your rate, the sooner the buyer will refinance. With this in mind, seller financing is usually offered at an interest rate slightly better than prevailing commercial rates. How much better? Generally speaking, it is smart to set the rate at one-quarter to three-quarters of 1 percent less than the prevailing rate for the same type of property. It is important to remember that interest rates vary depending on the property type and occupancy status. Residential property having one to four units, houses, condos, duplexes, triplexes, etc., usually fall into the standard or "conforming" mortgage rates. Conforming mortgage rates are what most people think of as regular mortgage rates. However, the mortgage rates on residential income properties are almost always higher and commercial properties higher still.

What interest rate you should charge will require a little homework on your part. Probably the easiest way to find out what is reasonable is to simply call a lender in your area and ask what rates would be available to you if you were to refinance the property yourself. If you are willing to accept a reasonable rate in the financing, you will create a win-win situation and you will probably not have to worry about your taxes being triggered by the buyer refinancing and paying off your loan early.

Assumption, Acceleration, and Due-on-Transfer Clauses

A seller considering an installment sale has to think, act, and protect himself or herself just like a commercial bank or other lending institution. That means you need to be comfortable with the property as an underlying security for the loan, be comfortable with the borrower's ability to repay the loan, and contractually protect yourself from potential future problems. How a mortgage note is drafted is very important. If you have never done it before, get professional help. If you are selling your property through a real estate agent, there probably will be an "arranger of financing" disclosure form you or your agent will need to provide to the buyer/borrower. The form discusses many of the issues that arise and provides valuable guidance on the types of issues that should be addressed in the mortgage note itself.

One consideration that must be addressed in negotiating the financing contract is what happens if the property is subsequently sold or transferred. The commercial bank approach is to include a provision in each mortgage note that accelerates the due date if the property is subsequently sold or transferred. These contractual clauses are called "due on sale," "due on transfer," or "acceleration provisions." Whatever the provision is called, the purpose is to provide a contractual requirement that the outstanding balance of the note be paid off if the property is sold or transferred. The reasoning for this is that lenders do not want the loans freely assumable by just anyone. When the loan was originally made, the lender checked out the buyer's credit history and ability to repay the loan. Presumably, the lender made the loan, in part, because it was comfortable with that particular borrower's ability to repay. However, if mortgages were freely assumable, the person assuming the note at a later time might not be as creditworthy as the original buyer/borrower. In commercial lending, this contractual provision usually works well. However, in seller financing there is the additional consideration of wanting to continue capital gains tax deferral. If the mortgage note contains a due-on-transfer provision and the property is subsequently sold, the note will be paid off and the liability for paying all the deferred capital gains taxes will be triggered. There is, however, a middle ground between leaving the note fully assumable and requiring the due-on-transfer provision.

Adding a qualified assumption provision to a seller-financed mortgage note is usually a good idea. After all, the goal for the seller/lender is to get a return from the investment, but also to continue the deferment of capital gains taxes. So, if the original buyer/borrower decides to sell the property and the next buyer/borrower is equally creditworthy, why not continue the loan and tax deferral? A qualified assumption should allow the buyer/borrower to offer the property for sale with "assumable financing," but still allow the seller full and sole discretion as to the acceptability and creditworthiness of the next potential buyer. Basically, the idea behind a qualified assumption clause is to indicate that the note holder would be willing to entertain assumption proposals, but is not obligated to allow the assumption. If the potential buyer is not acceptable or the note holder is not willing to allow the assumption, the new buyer would have to arrange other financing and the note would have to be paid off on sale or transfer as otherwise required in the due-on-transfer clause.

Prepayment Penalties

If a seller is trying to defer capital gains taxes by providing seller financing, then it stands to reason that the seller will not want the loan paid off early. Unfortunately, there are laws that prohibit the ability to contractually agree that the loan cannot be prepaid. Why? The laws were developed to help curtail unconscionable lending practices and unreasonable restraints on alienation. That's legalese which basically means you can't make a loan too one-sided and you can't make unreasonable restrictions that prevent a person from selling his/her property. The point is that there are laws that exist to control or limit what prepayment penalties are allowed. The extent of these laws and how they will affect you will depend on whether your property is categorized as consumer residential property or investment property.

Prepayment Penalties on Consumer Residential Properties

In determining allowable prepayment penalties, the first important factor is whether your note will be secured by residential property. Over the years, consumer protection statutes emerged to help curtail abusive lending tactics. Most of these laws are really targeted at predatory lenders who have a history of taking advantage of consumers. Nevertheless, these statutes do spill over to impact anyone offering financing on a property. These consumer protection statutes are in just about every state and directly restrict prepayment penalties on notes of residential property if all of the following are true:

1. The property is made up of one to four residential units. This would include all homes, condominiums, duplexes, triplexes, and quadruplexes.
2. The property will be owner occupied. *Owner occupied* means that the property is being used as the buyer/debtor's *primary residence.*
3. The note represents purchase money. The term *purchase money* simply means the note represented a portion of the total price paid for the property when originally purchased.

Generally, if all three of the above apply, there will likely be statutory legal restrictions on prepayment penalties. Each state has different laws. For example, at the time of this writing, California law limits prepayment penalties on residential, owner-occupied, purchase money notes to periods of not more that five years and limits the monetary penalty to an amount not more than six months interest on the amount of prepaid principal. California law also allows the borrower to prepay up to 20 percent of the outstanding balance of the note in any given year without *any* penalty.

There are mortgages in existence that have built-in prepayment penalties that exceed the penalty period or monetary penalties limited by state law. In some cases, the excessive prepayment penalties were simply drafting errors, but other times they look more intentional, perhaps as a bluff to discourage the uninformed debtor. Whatever the reason, an excessive prepayment penalty is unenforceable beyond what is allowed by the statute.

Prepayment Penalties on Investment and Commercial Properties

The consumer protection statutes described above are designed to do exactly that, protect *consumers*. Investors are usually considered more sophisticated and therefore do not need the type of protection afforded to the mom-and-pop consumer. As such, lending on investment property will not have the same statutory prepayment restrictions as residential, owner-occupied, purchase money loans. There are still going to be some legal restrictions on prepayment penalties, but there is a lot more freedom to make contractual agreements.

For our purposes here, the simplest definition of an investment property is any property that is not residential owner-occupied property. For example, you may carry the note on a single-family home, but as long as the buyer is not going to occupy it as a primary residence, it is considered investment property. Likewise, a *five*-unit residential property sold to someone who intends to live in it as his or her primary residence will still be considered investment property because it does not fit the *one- to four*-unit criterion.

When it comes to prepayment penalties, there is a significant advantage in seller financing of investment property. The amount and term of the prepayment penalty can be just about whatever you can negotiate. You may still face some legal restrictions, but what is legally acceptable will be much more helpful in deterring an early pay-off. In fact, one California court ruled that a 50 percent prepayment penalty was not unreasonable when the seller carrying the mortgage faced significant tax consequences if the note was paid off early. Again, each state is going to have a different view as to what is reasonable, so you need to check with a local real estate attorney. Amazingly, most real estate advisors mistakenly apply the consumer protection prepayment penalty rules to investment property situations. Make sure your advisor knows the difference.

Being able to negotiate a 10 to 15 percent prepayment penalty in a note can make a huge difference in the desirability of the installment sale option. How huge a difference? Let's take a look.

☛ **Example:** Paul sold a triplex to Mike, an investor who did not intend to occupy the property. The terms were that Mike would put down 20 percent and Paul would carry a note for the 80 percent balance for ten years at 8 percent with interest-only payments. The principal of the note was initially $200,000 and Paul had a 50 percent gross profit ratio (meaning 50 percent of the note's face value represented capital gain). Paul was only willing to sell the property if he could defer the taxes long term. Paul and Mike agreed to a 10 percent prepayment penalty if Mike paid off the note early.

In the example above, if Mike pays off the note within the first ten years, it would trigger Paul's capital gains taxes. With a 50 percent gross profit ratio on the note, Paul would be responsible for paying capital gains tax on $100,000. If we assume the combined state and federal taxes will be 20 percent, the tax would be $20,000. However, Paul and Mike agreed to a prepayment penalty of 10 percent, so if the note is paid early, Mike will have a penalty of $20,000 ($200,000 × 10 percent). In this case, the penalty was set to equal the amount of the taxes triggered. If Mike does pay off the note early, Paul will lose the income that would have come from the deferred capital gain, but is compensated by having the penalty amount available to pay his pre-maturely triggered taxes. In some situations, this may be a very agree-able win-win scenario for both seller and buyer. The buyer is not going to want to pay off the loan early unless some situation arises that makes it financially worthwhile; the seller may not want to lose his projected stream of income, but if he does, he is compensated for the taxes by the penalty.

Prepayment penalties may help discourage an early pay-off but it can never guarantee it. Depending on the situation, the sting of a pre-payment penalty can easily be outweighed by the economic benefit of selling or refinancing the property. As mentioned earlier, the best way to prevent the borrower from refinancing is to make sure the terms of your financing are equal to or better that those available in the open market.

How and When the Taxes Are Paid

Each year that you receive payments you report them on your tax returns. The payments are broken down into three components:

1. Interest income
2. Return of your adjusted basis on the property
3. Gain on the sale

The interest income is treated and reported as you would any other source of interest income. The return of your adjusted basis on the property is not taxed at all because it represents the return of your dollars invested in the property. And the gain on the sale is taxed at the capital gains and/or recapture of depreciation tax rate.

☛ **Example:** Chuck has a piece of vacant land he wants to sell. He originally paid $50,000 for it. Chuck sells the property for $200,000 with the buyer paying $75,000 down. Chuck carries back (finances) the remaining $125,000, amortized over 30 years with interest at 7 percent; monthly payments are $831.63. During the first year, the buyer makes 6 payments at the $831.63, in addition to $75,000 down. Chuck is able to defer some of the capital gains tax on the property, but will owe taxes on the payments received that year (including the down payment). Chuck will report the sale of the property on his 1040 for that taxable year along with any payments received on IRS Form 6252.

In the example above, the payments that Chuck received will be broken down into the three components by first calculating "gross profit percentage" and then figuring the interest paid. In this simple example the gross profit percentage is calculated as follows:

Sales Price:	$200,000
Cost:	–$ 50,000
Gross Profit:	$150,000

The gross profit percentage here equals $150,000 divided by $200,000, or 75 percent, which means that 75 percent of every dollar of *principal* is profit and will be taxed at the capital gains tax rate. That does *not* mean that 75 percent of every dollar of payments received, but rather 75 percent of that portion of the payments received that represent principal. Remember, a large portion of the monthly payments will be interest, not principal. The other 25 percent of every dollar of principal will be tax-free as it represents your return of dollars invested (cost). We get the third component, interest, by consulting a standard amortization table.

So in the first year, Chuck got $75,000 down plus $4,989.78 (6 payments of $831.63); $4,365.96 is interest; $623.82 is principal. In this case, the down payment plus 75 percent of the principal will be taxed as capital gain, 25 percent of the principal is a tax-free return of capital, and $4,365.96 is taxable interest income.

Now, let's complicate matters slightly with a more realistic situation—a 6 percent commission and $1,000 escrow fee is required. The gross profit ratio would look like this:

Contract Price:	$200,000
Cost:	-$ 50,000
Expenses:	-$ 13,000
Gross Profit:	$137,000

The gross profit ratio equals $137,000 divided by $200,000, or 68.5 percent (see Figure 11.2, line 19). The seller pays tax on 68.5 percent of every principal payment received, even though all of the costs of the sale are paid in the first year. In the first year, the seller reports $75,000 down plus $624 principal (Figure 11.2, line 22) with 68.5 percent of this total ($51,802) representing taxable installment sale income (Figure 11.2, line 26). Eventually, the seller will get the full $200,000 of principal (before payment of selling expenses of $13,000), of which $137,000 is taxable just as if he had made an outright sale.

It is possible that the tax due is more than the payments actually received by the seller in the year of the sale (as all payments go first to cover expenses of sale). If the property in the previous example had been mortgaged for $35,000 and had closing costs of $13,000 with the buyer paying $50,000 down, the seller would net $2,000 at close of escrow.

Down Payment:	$ 50,000
Mortgage Pay-off:	-$ 35,000
Commissions, etc.	-$ 13,000
Net to Seller	$ 2,000

Contract Price:	$200,000
Cost:	-$ 50,000
Expenses:	-$ 13,000
Gross Profit:	$137,000

FIGURE 11.2 Chuck's IRS Form 6252

Form **6252** Department of the Treasury Internal Revenue Service	**Installment Sale Income** ► Attach to your tax return. ► Use a separate form for each sale or other disposition of property on the installment method.	OMB No. 1545-0228 **200**_ **79**

Name(s) Shown on Return	Identifying Number
CHUCK	000-00-0000

1 Description of property ► INVESTMENT PROPERTY

2a Date acquired (month, day, year) ► 6/30/86   **b** Date sold (month, day, year) ► 6/30/0_

3 Was the property sold to a related party (see instructions) after May 14, 1980? If 'No,' skip line 4 .... ☐ Yes ☒ No

4 Was the property you sold to a related party a marketable security? If 'Yes,' complete Part III. If 'No,' complete Part III for the year of sale and the 2 years after the year of sale .... ☐ Yes ☐ No

Part I   **Gross Profit and Contract Price.** Complete this part for the year of sale only.

5	Selling price including mortgages and other debts. **Do not** include interest whether stated or unstated	**5**	200,000.
6	Mortgages, debts, and other liabilities the buyer assumed or took the property subject to (see instructions)	**6**	
7	Subtract line 6 from line 5	**7**	200,000.
8	Cost or other basis of property sold	**8**	50,000.
9	Depreciation allowed or allowable	**9**	
10	Adjusted basis. Subtract line 9 from line 8	**10**	50,000.
11	Commissions and other expenses of sale	**11**	13,000.
12	Income recapture from Form 4797, Part III (see instructions)	**12**	
13	Add lines 10, 11, and 12	**13**	63,000.
14	Subtract line 13 from line 5. If zero or less, **do not** complete the rest of this form (see instructions)	**14**	137,000.
15	If the property described in line 1 above was your main home, enter the amount of your excluded gain (see instructions). Otherwise, enter -0-	**15**	0.
16	**Gross profit.** Subtract line 15 from line 14	**16**	137,000.
17	Subtract line 13 from line 6. If zero or less, enter -0-	**17**	0.
18	**Contract price.** Add line 7 and line 17	**18**	200,000.

Part II   **Installment Sale Income.** Complete this part for the year of sale **and** any year you receive a payment or have certain debts you must treat as a payment on installment obligations.

19	Gross profit percentage. Divide line 16 by line 18. For years after the year of sale, see instructions	**19**	0.6850
20	If this is the year of sale, enter the amount from line 17. Otherwise, enter -0-	**20**	0.
21	Payments received during year (see instructions). **Do not** include interest, whether stated or unstated	**21**	75,624.
22	Add lines 20 and 21	**22**	75,624.
23	Payments received in prior years (see instructions). **Do not** include interest, whether stated or unstated	**23**	
24	**Installment sale income.** Multiply line 22 by line 19	**24**	51,802.
25	Enter the part of line 24 that is ordinary income under recapture rules (see instructions)	**25**	
26	Subtract line 25 from line 24. Enter here and on Schedule D or Form 4797 (see instructions)	**26**	51,802.

Part III   **Related Party Installment Sale Income.** **Do not** complete if you received the final payment this tax year.

27 Name, address, and taxpayer identifying number of related party

28 Did the related party resell or dispose of the property ('second disposition') during this tax year? .... ☐ Yes ☐ No

29 If the answer to question 28 is 'Yes,' complete lines 30 through 37 below unless one of the following conditions is met. Check the box that applies.

a ☐ The second disposition was more than 2 years after the first disposition (other than dispositions of marketable securities). If this box is checked, enter the date of disposition (month, day, year) .... ► _____

b ☐ The first disposition was a sale or exchange of stock to the issuing corporation.

c ☐ The second disposition was an involuntary conversion and the threat of conversion occurred after the first disposition.

d ☐ The second disposition occurred after the death of the original seller or buyer.

e ☐ It can be established to the satisfaction of the Internal Revenue Service that tax avoidance was not a principal purpose for either of the dispositions. If this box is checked, attach an explanation (see instructions).

30	Selling price of property sold by related party	**30**	
31	Enter contract price from line 18 for year of first sale	**31**	
32	Enter the **smaller** of line 30 or line 31	**32**	
33	Total payments received by the end of your 2001 tax year (see instructions)	**33**	
34	Subtract line 33 from line 32. If zero or less, enter -0-	**34**	
35	Multiply line 34 by the gross profit percentage on line 19 for year of first sale	**35**	
36	Enter the part of line 35 that is ordinary income under recapture rules (see instructions)	**36**	
37	Subtract line 36 from line 35. Enter here and on Schedule D or Form 4797 (see instructions)	**37**	

Form **6252**

In this scenario the gross profit ratio is $137,000 divided by $200,000, or 68.5 percent. The seller must pay taxes on $34,250 of the $50,000 even though he or she only netted $2,000.

If the buyer assumes (or takes the property subject to) the seller's mortgage, the contract price is reduced. If the mortgage assumed by the buyer is $35,000, closing costs are $13,000, and the buyer pays $15,000 down, the seller nets $2,000.

The seller's gross profit ratio is:

	Gross Profit	Contract Price
Sales Price:	$200,000	$200,000
Mortgage:		–$ 35,000
Contract Price:		$165,000
Cost	–$ 50,000	
Expenses:	–$ 13,000	
Gross Profit:	$137,000	

The gross profit ratio would be 83 percent ($137,000 ÷ $165,000), which means that the seller pays tax on 83 percent of every principal payment (Figure 11.3, line 19).

The seller's first year profit is $12,455 (83 percent of $15,000), even though he only nets $2,000 (see Figure 11.3). Confused yet? Not to worry, this is pretty run-of-the-mill stuff for your accountant. What is important is the concept that the payments received will actually be made up of components that will be taxed or not taxed according to what they represent.

Once again, the seller will eventually get the whole $200,000 of principal, a percentage of which is taxable just as it would have been in an outright sale. So, why do it? The obvious advantage in doing the installment sale is the ability to spread the tax due over a long period of time. But more important is what that tax money does for you while you are still "holding" it. *It earns interest.*

Let's take a look at a fairly typical economic situation. Generally speaking, there is about a three- to four-point spread between mort-

FIGURE 11.3 Chuck's IRS Form 6252

Form **6252**	**Installment Sale Income**	OMB No. 1545-0228
Department of the Treasury Internal Revenue Service	▶ Attach to your tax return. ▶ Use a separate form for each sale or other disposition of property on the installment method.	**200__** 79

Name(s) Shown on Return	Identifying Number
CHUCK	000-00-0000

1 Description of property ▶ INVESTMENT PROPERTY

2a Date acquired (month, day, year) ▶ 6/30/86 **b** Date sold (month, day, year) ▶ 6/30/0_

3 Was the property sold to a related party (see instructions) after May 14, 1980? If 'No,' skip line 4 . . . . ☐ Yes ☒ No

4 Was the property you sold to a related party a marketable security? If 'Yes,' complete Part III. If 'No,' complete Part III for the year of sale and the 2 years after the year of sale . . . . ☐ Yes ☐ No

Part I Gross Profit and Contract Price. Complete this part for the year of sale only.

5	Selling price including mortgages and other debts. **Do not** include interest whether stated or unstated	**5**	200,000.
6	Mortgages, debts, and other liabilities the buyer assumed or took the property subject to (see instructions)	**6**	35,000.
7	Subtract line 6 from line 5	**7**	165,000.
8	Cost or other basis of property sold	**8**	50,000.
9	Depreciation allowed or allowable	**9**	
10	Adjusted basis. Subtract line 9 from line 8	**10**	50,000.
11	Commissions and other expenses of sale	**11**	13,000.
12	Income recapture from Form 4797, Part III (see instructions)	**12**	

13	Add lines 10, 11, and 12	**13**	63,000.
14	Subtract line 13 from line 5. If zero or less, **do not** complete the rest of this form (see instructions)	**14**	137,000.
15	If the property described on line 1 above was your main home, enter the amount of your excluded gain (see instructions). Otherwise, enter -0-	**15**	0.
16	**Gross profit.** Subtract line 15 from line 14	**16**	137,000.
17	Subtract line 13 from line 6. If zero or less, enter -0-	**17**	0.
18	**Contract price.** Add line 7 and line 17	**18**	165,000.

Part II Installment Sale Income. Complete this part for the year of sale **and** any year you receive a payment or have certain debts you must treat as a payment on installment obligations.

19	Gross profit percentage. Divide line 16 by line 18. For years after the year of sale, see instructions	**19**	0.8303
20	If this is the year of sale, enter the amount from line 17. Otherwise, enter -0-	**20**	0.
21	Payments received during year (see instructions). **Do not** include interest, whether stated or unstated	**21**	15,000.
22	Add lines 20 and 21	**22**	15,000.
23	Payments received in prior years (see instructions). **Do not** include interest, whether stated or unstated	**23**	
24	**Installment sale income.** Multiply line 22 by line 19	**24**	12,455.
25	Enter the part of line 24 that is ordinary income under recapture rules (see instructions)	**25**	
26	Subtract line 25 from line 24. Enter here and on Schedule D or Form 4797 (see instructions)	**26**	12,455.

Part III Related Party Installment Sale Income. Do not complete if you received the final payment this tax year.

27 Name, address, and taxpayer identifying number of related party

28 Did the related party resell or dispose of the property ('second disposition') during this tax year? . . . . ☐ Yes ☐ No

29 If the answer to question 28 is 'Yes,' complete lines 30 through 37 below unless one of the following conditions is met. **Check the box that applies.**

a ☐ The second disposition was more than 2 years after the first disposition (other than dispositions of marketable securities). If this box is checked, enter the date of disposition (month, day, year) . . . . ▶ _____

b ☐ The first disposition was a sale or exchange of stock to the issuing corporation.

c ☐ The second disposition was an involuntary conversion and the threat of conversion occurred after the first disposition.

d ☐ The second disposition occurred after the death of the original seller or buyer.

e ☐ It can be established to the satisfaction of the Internal Revenue Service that tax avoidance was not a principal purpose for either of the dispositions. If this box is checked, attach an explanation (see instructions).

30	Selling price of property sold by related party	**30**
31	Enter contract price from line 18 for year of first sale	**31**
32	Enter the **smaller** of line 30 or line 31	**32**
33	Total payments received by the end of your 2001 tax year (see instructions)	**33**
34	Subtract line 33 from line 32. If zero or less, enter -0-	**34**
35	Multiply line 34 by the gross profit percentage on line 19 for year of first sale	**35**
36	Enter the part of line 35 that is ordinary income under recapture rules (see instructions)	**36**
37	Subtract line 36 from line 35. Enter here and on Schedule D or Form 4797 (see instructions)	**37**

Form **6252**

gage rates and stable investment rates like certificates of deposit (CDs). So, when mortgage rates are around 7 percent, CDs will be paying around 3 percent to 4 percent. For that reason alone, "investing" money by carrying the mortgage on a property seems to make good financial sense.

There are, of course, risks and lack of liquidity factors to be considered, but if you are comfortable with the risk and are looking for a long-term investment, financing the property would seem the better choice. How much better? The return on $100,000 at 7.5 percent is $7,500 per year while the return on $100,000 in CDs or Treasury bills at 4 percent is $4,000 per year. That is a yearly difference of $3,500. Sounds fairly straightforward, but that's not really an apples-to-apples comparison. Remember, if you are investing $100,000 of deferred gain, you are getting a return not only on your money but also on the portion that is represented by what you would have had to pay to the IRS in an outright sale. So, if you were in California, you would have a capital gains tax liability on $100,000 of approximately $24,300 between state and federal taxes. In an outright sale, the dollars available to you after paying the taxes would only be $75,700. So the true comparison is really between $100,000 invested or $75,700 invested.

Even if you were able to get the exact same rate of return on your investments, the return would be larger based on the larger principal drawing a return. The difference between these two over a ten-year period at 7.5 percent return is approximately $18,225. Looking at it another way, the tax-deferred investment provided a 42 percent greater return than the after-tax investment. That's definitely a millionaire's tax secret worth knowing.

CHAPTER 12

Hybrids–Combining Tax Strategies

"Income tax returns are the most imaginative fiction being written today."

Herman Wouk

The Best of Both Worlds–Combining an Installment Sale with an Exchange

Sometimes to meet your objectives, the best alternative is to combine two or more of the tax-deferral or elimination tools to meet your specific needs. One of the more common combinations is the 1031 exchange used in conjunction with an installment sale. Two of the main reasons for using this combination of tools are to reduce the level of real estate investment as a whole and to reduce an owner/manager's workload but maintain a stream of income into the foreseeable future.

The most widespread reason for a hands-on investor to combine a 1031 exchange with an installment sale is retirement. Most find the idea of easing the workload *and* maintaining a stream of income from the tax-deferred profit very appealing. Others see the combination as a flexible and manageable "exit strategy" from being a landlord altogether. Whatever the reasons, the 1031 exchange combined with an installment sale is an effective tool and has been gaining popularity in recent years.

Legal Status and Possible Complications

Under the Internal Revenue Code, a taxpayer may combine the two tax-deferral methods to completely defer capital gains tax. However, there are some less than intuitive rules you need to take into consideration.

When combining an exchange with an installment sale note, the IRS has the following three rules that apply:

1. The contract price is reduced by the fair market value of the like-kind property received in the trade.
2. The gross profit is reduced by any gain on the trade that can be postponed.
3. Like-kind property received in the trade is not considered payment on the installment obligation.

The net effect of these rules is to shift more of the capital gain into the installment sale portion of the transaction. The following is based on an example provided by IRS Publication 537:

☞ **Example:** In 2004, Gordon trades property with an installment sale basis of $400,000 for like-kind property having a fair market value of $200,000. He also receives an installment note for $800,000 in the trade. Under the terms of the note, he is to receive $100,000 (plus interest) in 2005 and the balance of $700,000 (plus interest) in 2006. Gordon's selling price is $1,000,000 ($800,000 installment note plus $200,000 fair market value of like-kind property received). His gross profit is $600,000 ($1,000,000 minus $400,000 installment sale basis). The contract price is $800,000 ($1,000,000 minus $200,000). The gross profit percentage is 75 percent ($600,000 divided by $800,000). He reports no gain in 2004 because the like-kind property he receives is not treated as a payment for figuring gain. He reports $75,000 gain for 2005 (75 percent of the $100,000 payment received) and $525,000 gain for 2006 (75 percent of the $700,000 payment received).

As you can see, the first rule (the contract price is reduced by the fair market value of the like-kind property received in the trade) acts to effectively increase the gross profit percentage on the installment note payments. If the property had been sold by installment sale alone, the gross profit percentage would have been 60 percent ($600,000 divided by $1,000,000). On the other hand, if the exchange property had a fair market value of $400,000, the gross profit percentage would be 100 percent ($600,000 divided by $600,000). Does it really matter? Yes, it does if you are trying to plan what your yearly capital gains taxes will be from the installment sale payments.

Presumably the IRS created this shifting or reallocation rule to set the tax payments in motion for receipt sooner rather than later. After all, an installment sale has set payments and a foreseeable repayment schedule, so the higher the gross profit ratio, the faster the gain is received and the taxes become due. On the other hand, the reallocation rule forced additional adjusted basis to the replacement property (up to its fair market value) thereby minimizing the gain that would have qualified for the indefinite deferral of an exchange. In the IRS's example above, the basis exceeded the fair market value of the property received, so no portion of the gain is allocated to the exchange replacement property and no gain is being "indefinitely" deferred by the like-kind exchange portion of the split. Score one for the IRS? Maybe. Let's change the facts a little to see how the taxpayer might come out ahead (changes italicized):

☛ **Example:** In December 2004, Gordon trades property with an installment sale basis of $400,000 for like-kind property having a fair market value of *$400,000.* He also receives an installment note for *$600,000* in the trade. Under the terms of the note, he is to receive *regular amortized payments with a balloon due in ten years (30 due in 10)*. Gordon's selling price is $1,000,000 (*$600,000* installment note plus *$400,000* fair market value of like-kind property received*)*. His gross profit is $600,000 (*$1,000,000* minus $400,000 installment sale basis*)*. The contract price is *$600,000 ($1,000,000 minus $400,000)*. The gross profit percentage is *100 percent ($600,000 divided by $600,000)*. He reports no gain in 2004 because the like-kind property he receives is not treated as a payment for figuring gain. He reports *100 percent of the principal repayment as gain as he receives the future payments*.

The main change made in the example was that we made Gordon's replacement property equal to the adjusted basis ("installment sale basis") of the relinquished property. Now, after applying the IRS's reallocating rules, the entire adjusted basis of the relinquished property is assigned to the replacement property and the gross profit ratio on the installment sale portion is now 100 percent. See Figure 12.1.

At first glace, this doesn't seem very desirable. Gordon's replacement property is not deferring *any* of the capital gain and the installment sale principal payments received in the future have to be reported as 100 percent taxable. However, there is a bright side for Gordon.

Looking at these results from a different perspective, Gordon might find his position *very* desirable. First, consider the fact that the installment note has a very secure 60 percent loan-to-value ratio ($600,000 note on a $1,000,000 property). Normally, to get that type of a loan-to-value ratio, Gordon would have had to get $400,000 cash as the down payment—all of which would have been immediately taxable. Gordon saved $80,000 to $120,000 in immediate capital gains taxes depending on his state tax rate (15 percent for federal plus his state tax rate). Second, and perhaps more important, Gordon succeeded in doing something most investors are always trying to accomplish, he separated his original investment from his profit. Gordon has

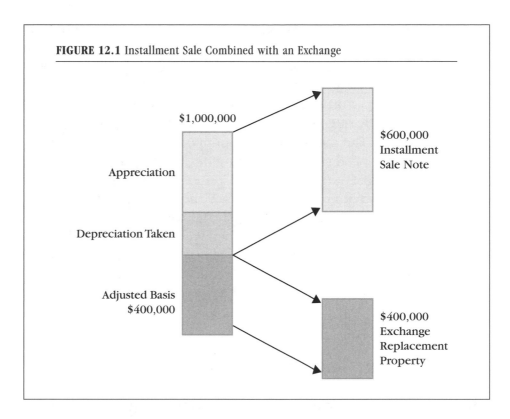

FIGURE 12.1 Installment Sale Combined with an Exchange

$1,000,000

Appreciation

Depreciation Taken

Adjusted Basis
$400,000

$600,000
Installment
Sale Note

$400,000
Exchange
Replacement
Property

a $600,000 installment note made up of all tax-deferred profit and a $400,000 property with a $400,000 adjusted basis.

Interestingly, if Gordon were to hold the replacement property received in the exchange portion of this scenario a few years and then sell it outright, he would have minimal taxes on the sale. Remember, the allocation shifting rules forced the full basis of the relinquished property to the replacement property. Also remember that a capital gain is the difference between sales price and the adjusted basis. So in Gordon's case, if the market value of his $400,000 replacement property remained constant, there would be very little or no gain upon a subsequent sale of the property.

Keep in mind, the IRS will disallow the exchange portion of Gordon's 1031 exchange combined with an installment sale if it was his "intent" at the time of the exchange to sell off the replacement property and cash out. However, if Gordon intended to hold the property for use in business or investment, but some unforeseeable circumstance arose and Gordon needed to cash out, he could do so without triggering significant taxes. Also, if the replacement property were held for a sufficient time before being sold, the exchange would not usually be questioned. How long is a "sufficient" time? There is no firm answer. The conventional wisdom is that two years is long enough, but the IRS has resisted confirming or disputing any definite period.

There is one additional potential issue in combining 1031 exchanges with installment sales. If the properties involved have existing mortgages, there are mortgage-over-basis considerations and mortgage boot issues that will need to be taken into account. The mere fact that there are existing mortgages should not discourage you, but it does complicate the analysis enough to necessitate getting expert advice from a qualified tax professional or real estate tax attorney.

Other Combinations to Consider

In the right circumstances, combining an exchange with an installment sale is a very useful tax-planning technique. This type of hybrid planning is becoming more popular as investors learn that it is possible. Unfortunately, many advisors simply don't think outside of the box. You do have choices. Other possible hybrid strategies might include part private annuity trust and part exchange, or maybe part exchange and part charitable annuity trust, or maybe part installment sale and part tenant-in-common exchange, and so on. Make sure you pick an advisor who can show you all of your possible alternatives.

CHAPTER 13

Private Annuity Trusts

"There is nothing wrong with a strategy to avoid the payment of taxes. The Internal Revenue Code doesn't prevent that."

William H. Rehnquist

What Is a Private Annuity Trust?

A private annuity trust is a vehicle in which the seller can sell appreciated real estate, create a stream of income for life, and defer the capital gains taxes. The concept stems from, but is quite different from, commonly known insurance company annuities. The annuity structure is basically the same, but a private annuity, like the name suggests, is between private parties. In most cases, private annuities are between parents and children although that is not a requirement. In its simplest description, a private annuity is where one person (the annuitant) gives another person or entity (the obligor) a lump sum of money or an asset in exchange for the promise to provide a stream of payments in the future (an annuity contract). A private annuity trust is simply a specially designed trust set up to provide an entity to protect the assets for the future beneficiaries and to give succession continuity in case something happens to the named trustee(s).

Assets transferred to the private annuity trust in exchange for an annuity contract can be just about anything of value, including appreciated real estate. Most importantly, where appreciated real estate is exchanged for the private annuity contract, no capital gains tax is triggered. The tax liability works something like an installment sale. The obligation to pay the capital gains tax and recapture of depreciation are deferred until the future payments are actually received by the annuitant (seller). But unlike installment sales, there are no risks of having to foreclose or having the buyer pay off the note early and trigger the full/immediate capital gains tax liability.

Another significant advantage of the private annuity trust is the ability to defer receipt of the payments. Because it is an annuity, the IRS allows you to defer receiving payments for any length of time up to the age of 70½. Because no tax is due until you start to receive payments, deferring the payments results in deferring the tax liability. This is where private annuity trusts really shine as a tax-planning device. The fact that you can defer payment of the capital gain allows the trust to invest and earn income from the funds that would otherwise have gone to the government.

☛ **Example:** Jeff and Shannon are married and own an apartment building that they bought for $100,000 15 years ago. The apartment building has a present value of $500,000 and an adjusted basis of $50,000. They would like to sell the building but know they face state and federal taxes of approximately $135,000. As would be anticipated, they are not excited about paying the taxes and are looking for an alternative. They no longer wish to be landlords, so they have ruled out a 1031 exchange and they are uncomfortable with the risks associated with an installment sale. Jeff and Shannon are both 55 years of age and have two adult children. Jeff and Shannon intend to retire at 65 and are presently financially secure and have no immediate need for the money from the sale of the property. Jeff and Shannon decide to create a private annuity trust and make their two adult children the cotrustees and the beneficiaries. They then transfer the apartment building to the trust in exchange for a private annuity contract with a present value of $500,000 with the beginning payment deferred until they reach 65 years of age. Once the property is transferred to the trust, the trustees (the children) authorize the sale, sell the property, and place the proceeds from the sale in a trust investment account where the trust principal will continue to grow until Jeff and Shannon reach 65 years. At that time, the trust will begin making the scheduled annuity payments to Jeff and Shannon according to the terms of the annuity contract. Once the annuity payments begin, Jeff and Shannon will have to recognize, report, and pay the capital gains tax on a portion of each payment received.

This is a very simplified summary of how a private annuity trust works, but it shows how they are commonly used. Private annuity trusts are sophisticated tax and estate planning devices and in the right situations they are excellent tax deferral and investment tools. Unlike installment sales and 1031 exchanges, this is one deferment tool that requires you get professional assistance and strictly adhere to the IRS rules.

A Millionaire's Tax Secret

Private annuity trusts have been around for some time but are not well known. Many of the major investment houses have used private annuity trusts for wealthy clients' tax and estate planning. Additionally, some estate planning attorneys and sophisticated financial planners are also aware of private annuity trusts. However, most people do not look to sophisticated attorneys or financial planners when considering the sale of property. Instead, the primary source of information and tax advice on real estate matters usually comes from the local real estate professional. Unfortunately, there are very few real estate professionals who are aware of private annuity trusts or understand how they work. Unlike installment sales and 1031 exchanges, the real estate community has not caught on to this option for tax deferral. The primary reason real estate professionals fail to embrace the use of private annuity trusts is probably the level of complexity, the need to bring in additional advisors, and the formalities required. Nevertheless, as more baby boomers hit retirement age looking for stream-of-income alternatives, real estate professionals will get up to speed on private annuity trusts or start losing business to the more savvy among them who are.

Given the right circumstances and investor objectives, the private annuity trust can be one of the most useful tax and planning vehicles available. They may not be well known now, but they will probably be commonplace in the not-so-distant future.

A Specialty Plan Tool

The foundation of a private annuity trust is simply a contractual annuity agreement and an irrevocable trust to provide structure. Some of the organizations, which specialize in financial and estate planning products, have tried to give a proprietary feel to private annuity trusts by giving them slightly different names. In addition, you may find advisors who want to combine private annuity contracts with other types of planning devices. Some of these get pretty extravagant, like "offshore trusts" or "international business companies." While there might be valid reasons for this type of extravagant tax and estate planning, they get a little too fancy (and questionable) for my liking. I tend to discourage clients from getting too complicated. On a tax planning complexity scale of one to ten, a basic private annuity trust is somewhere around the four to five range making it not too difficult for the average investor to understand.

Although you may find private annuity trusts called different names, the main structure will always include the basic components of a private annuity contract and an irrevocable trust.

Both Estate and Capital Gains Tax Advantages

Private annuity trusts have estate planning as well as tax-deferral advantages. The primary focus of this book is tax secrets in real estate investing; however, it would be appropriate here to also mention the estate planning benefits.

If capital gains taxes are considered bad, then estate taxes are worse. At the time of this writing, the estate tax exemption amount is $1,500,000 per person rising incrementally over the next six years and then set to revert to $1,000,000 in 2011. The current $1,500,000 exemption sounds like a lot, but anyone who has a home and a couple of investment properties gets to that level pretty fast and is probably facing some estate taxes. For those people, the tax on assets above the exemption amount starts at 37 percent and quickly moves up to 50 percent. If that's not enough motivation to do estate planning, consider the *additional* 55 percent generation-skipping tax that applies to estates passing directly to grandchildren. That means that $1,000,000 of estate-taxable assets passing from parents to children will incur between $370,000 and $500,000 in taxes. Those same assets passing to grandchildren will, in essence, be taxed again under the application of the generation-skipping tax with the end result being that the tax can eat up approximately 75 percent of the total value. There are exemptions, exclusions, and the like, but once you use those up, the remaining estate faces hefty taxation.

A private annuity trust can significantly reduce estate tax liability by removing an asset from your estate. By transferring the asset into a private annuity trust in exchange for a private annuity contract, you have sold the property. Thus, you no longer own the asset and it will not be considered a part of your estate for taxation purposes. The private annuity contract you received in exchange for the property is only set for lifetime payments; it has no value upon your death, so again, it is not counted as part of your estate.

☛ **Example:** Theresa is a 60-year-old widow. She has one child, Don. Theresa's long-time home and stock investments together equal approximately $1,500,000. In addition, about 20 years ago, Theresa inherited an investment property currently valued at $1,000,000 and it has an adjusted basis of 200,000. If Theresa were to pass away in a year where the exemption amount was $1,500,000 and her son were to inherit the whole estate, the end result would look something like this:

Home and Stock	$1,500,000
Investment Property	$1,000,000
Total Estate	$2,500,000
Less Estate Tax Exemption	($1,500,000)
Net Taxable Estate	$1,000,000
Less Approximate Estate Tax	($ 399,000)
After-Tax Estate	$1,901,000

As you can see, the estate taxes would be approximately $399,000. If instead, Theresa had transferred the investment property into a private annuity trust with her son as the trustee and beneficiary, the estate would have had *no* estate tax due. The $1,500,000 value in home and stock investments would have been protected by the $1,500,000 exemption and the investment property would no longer be in the estate at all. The investment property would pass outside the estate to her son as the beneficiary of the trust. There would still be a reckoning for the deferred capital gains tax, but the tax savings overall would be very significant.

The estate tax savings is certainly a consideration, but most people creating private annuity trusts are doing so to defer the capital gain and generate a stream of income. Using Theresa's situation from the

---

FIGURE 13.1 The Benefit of a Private Annuity Trust

Proposed Transfer Date:	12/2005
Projected §7520 Rate:	6.00%
FMV of Property:	$1,000,000
Client's Basis:	$200,000
Payment Period:	Monthly
Payment Timing:	End
Number of Annuitants	1
Theresa's Age:	60
Annuity Factor:	10.8279
Payout Frequency Factor:	1.0272
Annual Payout:	$89,909
Monthly Payment:	$7,492
Single Life Expectancy:	24.2 Years
Life Expectancy Adjustment Factor:	0.0
Tax-Free Portion:	$8,264
Capital Gain Portion:	$33,058
Ordinary Income Portion:	$48,586

Illustration courtesy of Accountant Matt Crammer, Crammer Accountancy, 562-923-9436

previous example, the income generated from the private annuity trust for Theresa would be projected at $7,492 per month for life. Figure 13.1 is how Theresa's situation would appear in a financial illustration.

Structure and Implementation

Structure

A private annuity trust is an irrevocable nongrantor trust. That means that once it is set up and funded, it is difficult and costly to change. The trust itself has to be established for the benefit of someone other than the property seller, usually the seller's children or family, and there are very specific rules and IRS requirements that must be followed. Once the trust is established, the seller transfers ("sells") the property to the trust in exchange for a private lifetime annuity contract. The seller now becomes an annuitant, meaning the seller is due annuity payments and the trust becomes the obligor, meaning that the trust is now obligated to make the annuity payments. No tax is due on the transfer of the property into the trust because the tax is deferred much like an installment sale. The trustee of the trust has all the responsibility and authority for the property thereafter. The trustee then sells the property. No tax is due on the trust sale of the property because what the trust paid for the property (the present value of the annuity contract) and the amount of the market sale will be equal so there is no gain to be taxed. The proceeds from the sale then go into the trust investment accounts or other investment vehicles established by the trust. The trustee then has the responsibility to manage the investments and to make the annuity payments to the annuitant at the predetermined times. The annuity payments are for the lifetime of the annuitant and when the annuitant passes away, the trustee will have the responsibility of distributing the remaining trust assets/money to the predetermined beneficiaries which are usually (but not necessarily) the family members. The IRS requires the lifetime annuity payments to be based on the average life span of 85 years of age. The annuity payments can be set for an individual life span or in the case of a husband and wife; can be set to make payments until both pass away. See Figure 13.2.

Establishing a Private Annuity Trust

The first step is to get knowledgeable legal and tax advice. A qualified advisor will be able to give you the pros and cons of a private annuity trust as they will impact your specific situation. Do not rely on the financial "advisors" who would like to manage the trust money. Do not rely on the companies who want to sell you a whole bunch of different planning and financial tools. As a matter of fact, do not rely on the general descriptions and examples given in this book. Each per-

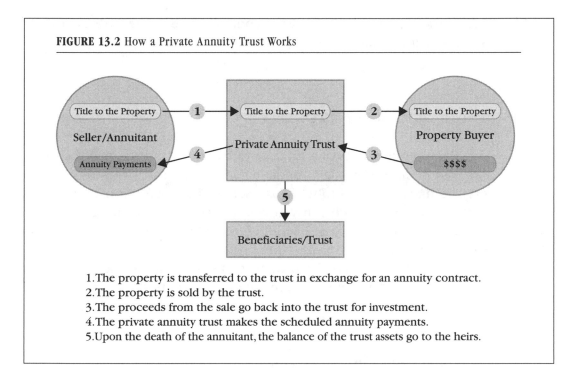

FIGURE 13.2 How a Private Annuity Trust Works

Title to the Property — 1 → Title to the Property — 2 → Title to the Property

Seller/Annuitant — Private Annuity Trust — Property Buyer

Annuity Payments ← 4 — 3 ← $$$$

5 ↓

Beneficiaries/Trust

1. The property is transferred to the trust in exchange for an annuity contract.
2. The property is sold by the trust.
3. The proceeds from the sale go back into the trust for investment.
4. The private annuity trust makes the scheduled annuity payments.
5. Upon the death of the annuitant, the balance of the trust assets go to the heirs.

son's situation is different and there is no substitute for good *situation-specific* legal and tax advice. Okay, with that said, after getting the appropriate advice, the establishment of the private annuity trust is fairly straightforward. Your advisor should be able to provide you with financial illustrations to explain exactly how your private annuity contract would work for you. Once you approve the financials, you will need a knowledgeable attorney to create the trust structure. Then you and your selected trustee will need to execute and notarize the appropriate documents. Once that is done, the trust will exist and the property can be transferred to it in exchange for an "estimated" private annuity contract. The contract is only estimated because the trust sale of the property has not occurred yet so the actual net proceeds from the sale can only be estimated until the sale is completed. Upon the completion of the sale, the trust will issue a replacement private annuity contract based on the actual confirmed net proceeds. At that point, establishing of the private annuity trust is complete and the trustee is now responsible for managing the proceeds from the sale.

Transfer and Sale of the Property

One requirement of a valid private annuity trust is that the property not be listed for sale or under a contract for sale prior to the property being transferred to the trust. Why? The conventional wisdom is that the IRS is okay with private annuity trusts as planning tools, but not as tax avoidance tools. Therefore, one of the factors taken into consideration if they scrutinize your private annuity trust will be if the property was already in the process of a sale. Some advisors say this is an easy rule to get around and that may be true, but why not just do it right to begin with? Talk to your advisor. The proper sequence of transfer and sale would be as follows:

1. The seller establishes the trust.
2. The seller transfers the property to the trust in exchange for the annuity contract.
3. The trustee (not the seller) would then list the property for sale.
4. The trustee (not the seller) would execute the contract for sale and all escrow/closing documents.
5. The escrow or closing agent must issue the closing proceeds in the name of the private annuity trust and the proceeds become trust funds.

Thereafter, the trustee is responsible for the management of the trust funds and making the annuity payments as prearranged in the trust and annuity contract.

Maximizing the Tax Deferral

One of the best characteristics of the private annuity trust is the annuitant's ability to defer the payments. What that means is that the person establishing the private annuity trust can legally defer receipt of any payments up to 70½ years of age. If you are 50 at the time you establish the private annuity trust, you can defer the payments for 20½ years. This becomes an amazing feature when you recall that the capital gains taxes are deferred until the annuitant actually starts receiving the payments. That means that in the above example, the trustee *you* selected can *invest* the entire proceeds of the sale (now trust funds) for the benefit of the trust for 20 years before having to pay out one dollar in annuity payments.

If a lightbulb did not just go on in your head, you should stop, back up, and reread the last paragraph. Okay, let's see what could happen based on a 20-year deferral.

☞ **Example:** Mike is 50 years old. He owns an apartment building valued at $725,000 and he still owes $300,000 on the mortgage and has an adjusted basis of $300,000. He establishes a private annuity trust and transfers the apartment building to it in exchange for a private annuity contract. The private annuity contract specifies that the lifetime payments be deferred until he reaches 70 years of age. The trustee of the trust sells the property and after selling expenses (hypothetically $25,000) and paying off the mortgage ($300,000), the net proceeds that go into the trust are $400,000. All capital gains taxes are deferred until Mike starts receiving payments. The trust now wisely invests the money and over the 20-year deferment period is able to earn an average after-tax return of 10 percent per year. That means when Mike starts receiving his private annuity payments the trust principal could have grown to approximately $2,931,229.45.

That's the magic of deferring payments coupled with compound interest. Although this sounds too good to be true, it's not really. A private annuity trust can be structured to work just like an IRA or other retirement investment vehicle. In fact, one of the more common advantages for starting a private annuity trust is to "catch up" or supplement retirement planning. The rate of return built into the example above is not unrealistic for long-term investments and many commonly traded mutual funds are expected to exceed this average over ten-year periods. However, the trust is not locked into mutual fund investing. The trust has great flexibility in investment options.

Reinvestment within the Trust

The structure of a private annuity trust is just that, private. So how the trust invests is up to the trustee and the directions drafted into the trust at inception. The fact that your trustee has the freedom to choose how the money is invested is one really good reason you need to be able to absolutely rely on the person you choose as trustee. Most people choose a family member, usually a son or daughter, who will be the beneficiary of the trust if the annuitant passes away. Who you choose is up to you. If your children are not as financially savvy or responsible as you would like, you can always choose a professional trustee or a combination of family member and professional trustee to act jointly as cotrustees. Whoever you choose will have a fiduciary responsibility to invest the funds prudently, but "prudently" still leaves a great deal of flexibility. All of the traditional investments like stocks, bonds, and mutual funds are okay, but the trust can also buy commercial annuities, real estate, and just about anything else you can imagine.

Private Annuity Trusts Investing in Commercial Annuities

One of the best ways to invest money within a private annuity trust is to buy commercial annuities or appreciable assets. Remember, the private annuity trust structure, like all business and investment entities requires yearly tax filings and payment of taxes on the yearly income earned. So, for ease of management, security, and maximum tax deferral, a commercial annuity offers some advantages. Commercial annuities do not offer the growth potential of other types of investing, but they do provide security and additional tax deferral.

☞ **Example:** Carl is 55 years old and has a large piece of vacant land he bought 20 years ago for $100,000. A developer has been after him for some time to sell the land and the current market value is $500,000. Carl plans to retire in ten years and feels the market for the property is strong now but may not be in ten years. Carl decides to establish a private annuity trust and transfers the land to it in exchange for a private annuity contract with the lifetime annuity payments deferred until he is 65. The *trust* sells the land to the developer and uses the $500,000 proceeds to buy a commercial annuity with its payments also deferred for ten years. Now, when Carl retires at 65, the commercial annuity will start making payments to the private annuity trust which will in turn make the private annuity payments to Carl. Carl has deferred his capital gains tax on the sale of the land by selling it to the trust in exchange for the private annuity contract and because the trust bought a deferred commercial annuity, there is no taxable income for the trust to report until the commercial annuity begins making payments to the trust.

Is this legal? Yes, taxes are not being eliminated, only deferred. The trust will have to pay tax on the investment income when the payments start and Carl will have to pay the capital gains taxes and interest income tax when the private annuity payments begin. The IRS has not lost any money. They will get the capital gains tax and interest income taxes from you eventually. After all, it is safe to assume that the IRS will still be here after both you and I are gone.

Installment Sale or Private Annuity Trust? Sometimes Both

In most cases a private annuity trust is considered an alternative to an installment sale. Both an installment sale and a private annuity provide a stream of income and allow you to defer capital gains tax liability over a period of time. However, there are sometimes situations where a person may want to establish a private annuity trust, transfer the property to it in exchange for the private annuity contract, and then have the private annuity trust sell the property with installment sale terms. Why? Because by doing so, the two big drawbacks associated with installment sales are eliminated—the risk of early pay-off (triggering immediate tax) and the taxes due on the down payment.

☛ **Example:** Tom Smith owns a small shopping center he inherited from his parents 15 years ago. The current basis on the property is $300,000. He wants to sell it but the available financing for the property is tight and he knows to get full value he will have to offer seller financing terms. He does not really mind financing the property as long as the loan-to-value ratio is sufficient to reduce the risk of having to foreclose. The property is currently valued at $1,000,000 and Tom wants at least 30 percent down to feel comfortable with the risk. However, under an installment sale, Tom's accountant has told him that there will be approximately $100,000 in taxes due (state and federal) on the $300,000 down and that the buyer may refinance or sell the property in a few years, pay off the note, and trigger an immediate capital gain situation for Tom. Tom decides to establish a private annuity trust (The Smith Family Trust) and transfer the property to it in exchange for a private annuity contract deferring his taxes until the annuity payments start. The trust then sells the property to a buyer for the 30 percent down and 70 percent owner (now the trust) financing. The trust realizes no gain on the sale because what it paid for the property, the value of the annuity contract, and what the property sold for are the same. The trust now has the full $300,000 in cash to invest and a note for the other $700,000. All capital gains taxes are deferred until Tom starts receiving the annuity payments from the private annuity trust. Moreover, if the buyer subsequently sells or refinances the property and pays off the $700,000 note, there will be no triggering of capital gains taxes because there is no gain attributable to the sale by the trust.

As you can see, a private annuity trust combined with an installment sale does have some advantages. However, each situation needs to be well thought through because using this structure may create a second layer of taxation on the installment sale interest earned. There are ways to avoid this second layer of taxation, but you should discuss it at length with your tax advisor or attorney to make sure a private annuity will work for you.

Trust Investing—Keeping It in Your Family

One of the more interesting aspects of establishing a private annuity trust is that it becomes a family investment tool. Remembering that the trustee can be very flexible in the type of investments, it is easy to create some interesting advantages for family members or friends for that matter.

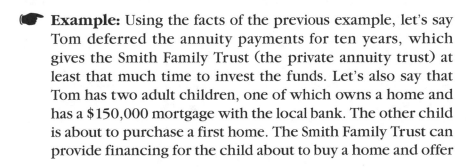 **Example:** Using the facts of the previous example, let's say Tom deferred the annuity payments for ten years, which gives the Smith Family Trust (the private annuity trust) at least that much time to invest the funds. Let's also say that Tom has two adult children, one of which owns a home and has a $150,000 mortgage with the local bank. The other child is about to purchase a first home. The Smith Family Trust can provide financing for the child about to buy a home and offer

to refinance the mortgage on the other child's home. The trust simply acts as any lender would in structuring the notes and interest at market rates. The end result would be that both children have their homes financed though the Smith Family Trust and all interest accumulating on those mortgages would be paid into the Smith Family Trust instead of the local bank. All homeowner mortgage deductions for the children remain exactly as they would if a commercial lender had made the loans. The notes can be structured to require each child to refinance their homes to pay off the notes in ten years so that the Smith Family Trust can start making the annuity payments to the annuitant (Tom Smith). However, the children may not need to refinance their homes at the ten-year point as long as the payments they make and the other assets of the trust are sufficient to make the monthly annuity payments to Tom.

This is a really great way to help out children or grandchildren who are buying a home. It is also a really good way to control the return on the trust investments and "keep it in the family." Family home mortgages are just one possibility. The Smith Family Trust, in the example above, could help the family in a lot of ways. It could provide financing for a family member to start a business, for a down payment on an apartment building, to finance (by loan) the cost of higher education, or just about anything else you can imagine.

Whatever investments the trust makes, the goal is to have the funds available to make the annuity payment to the annuitant when they come due. In that regard, the investments should always be economically and financially reasonable so that the trust can meet its obligations.

Legal Formalities and Requirements

Now that we have covered the potential benefits of establishing a private annuity trust, you might be thinking, "What's the catch?" Common sense says anything that sounds too good to be true, usually is. Up to this point, you have seen the positive features, potential for growth, and other opportunities associated with the private annuity trust. Now it's time to explore the less than desirable aspects.

Seller Cannot Be the Trustee

In the case of a private annuity, the annuity, by definition, must be an "unsecured promise" to make lifetime payments in exchange for a "lump sum payment." For the purpose of this book, that lump sum payment is made in the form of appreciated real estate instead of cash. The IRS has determined that if the promise to make lifetime payments is *in any way* "secured," then the promise to make the payments is more like a financing agreement than it is like an annuity. As such, the agreement would not qualify for the tax treatments afforded to annuities under the law. So in the simplest terms, if the seller retains *any* interest in or control over the property, the IRS will disallow the private annuity tax advantages. With that said, it becomes obvious why the person who establishes the private annuity trust (the annuitant) cannot be either a trustee or a named beneficiary of the trust agreement.

The requirement that private annuities be unsecured basically means that the annuitant has to give up all ownership and control over the property, and how the trust assets are invested after the property is sold. The trustees selected to manage the trust have to be absolutely trustworthy which is why private annuity trusts are usually intra-family planning tools. In most cases private annuity trusts are created by parents and managed by their adult children. However, that is not a requirement. Another option is to have the trust managed by a professional corporate trustee. Some people opt for having cotrustees by choosing both a family member and a professional trustee to serve jointly. The only rule is the trustee cannot be the annuitant, the spouse of the annuitant, or the fiduciary of an annuitant.

Annuity Must Be Unsecured

By definition, a private annuity is a lifetime series of payments under an unsecured contract. In the situation where real estate is given in exchange for an annuity, it is especially important to differentiate the private annuity from an installment sale for tax purposes. Both have tax-deferral characteristics, however, only an annuity has *payment*-deferral options and alternative investment opportunities. A private annuity also acts to remove the asset from your estate for estate tax purposes, where an installment sale note would still be an estate asset subject to estate taxes.

The requirement that a private annuity be unsecured is somewhat discomforting to many property owners because it means a loss of control over their asset. The structure of a private annuity trust requires the trustee to have control over the trust assets and the annuitant cannot have any overt control over the trustee. This seems like somewhat of a fiction, because most private annuity trusts have a family member or professional trustee, so some ability to influence the actions of the trustee will exist whether it is acknowledged or not.

Strict Guidelines and Formalities

To qualify for the benefits of a private annuity trust, the trust structure and annuity contract must conform to the IRS requirements. We have already looked at a few of these in the preceding sections: the annuity must be unsecured, the annuitant cannot be the trustee, the property must be transferred to the trust before it is sold, etc. However, the list of requirements is long and includes other items we have not yet discussed. The following are other requirements that need to be considered:

- The annuity interest rate must be set at an amount equal to the federally set rate (Sec 7520 rate) at the time the annuity contract is created. The federal rate changes each month.
- Payments may be deferred but must start by age 70½. An annuitant may structure the annuity contract so that scheduled payments are deferred for any period, but has to follow the minimal distribution rules providing that payments must begin by age 70½.
- The trust must have independent economic viability. This means that some portion of the fair market value of the asset (usually 7 to 9 percent) must be excluded from the annuity calculation and "gifted" to the trust. By doing this, the trust has an independent economic substance beyond annuity.
- Payments must be calculated on the life expectancy of the annuitant determined by actuary tables. In the case of a joint husband and wife annuity, the payments are based on the life expectancy of the younger, but the limit on the deferral period is based on the age of the older.
- The annuitant cannot control or influence the financial investment decisions of the trustee. Any control or influence and the arrangement will be seen as the annuitant retaining control over the assets and the annuity trust will fail.
- A private annuity with scheduled payments equaling less than the IRS's required present market value will be treated as a partial gift for tax purposes.

Costs to Create and Manage a Private Annuity Trust

Every method of deferring capital gains taxes has costs associated with its implementation. The private annuity trust is probably the most expensive because its structure is irrevocable and usually lasts many years, if not decades. Most of the costs are in the creation, but there are ongoing yearly tasks associated with properly maintaining the trust and filing the annual tax return. Many of these fees can be reduced or eliminated if your chosen trustee is competent and willing to personally perform the tasks. The following are the three main areas where expenses are incurred:

1. *Creation of the trust and annuity contract.* Private annuity trusts are not for the "do-it-yourselfer." You *will* need an attorney to set up your trust and draft the annuity contract. The attorney's fees should be in the $2,500 to $3,500 range and include drafting/executing the trust and annuity contract, as well as preparing and recording the deed transferring the property to the trust. Finding a knowledgeable attorney will be the real trick. Tax and estate planning attorneys will be your best bet, but understand that this area of law is very specialized. Even an experienced tax or estate planning attorney may have never been asked to do a private annuity trust. Don't let some new attorney use you as a training tool, hire only someone who has specific experience with private annuity trusts.

2. *Cost of managing trust assets.* If you are going to be using an adult child to manage the day-to-day affairs of the trust, you will be able to keep costs here to a minimum. If not, a professional trustee will charge a set fee based on the value of the trust assets. The fees are commonly around 1 to 1.5 percent for "money manager"–type duties, but may be a higher percentage on smaller trusts or a slightly lower percentage on trusts of over $1,000,000. Professional trustees that do more that just money management duties will usually charge a flat yearly fee based on the size of the trust and an hourly fee for services performed. As mentioned above, these fees may be partially avoided if your chosen trustee is an adult child who is able (and trustworthy) to handle and competently invest the money. If not, the fees charged by professional trustees

are well worth the expense and will let you sleep better at night.

3. *Accounting expenses.* This is another area where professional help is necessary. Trust accounting, especially private annuity trust accounting, is a specialty. Your local tax preparer is not going to understand how the yearly tax returns need to be handled. Get the appropriate help and you will avoid trouble in this area. Trust tax returns can run a few hundred dollars per year or more depending on the complexity of the trust investment activities.

Private Annuity versus an Installment Sale

A private annuity trust is similar to an installment sale in that they both create a stream of income from the tax-deferred sale of a property. Likewise, they are similar in how the taxes are eventually paid. In both, a private annuity sale and an installment sale, the capital gains taxes on the disposal of the property are deferred or spread out until the payments are actually received. In both cases, the monthly payments received are divided into three components: a percentage representing interest income, a percentage representing capital gain, and a nontaxable percentage representing recovery of the initial investment or basis. These percentages are established up front and do not change. In the years after, the taxpayer reports the amount of interest income and gain on his or her tax returns for payments received during that tax year.

While the above paragraph may seem to make the two alike, it is where the similarities end. While they both defer the payment of taxes, the risks and costs associated with each are significantly different. For example, installment sales are generally easier and less expensive to implement, but come with the risks associated with lending money and the possibility of an early pay-off triggering taxes. Private annuity trusts resolve both of those risks, but are more complicated and have a higher start-up cost and slightly higher yearly tax filing expenses. Additionally, each of these deferral methods has significant differences in its legal formalities, structure, estate planning applicability, and flexibility. Which method is better for you will depend on how well the tool meets your specific objectives.

Summary and Frequently Asked Questions

By creating a private annuity trust, you can sell appreciated property to the trust in exchange for a private annuity contract. The trust can then sell the property and reinvest the funds. Neither the transfer of the property to the trust or the subsequent sale of the property by the trust will trigger an immediate capital gains tax liability. The trust will then make lifetime payments to you and any remaining assets in the trust will pass to your heirs upon your death.

Private annuity trusts are a bit more complex than the other deferral methods we have looked at so far. The fact that they are slightly more complicated is exactly why the real estate community as a whole has yet to embrace them. However, that is changing because the average investor is becoming more sophisticated. Although there are significant pros and cons to consider, the private annuity trust is sure to grow into one of the more favored real estate exit strategies in the future.

This chapter has given an overview of private annuity trusts but is far from comprehensive. Regardless of how much I write or speak on private annuity trusts, I seem to always get asked the same questions, so here are the direct answers to the most frequently posed questions:

Q. Why have I never heard of private annuity trusts?

A. The private annuities are not highly touted in the real estate community because of the relative complexity. However, finding a knowledgeable attorney or accountant should be fairly easy. Also, you can find a lot of information on the Internet by doing a search for "private annuity."

Q. Why aren't the taxes triggered when I sell the property to the trust?

A. You are receiving a lifetime annuity contract from the trust as payment. There is no way to accurately determine how many payments will be made during your lifetime, so the IRS has decided it is better to tax you as the payments are received.

Q. What happens if the trust runs out of money before I die?

A. You would have the option to sue the trust for breach of the annuity contract. But if the trust has exhausted its assets, there would be no point.

Q. What happens if I die younger than the (85-year-old) life expectancy used in calculating the annuity payments?

A. The existing trust assets pass to your heirs as you arranged in the trust. The unpaid portion of the deferred capital gains tax would become due at that time.

Q. Can I have the trust pay the annuity to both my spouse and me?

A. Yes, second-to-die or joint annuities for spouses are common.

Q. Who should be the trustee?

A. Typically, the trustee is one of your children or one of the beneficiaries of the trust. You may also choose a professional trustee, an accountant, an attorney, or a combination of professionals and/or children. However, neither you nor your spouse can act as trustee.

Q. How much does it cost to set up a private annuity trust?

A. Fees vary, but in the neighborhood of $2,500 to $3,500 should be expected.

Q. How long does it take to get the trust established and ready to go?

A. That would depend on how busy your attorney is, but you should usually plan on about 20 to 30 days.

Q. If my property is already on the market can I still do a private annuity trust?

A. Yes, but see your advisor for more information.

Q. Are there any rules on how the trust has to invest the proceeds from the sale of the property?

A. Yes, but there is a great deal of flexibility. For example, investments in stocks, bonds, mutual funds, real estate, mortgage notes, certificates of deposit, commercial annuities, and more are all allowed.

Q. Does the trust have to pay taxes on the income from investments?

A. Yes. The tax rates are generally higher than the rates for personal income. For this reason, financial and tax planning is important to minimize or eliminate taxes at the trust level.

Q. If I don't need the monthly annuity payments now can I defer them?

A. Yes. Private annuity payment deferral options follow some of the same rules as retirement accounts. You may defer receipt of payments (and the tax liability that goes along with them) up to the age of 70½.

Q. If I own more than one property, can I add additional properties to the private annuity trust at a later date?

A. Yes. The private annuity trust "pays" you for each property by means of an annuity contract. A single annuity contract may cover more than one property if the properties are sold within a month or so of each other. However, to add a property at a later date, an additional annuity contract must be created for the new property or properties. Each annuity contract will stand on its own and may have different deferral periods.

Q. What if I change my mind and want to change the deferral period after the original annuity contract is created?

A. You can amend to receive payments sooner, but you cannot change the annuity contract to defer the payments for a later date.

Q. I like the idea of the private annuity trust, but I wanted some cash out of the sale. Can I do that?

A. Yes. You can allocate a fractional portion of the property to the private annuity trust with the remaining portion paid out to you at the closing. However, keep in mind that you will have to pay taxes on any capital gain not deferred. Along those same lines, you can also combine a private annuity trust and a 1031 exchange by allocating a portion of the property you are selling for each purpose. See your advisor.

Where to Get More Information about Private Annuity Trusts

Private annuity trusts are probably considered one of the true tax secrets out there. Not because anyone is trying to keep them secret, but rather because they are not well known or understood. There seem to be a lot of professional money managers promoting private annuity trusts, but, of course, that's because they want to get paid to manage the money once it's in the trust. There's nothing wrong with a trustee hiring a money manager to handle the trust investments once the decision is made to actually do a private annuity trust. However, I always recommend getting a more unbiased advisor when considering whether a private annuity trust is a good idea in the first place. I generally recommend consulting an attorney or an accountant rather than an investment manager. Unfortunately, it may not be easy to find an attorney or accountant that actually has this specialized experience. You may be able to find one in your own area, but if not, the accountant I recommend is Matthew Crammer of Crammer Accountancy. Matt's contact information is listed in the Recommended Advisors section at the back of this book.

You can find more information on the Internet at http://www .privateannuitytrusts.com.

Charitable Remainder Trusts

"The ancient Egyptians built elaborate fortresses and tunnels and even posted guards at tombs to stop grave robbers. In today's America, we call that estate planning."

Bill Archer

Introduction to Charitable Remainder Trusts

Charitable remainder trusts are generally associated more with estate planning than with real estate investment strategies. For that reason, it is common for average investors to mistakenly overlook charitable remainder trusts. But as you are about to see, this is a great planning tool that can accomplish the following:

- Eliminate capital gains tax.
- Create a reliable stream of income to one or more persons during their lifetimes.
- Provide an immediate income tax charitable deduction.
- Avoid future taxes at the estate level.
- Support your choice of a worthwhile charity.

A charitable remainder trust is simply an irrevocable trust that you create to hold assets that will be donated to a charity or charities in the future. The trust takes ownership of the appreciated real estate, sells it, and invests the proceeds. The trust specifies that you (or you and your spouse) are entitled to a stream of income from the invested assets for your lifetime(s) and names the charity as the remainder beneficiary upon your death. This allows you to receive lifetime scheduled income from the trust and, upon your death, the remaining assets pass to your chosen charity.

Many people do not understand the advantages of charitable remainder trusts. In fact, a common initial reaction is "Why would I want to give my property away?" This type of negative response is why many real estate and financial advisors don't even bother to discuss the option. That's unfortunate because sometimes a charitable remainder trust is the perfect tool to meet the property investor's objectives.

It's hard to understand the advantages without looking at financial projections of the impact. Each situation is different and your own financial impact needs to be analyzed for you by someone qualified to advise you. However, the next section will show you a stream of income and income tax deduction illustration so you will get a general idea how charitable remainder trusts work financially.

Stream of Income Illustration

When considering a charitable remainder trust, start by getting a picture of how the financial and tax benefits will work. Most charitable and financial advisors will have computer software that can give you a detailed analysis of the financial impact. Figures 14.1 to 14.3 include a sample financial illustration provided by an accountant. It is based on the following situation.

☛ **Example:** A single man, 65 years of age, is considering the transfer of a $1,000,000 apartment building to a charitable remainder annuity trust. The apartment building has an adjusted basis of $75,000. His current yearly income (prior to

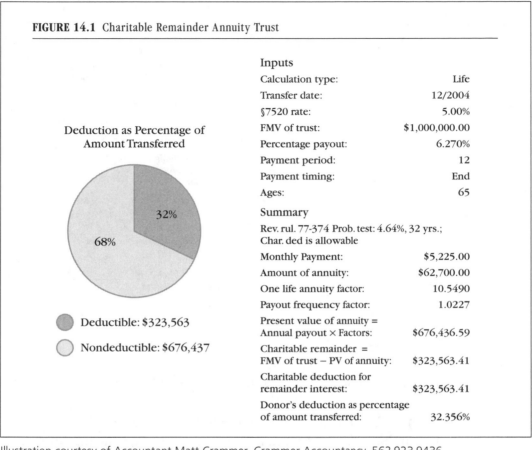

FIGURE 14.1 Charitable Remainder Annuity Trust

Deduction as Percentage of Amount Transferred

32%

68%

● Deductible: $323,563

○ Nondeductible: $676,437

Inputs

Calculation type:	Life
Transfer date:	12/2004
§7520 rate:	5.00%
FMV of trust:	$1,000,000.00
Percentage payout:	6.270%
Payment period:	12
Payment timing:	End
Ages:	65

Summary

Rev. rul. 77-374 Prob. test: 4.64%, 32 yrs.; Char. ded is allowable

Monthly Payment:	$5,225.00
Amount of annuity:	$62,700.00
One life annuity factor:	10.5490
Payout frequency factor:	1.0227
Present value of annuity = Annual payout × Factors:	$676,436.59
Charitable remainder = FMV of trust − PV of annuity:	$323,563.41
Charitable deduction for remainder interest:	$323,563.41
Donor's deduction as percentage of amount transferred:	32.356%

Illustration courtesy of Accountant Matt Crammer, Crammer Accountancy, 562-923-9436

the trust) is $150,000 and he wants the charitable remainder annuity trust to provide a stream of income for his lifetime. His combined federal and state capital gains tax rate is 24.3 percent and the Section 7520 rate is 5 percent.

Although the information in these figures looks complicated, it's really not. In summary, the person in this illustration would receive a monthly income of $5,225 from the charitable remainder annuity trust for as long as he lives. He would be able to take a charitable gift income tax deduction of $75,000 in each of the first four years, saving him a

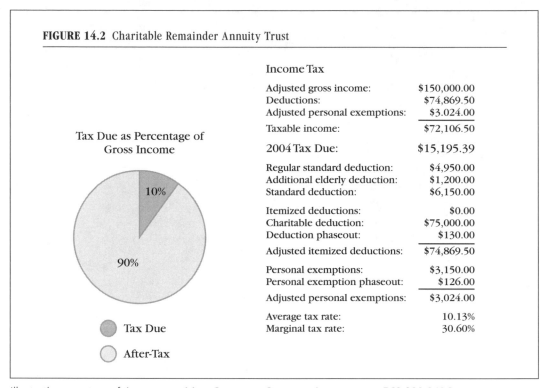

FIGURE 14.2 Charitable Remainder Annuity Trust

Tax Due as Percentage of Gross Income

- Tax Due
- After-Tax

Income Tax

Adjusted gross income:	$150,000.00
Deductions:	$74,869.50
Adjusted personal exemptions:	$3,024.00
Taxable income:	$72,106.50
2004 Tax Due:	$15,195.39
Regular standard deduction:	$4,950.00
Additional elderly deduction:	$1,200.00
Standard deduction:	$6,150.00
Itemized deductions:	$0.00
Charitable deduction:	$75,000.00
Deduction phaseout:	$130.00
Adjusted itemized deductions:	$74,869.50
Personal exemptions:	$3,150.00
Personal exemption phaseout:	$126.00
Adjusted personal exemptions:	$3,024.00
Average tax rate:	10.13%
Marginal tax rate:	30.60%

Illustration courtesy of Accountant Matt Crammer, Crammer Accountancy, 562-923-9436

total of $77,734 in those years. In the fifth year, he would get a remaining charitable gift income tax deduction of $23,563, saving him an additional $4,652. His total capital gains tax savings would be $82,386.

How the Immediate Income Tax Deduction Works

As you saw in the previous section, you will be able to take a charitable gift income tax deduction that can be used to reduce your immediate income tax liability. The amount of the income tax deduction and actual benefit will depend on two factors; the estimated value to the charity and the type of charity.

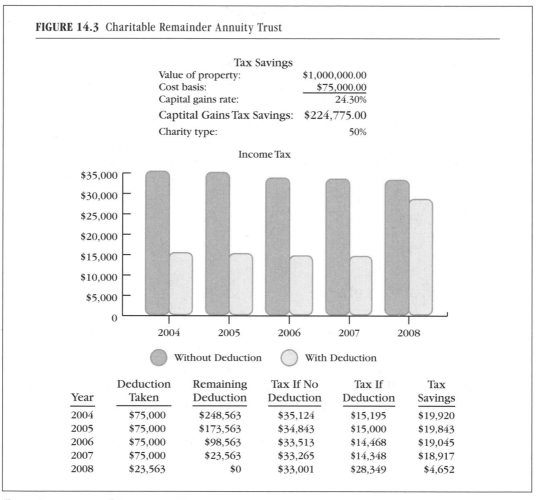

FIGURE 14.3 Charitable Remainder Annuity Trust

Tax Savings

Value of property:	$1,000,000.00
Cost basis:	$75,000.00
Capital gains rate:	24.30%
Captital Gains Tax Savings:	$224,775.00
Charity type:	50%

Income Tax

Without Deduction   With Deduction

Year	Deduction Taken	Remaining Deduction	Tax If No Deduction	Tax If Deduction	Tax Savings
2004	$75,000	$248,563	$35,124	$15,195	$19,920
2005	$75,000	$173,563	$34,843	$15,000	$19,843
2006	$75,000	$98,563	$33,513	$14,468	$19,045
2007	$75,000	$23,563	$33,265	$14,348	$18,917
2008	$23,563	$0	$33,001	$28,349	$4,652

Illustration courtesy of Accountant Matt Crammer, Crammer Accountancy, 562-923-9436

The total amount of the income tax deduction allowed will be based on the projected value of the remainder interest of the property donated to the trust. There are specific formulas used to determine the deduction you will get. Basically, in a lifetime annuity trust, the younger you are, the lower the charitable deduction will be because it is anticipated that the trust will have to make more lifetime payments to you thereby reducing the amount that eventually goes to the charity.

The amount of the income tax deduction will also depend on the type of charity you choose. Most public charities are classified as 50 percent charities, and you may deduct charitable contributions to the extent they do not exceed 50 percent of your adjusted gross income. Certain organizations, such as war veterans' organizations, fraternal orders, and private foundations, are classified as 30 percent charities. When making contributions to these charities, you may deduct gifts to the extent they do not exceed 30 percent of your adjusted gross income. Any unused part of the deduction can be carried forward for up to five years.

Philanthropic Advantages

It's always nice to come out ahead financially, but many times the true motivation to do a charitable remainder trust is to support a favorite charity, university, or your church. If your motivation is primarily philanthropic, the best part of a charitable remainder trust is the ability to benefit from the asset while you are still alive and make a current day commitment to give. Many charities rely on this type of gifting to survive and your charitable gesture will be appreciated.

How the Trust Structure and Property Sale Works

Figure 14.4 shows the property title transfer and money flow in a typical charitable remainder trust. As you will see, the structural characteristics are fairly easy to understand. In the subtopics following Figure 14.4 we are going to take a closer, but basic look at how charitable remainder trusts work.

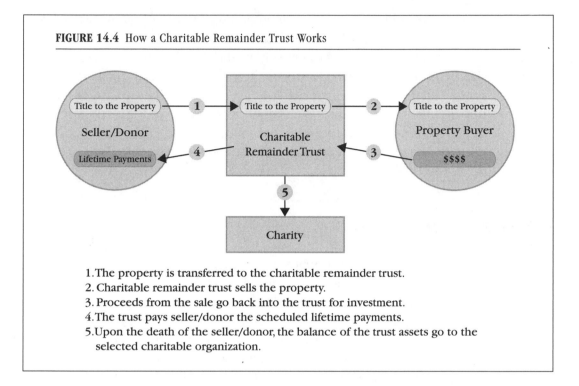

FIGURE 14.4 How a Charitable Remainder Trust Works

1. The property is transferred to the charitable remainder trust.
2. Charitable remainder trust sells the property.
3. Proceeds from the sale go back into the trust for investment.
4. The trust pays seller/donor the scheduled lifetime payments.
5. Upon the death of the seller/donor, the balance of the trust assets go to the selected charitable organization.

Structure of the Trust

As the name implies, a charitable remainder trust is a *trust*. A trust is simply an entity created for you to hold and manage assets. The legal specifics are beyond the scope of this book and you would be well advised to get an attorney to properly draft the documents for you. However, don't let the legal side of this discourage you. Charitable remainder trusts are considered pretty commonplace for trust and estate planning attorneys.

Unlike commonly known and used revocable living trusts, a charitable remainder trust is irrevocable, which means that once it is created and in operation you cannot change your mind. For that reason, it is prudent to get good advice and make sound decisions up front.

Once the trust itself has been created, you will transfer the property into the trust. It is important not to put the property on the market or begin the process of selling until the trust has been created and the property transferred into the trust. Nevertheless, if you have already started the sale process, it is possible to back up and create the necessary structure and documentation, although strictly speaking you are not supposed to. If you have already sold the property and the escrow has closed, it is too late to use a charitable remainder trust to defer the taxes.

Sale of the Property

Once the property has been transferred to the trust, the trust owns it. It is the trustee you selected (usually you as trustee) who will need to sign the listing agreement, sale contract, escrow/closing instructions, and any other transactional documents on behalf of the trust. When the sale is completed, the proceeds from the sale must go to the trust for investment and management under the terms of the trust. When the trust sells the assets, there will be no capital gains tax because a charitable remainder trust is exempt from capital gains tax.

Investment of Funds

Once the asset has been sold, the trustee reinvests the proceeds for growth and to provide the lifetime income stream(s) you established in the terms of the trust. The amount and type of payments you receive will depend on the choices you made at the time you set up the trust.

There are many charitable organizations that will act as trustee of a charitable remainder trust if they are named as a beneficiary. In fact, most will want to control the process of designing the trust, selling the property, investing the funds, and making the lifetime payments to you. However, there is no requirement that you have a charitable organization act in any of those capacities. You may choose just about anyone you want, including yourself, to act as trustee and administer the trust's affairs.

Income for Life

Once the property is sold and the sale proceeds are invested by the trust, the trust will be responsible for paying you and any copayee named in the scheduled payments. How you structure the payments is a matter of your own preference. Depending on your choice of payment options, your charitable remainder trust will be either a charitable remainder unitrust (CRUT) which has variable payments calculated as a percentage of the trust assets, or a charitable remainder annuity trust (CRAT) which has fixed payments regardless of the trust's investment performance. We will look closer at both CRUTs and CRATs below.

Remainder to the Charity

The end result of a charitable remainder trust is that the remaining assets of the trust eventually go to your chosen charity when the person (or persons) receiving lifetime income payments passes away.

Charitable Remainder Trust Types

Charitable remainder trusts have been around for a long time and are more common than most people think. There are two basic structures for charitable remainder trusts, the annuity trust and the unitrust. For a charitable remainder trust to be valid, the regulations require that it be either an annuity trust or a unitrust and not a hybrid or blending of the two. As you will see, the basic difference between these two is how the stream of income for the donor is calculated.

Charitable Remainder Annuity Trust (CRAT)

A charitable remainder annuity trust is structured to pay the donor a *fixed* amount each year for the donor's lifetime or for a term of years, with the property remaining in the trust passing to the charity upon the donor's death. The payments can be set up to pay the donor and spouse during their joint lifetimes and can even go to other persons like children or grandchildren.

The annuity payments can initially be set as a fixed amount of the initial value of the assets in the trust or can be set as a fixed sum. The annual payments must be set no lower that 5 percent and no higher than 50 percent. As a practical matter, most CRAT payments are set at an annual payout of somewhere in the range of 5 to 15 percent. Once set, the payments cannot be changed regardless of future inflation or investment performance of the trust.

Charitable Remainder Unitrust (CRUT)

A charitable remainder unitrust is structured to pay the donor a *percentage* of the fair market value of the trust assets each year for the donor's lifetime or for a term of years, with the property remaining in the trust passing to the charity upon the donor's death. Here again, the payments can be set up to pay the donor and spouse during their joint lifetimes and can go to other persons like children or grandchildren.

There are at least four variations possible for structuring how a CRUT will pay out:

1. *Type I—Standard (CRUT)*. A standard CRUT pays a flat fixed percentage of the net fair market value of trust assets. The pay-

ments are made regardless of trust earnings and are usually intended to come from income, but will be made from trust principal when necessary.

2. *Type II—Net income or income only (NICRUT).* This is a simple variation of the standard charitable remainder unitrust. The "net income" or "income only" simply means that the payout is limited to the lesser of the standard unitrust specified percentage or the actual trust income. Unlike the standard unitrust, a NICRUT must have income to make payments; no invasion of principal is allowed. Trust income is usually defined as interest, dividends, rents, and royalties, but would preclude annual payments being made from capital gain or trust principal. This payout structure is commonly referred to as an income only, net income, or Type II unitrust.

3. *Type III—Net income with make-up (NIMCRUT).* The NIMCRUT structure works just like the NICRUT above, except that the trust may make payments from trust income in excess of the standard unitrust specified percentage to make up for deficiencies in prior years. This payout structure is referred to as a net income with make-up or Type III unitrust.

4. *Type IV—FLIP CRUT.* The FLIP CRUT is generally used for a gift of property that will not generate any income until it is sold, such as vacant land. Like a NICRUT, the FLIP CRUT is initially structured for payments of the lesser of the net income or standard unitrust specified percentage. The result is that during the period before the sale, the "income only" provision eliminates the need for the trust to make payments if no cash/income is available. On some established triggering event, usually the sale of the property, the income only provision ceases and the unitrust payout structure changes or "flips" to set itself to the specified payout percentage exactly like a standard CRUT.

Are you confused yet? If so, don't worry about it. The main difference between the CRAT and the four variations of a CRUT are simply how the payout is structured. Just remember that the CRAT structure pays the donor a *fixed* amount each year, regardless of inflation or changes in the value of trust assets. The various CRUT structures pay out a set *percentage* of the annually determined fair market value of the trust assets.

Which is better? It depends on what you want. The annuity structure provides the security of fixed payments in a declining market, but risks the depletion of the trust assets. The unitrust structure provides a hedge against inflation, but risks lower payments if the total value of trust assets goes down.

Legal Requirements

It is important to follow the IRS requirements for structure and form on charitable remainder trusts. In all likelihood, if you are going to do a charitable remainder trust you will be using either your own attorney or one provided by the charity to draft the necessary documents and advise you. This is an area of tax planning and law that needs careful attention to detail and full consideration before you act. Most advisors will be able to walk you through the issues that affect you specifically, but the following are some considerations common in most charitable remainder trusts.

Irrevocability

All charitable remainder trusts are required to be irrevocable. This means that once the trust is created and the property transferred to the trust, there is no going back. It is possible to seek court-assisted modifications to the structure of the trust, but there will have to be a good reason and the costs associated with making changes are usually prohibitive.

Mortgage Issues

If you have an existing mortgage on the property being considered for a charitable remainder trust you may not be able to use it. The IRS has taken the position that mortgaged property does not qualify for charitable remainder trust tax treatment. Why? At first, this rule doesn't seem to make sense because in most cases the property being transferred into the trust is going to be sold anyway. So why not just calculate the value of the charitable remainder trust (and gift) on the net proceeds after the mortgage is paid off? Seems to make sense, but this example will illustrate the problem.

☞ **Example:** Christina has an eight-unit apartment building she is thinking about selling. She bought it a long time ago and has a current adjusted basis on it of $100,000. The property has a fair market value of $400,000 and Christina has calculated her capital gains taxes if she sells outright at about $100,000. The building is currently owned free and clear. Christina decides to take a 75 percent loan-to-value mortgage out on the property and puts the proceeds ($300,000) from the mortgage in her bank. Christina now plans to gift the property to a charitable remainder trust.

If there were no rule against mortgaged properties in charitable remainder trusts, Christina's trust would have a net value of $100,000 ($400,000 sales price less the mortgage pay-off of $300,000) and Christina would receive the stream of income from the trust for her lifetime with the remainder going to the designated charity. What has really happened here is that Christina has been able to pull out $300,000 of tax-free money (the loan proceeds) and then donate the property's remaining equity, which would have otherwise been tax dollars, to charity. Obviously, the IRS caught on to this creative planning pretty fast and put a stop to it by not allowing mortgaged property to qualify.

If you do have mortgaged property that you would like to use for a charitable remainder trust, speak to a charitable remainder trust attorney or one of the larger charities in your area. Depending on the value of the asset and the amount of the mortgage, there are still ways to get around no-mortgage rules. Also, you may want to consider the alternative of a private annuity trust with a charitable beneficiary. Private annuity trusts do not have a no-mortgage restriction.

Seller as Trustee

For the purposes of this book, the function of a charitable remainder trust is to hold and invest the tax-free proceeds from the sale of a property and pay the lifetime stream of income to the seller/donor. In most cases, the seller/donor is going to want to retain some control over how those sale proceeds are invested. The person granted the authority to manage the trust investments is the trustee. Generally, the trustee can be any person, including the donor, a donor's relative, a financial advisor, accountant, attorney, etc. There can also be cotrustees, for example, a husband and wife, a parent and child, or any relative and a professional advisor.

There are some trustee powers, which, if retained, will cause problems with how the IRS views the tax-exempt status of the trust. These issues usually do not arise in the garden-variety situation where the trust simply sells the property and invests the proceeds. Your charitable remainder trust advisor can tell if your specific situation will create any restrictions on you being the trustee.

Payment and Term Restrictions

Usually the person starting the charitable remainder trust will want to maximize the stream of income from the trust and the immediately available charitable deduction from the gift. There are many factors that come into play in calculating just how to maximize the benefits. The income stream, who gets it, and for how long will be up to you, but there are limits and controlling factors. Whether you choose the annuity format or one of the various unitrust structures, every charitable remainder trust has the following four restrictions in common:

1. *Minimum and maximum distributions.* In structuring the income stream for an annuity format, the annual distribution has to be no less than 5 percent or no more that 50 percent of the fair market value of the assets initially transferred to the trust. Similarly, for a unitrust, the annual distribution must be no less than 5 percent or no more than 50 percent of the total trust assets valued annually.

2. *Stream of income duration restrictions.* Both annuities and unitrusts can be set up to create a stream of income for the lifetime of any person living at the time the trust is created. This would include the joint lifetimes of husband and wife. A charitable remainder trust may also be structured to create a stream of income for a set term of years rather than based on a lifetime. If structured for a set term, the period may not exceed 20 years. Instead of paying to an individual, the stream of income from a charitable remainder trust may go to another trust, a partnership, or a corporation, but only under a set-term structure and not exceeding 20 years.

3. *Projected benefit to charity.* Every charitable remainder trust must be structured from the outset to provide that after all the anticipated stream of income payments are made, a minimum of 10 percent of the fair market value of the initial trust assets will still go to the charity. This is an initial projection only and the trust will not fail in later years if the investment performance fails to keep pace. The projected benefit to charity rule is based on payment amounts and actuary tables.

4. *Probability of exhaustion.* No charitable remainder trust may be structured in a way that results in a greater than 5 percent chance that the trust will run out of money before making the remainder gift to the charity. This rule applies to both trust structures but is more applicable to lifetime payments under

an annuity format. The probability of exhaustion rule limits the risk that the donor will outlive his, her, or their actuarial life expectancies.

The first rule states that the annual payout can be set anywhere from a minimum of 5 percent to a maximum of 50 percent. This sounds as if it leaves a tremendous amount of leeway. In reality, however, the other rules limit the payout by requiring an amount still be available for the charity when all is said and done. When the payments are set for life, the age of the donor will be the most significant limiting factor.

Disadvantages

Irrevocability

The concept of a charitable remainder trust is basically that a donor makes a present or completed gift to a charity, but retains a lifetime benefit from the asset before the charity actually gets it. The key words here are "present or completed gift," meaning that once you transfer the asset to the trust, you cannot take it back or change your mind. Only a present or completed gift qualifies for the charitable deduction and other tax advantages we have explored. For the IRS to treat the transfer into the trust as a "present or completed gift," the trust itself cannot be amendable or revocable.

This irrevocability requirement applies primarily to the financial structure of the trust and the gift itself. A donor may retain the right to remove a bad trustee and even to change the ultimate charitable recipient of the gift. It is common that people like the idea of charitable remainder gifts, even if they are not sure which charity they will want to ultimately benefit. There is also the possibility that a named charity might cease to function or change its philanthropic purposes to something different than what the charitable remainder gift donor had in mind. For these reasons, a charitable remainder trust may contain provisions allowing the donor to amend to change charities. However, other than these few exceptions the trust must be irrevocable.

Family Inheritance Considerations

Another of the distinct disadvantages of a charitable remainder trust is that the trust assets go to charity upon the donor's death rather than to the donor's children or family. This may not matter if the donor has sufficient other assets for inheritance purposes or has an overriding desire to benefit the charity. But for many people, family inheritance considerations will discourage the use of charitable remainder trusts.

Charities have always faced this issue and have come up with a few ways for you to either soften the blow or completely replace the asset for heirs. In the following sections we will look at the two primary methods of making the gift *and* leaving something for your heirs.

Ways to Solve the Family Inheritance Issue

The most crucial disadvantage of charitable remainder trusts is that the principal of the trust (the remainder) will ultimately go to charity rather than to the donor's family or children. To overcome this result or to lessen its impact, planners have come up with two possible ways to replace the donated asset.

Wealth Replacement Trusts

One possible solution is to create a wealth replacement trust. A wealth replacement trust is basically designed to purchase and con-

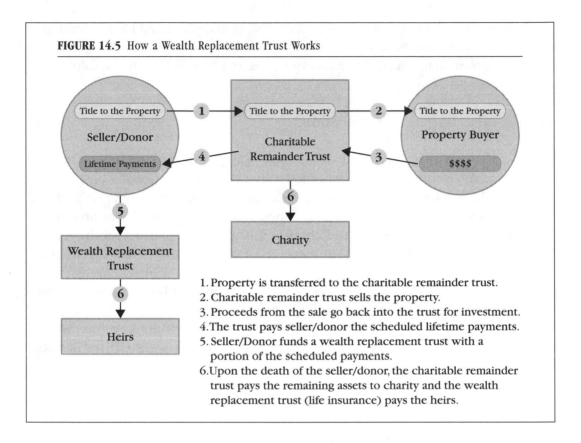

FIGURE 14.5 How a Wealth Replacement Trust Works

1. Property is transferred to the charitable remainder trust.
2. Charitable remainder trust sells the property.
3. Proceeds from the sale go back into the trust for investment.
4. The trust pays seller/donor the scheduled lifetime payments.
5. Seller/Donor funds a wealth replacement trust with a portion of the scheduled payments.
6. Upon the death of the seller/donor, the charitable remainder trust pays the remaining assets to charity and the wealth replacement trust (life insurance) pays the heirs.

tinue paying the premiums on a life insurance policy that will pay a set amount upon the death of the donor or on the last to survive in the case of couples. The idea is that you use some of the income from the tax savings and perhaps a portion of the monthly income from the charitable remainder trust to purchase the insurance. The death benefit of the life insurance goes directly to the heirs as a replacement for the value of the asset transferred to the charitable remainder trust. See Figure 14.5.

The fact that the insurance death benefit goes *directly* to the heirs is of significant planning importance because it means it will not be included in the donor's estate upon death and is therefore not exposed to estate taxes. For a person with an estate in excess of the estate tax exemption, this type of planning can be a very smart move.

☛ **Example:** Rebecca has a piece of vacant land left to her by her father 25 years ago. The basis on the land is around $100,000 and the current market value is approximately $500,000. Rebecca is 55 years old, her net worth or estate is approximately $2 million, and her yearly income is $100,000. Rebecca would like to make a donation to the university she attended to be used for needy students. To accomplish that, Rebecca has decided to create a charitable remainder trust and donate the land to it. She also has two children to whom she wants to leave her estate, so she has decided to create a wealth replacement trust to purchase a $500,000 life insurance policy. She intends to fund the wealth replacement trust with the immediate income tax savings she will receive as a result of the charitable remainder gift. She has worked out all the legalities and has put her plan into motion.

In the above example, Rebecca has accomplished a lot through a fairly straightforward plan. Let's say Rebecca lives for two years and is then killed in an automobile accident. Let's also assume the estate tax exemption at the time of her death is $1,000,000. Given this scenario, Rebecca's plan would accomplish the following:

- Rebecca's transfer of the land into the charitable remainder trust netted her an immediate $30,000 income tax deduction in each of the two years she lived.
- Rebecca, as trustee of her charitable remainder trust, sold the land upon receipt and paid no capital gains tax. By doing so, Rebecca was able to turn a nonproducing asset into cash that could be invested to generate income for the charitable remainder trust, which would, in turn, make the scheduled payments to Rebecca.

- Rebecca was able to receive two years' worth of scheduled life-time income from the trust—approximately $59,500.
- When Rebecca passed away, the remainder of the trust assets went to the university, as Rebecca specified, to fund scholarships for needy students.
- Rebecca's two children each received an equal share of the $500,000 insurance death benefit without any tax liability.
- Rebecca's estate saved approximately $225,000 in estate taxes because the $500,000 piece of land was no longer part of the taxable estate. And because the children received the insurance payment directly from the wealth replacement trust, their net "inheritance" was $225,000 *higher* than if the charitable remainder trust and wealth replacement trust had never been created.

As you can see, results of combining a charitable remainder trust with a wealth replacement trust can be dramatic. Wealth replacement trusts can be combined with any type of charitable remainder structures. The biggest potential problem with the concept of a wealth replacement trust is the possibility that the donor may not be insurable or that the insurance may be prohibitively expensive. Additionally, there are formalities that must be followed to be sure the life insurance death benefit is not included in the donor's taxable estate. There also are the attorney's fees involved in setting up both trusts and some yearly accounting fees for filing the relatively simple yearly tax returns. But even with all this in mind, the combination of charitable remainder trust and wealth replacement trust can be a powerful tool in the right situations.

Income Accumulation Accounts

Another possibility is the simple concept of setting the annual income from the charitable remainder trust aside for the benefit of heirs. If you have sufficient income and you simply don't need the money from the trust payments, you can set up an investment account with the idea that it will pass to your heirs upon your death. You could also disburse a portion of the income to fund children's or grandchildren's college funds, retirement funds, or whatever.

Charity Selection Considerations—What If You Change Your Mind?

Some potential donors are uncomfortable with naming a charity because of the irrevocable nature of charitable remainder trusts. It is possible that the goals or purpose of a particular charitable organization may change. Likewise, a donor's charitable interests or desires may change. Because of this, it is sometimes hard for a donor to make a commitment. This is perhaps the best reason to have your own attorney draft your charitable remainder trust. After naming the initial charitable beneficiary or beneficiaries, it is possible to have a provision in the trust allowing the donor to add or substitute other charitable remainder beneficiaries and/or change the shares to any one or more them. Charities that provide attorney services to donors are not going to allow you that type of discretion.

Where to Get More Information about Charitable Remainder Trusts

Many of the larger charities and most universities have fundraising departments that will be happy to provide any information you might want. However, as explained above, many people prefer to retain some flexibility about where the remainder gift will ultimately go. If so, you will need to contact an attorney to draft your charitable remainder trust. But first, you will need to decide if the financial and tax aspects of a charitable remainder trust fit your needs. To do that, you will want to discuss your specific situation with an advisor and have a financial illustration prepared that shows you the dollars and cents of it all. You should be able to find a knowledgeable independent advisor/accountant in your area or you may choose to go directly to one of the larger charities. If not, the advisor I recommend is the same accountant I recommended for private annuity trusts: Matthew Crammer, of Crammer Accountancy. Matt's contact information is listed in the Recommended Advisors section at the back of this book.

CHAPTER 15

Primary Residence Exclusions

"The income tax has made liars out of more Americans than golf."

Will Rogers

What Is the Primary Residence Exclusion?

There is a significant difference between the tax liability on the sale of an investment property and the tax liability on the sale of a primary residence. The main reason for this difference is a capital gains exclusion/exemption created by the Tax Reform Act of 1997. Before the 1997 act, the tax laws provided a primary residence "rollover" provision that allowed a homeseller 18 months in which to reinvest the gains in another primary residence without triggering taxes. There was also a one-time, over 55 years of age, $125,000 exemption that was designed to let aging Americans buy down to smaller homes and not be taxed on the first $125,000 of profit. Both of these provisions became history when the Tax Reform Act took effect on May 6, 1997.

The new primary residence or "main home" exclusion is basically a $250,000 exemption for individuals and a $500,000 exemption for married couples when selling a primary residence. As long as the property qualifies, there are no more rollover or reinvestment requirements, no minimum age requirements, and the new exemption can be used as many times as you like, but not more frequently than once in a two-year period. The actual IRS rule is as follows:

> You can exclude the entire gain on the sale of your main home up to

1. $250,000 or
2. $500,000 if all of the following are true:
   a. You are married and file a joint return for the year.
   b. Either you or your spouse meets the ownership test.
   c. Both you and your spouse meet the use test.
   d. During the two-year period ending on the date of sale, neither you nor your spouse excluded gain from the sale of another home.

What Property Qualifies as a Primary Residence

There are two tests to determine whether a property qualifies for the $250,000/$500,000 primary residence exemption. To be entitled to the exclusion you must have

1. owned the home for at least two years of the last five years, and
2. lived in the home as your primary residence for at least two years of the last five years.

These two requirements are referred to as the "ownership test" and the "use test" or requirements. There are some exceptions to the two-year ownership and use requirements that will be discussed below, but as a general rule both these conditions must be met for the property to qualify for the exemption. Additionally, even if the property qualifies, you may be disqualified if you or your spouse has taken the exemption on another property within the last two years.

IRS publications refer to a primary residence as a "main home" (this book will use the two terms *primary residence* and *main home* interchangeably throughout). A main home is not necessarily a traditional "house." A main home can also be a mobile or motor home, a boat that qualifies as a residence, a co-op apartment, or a condominium. Likewise, a fractional percentage of an investment property that is used as a primary residence may also qualify.

How the Required Two-Year Time Period Is Calculated

One of the commonly misunderstood areas of the primary home exemption is how the time periods are calculated to meet the ownership and use tests. For the average person who has owned and lived in their home for the past two or more consecutive years, there is usually no question of qualifying for the exemption. However, calculating the time period becomes a little more difficult in situations where the use has not been continuous, the exemption has been previously claimed, or where one of the spouses does not meet one of the tests.

The general rule is that a taxpayer must have owned and lived in the home for two of the last five years. It does not matter *which* two of the last five years or that the two years are contiguous.

☛ **Example 1:** Anne moved to Denver three years ago from Los Angeles. When she moved, she decided to rent her Los Angeles home for a time instead of selling it. She had owned and lived in the Los Angeles home for many years including the two years immediately prior to moving to Denver. Anne recently completed the sale on the Los Angeles home. Although Anne has not lived in the Los Angeles home for three years, she will still qualify for the primary home exemption on its sale.

☛ **Example 2:** Sally has had a beach house in New Jersey for three and a half years. Two years ago she moved to New York City after having lived in the beach house as her main home for 18 months. She has continued to use the beach house on the weekends and holidays while living in the city. Currently, she is planning to rent her city home and move back to the beach house for six months and then relocate to the West Coast. After Sally lives in the beach house for six more months, each of her homes will qualify for the exemption unless both are sold within a 24-month period. Before Sally relocates she intends to sell the beach house and use her primary home exemption to avoid taxes on the profit. She also plans to sell the city home two years later and use the primary home exemption *again* to avoid taxes on the profit from that sale. Sally will qualify for both exemptions because she will be able to show that she meets the criteria for both homes and did not try to use the exemption more than once in a two-year period.

☞ **Example 3:** Don and Julie were married about a year ago. Prior to getting married they both owned their own homes. When they got married, they decided to live in Julie's home and Don sold his using the primary residence exemption to shield him from taxes on the gain. Currently Don and Julie have decided that they need a bigger home and want to sell Julie's house and relocate. The estimated gain on Julie's house is $400,000 and they plan to use the "married couple" primary residence exemption of $500,000 to shield them from taxes on the gain. Unfortunately, they do not qualify for the full married couple exemption because Don does not meet either the ownership or the use tests. Julie does meet both tests and could file a separate tax return and claim her exemption, but that would only shield $250,000 of the $400,000 anticipated gain. Don and Julie's two main alternatives are:

1. Wait one more year so they both qualify and use the married couple $500,000 exemption at that time.
2. Sell now using only Julie's $250,000 exemption (filing separate tax returns) and pay the taxes on the other $150,000 of gain.

Don and Julie's situation above would not normally pose too much of a problem because it will usually take a few months in the process of selling and locating a replacement home. That means that Don and Julie can start the process in about nine months and time the closing of the property for a day or two after the two-year mark.

In most cases, figuring whether the property (and taxpayer) qualify for the exemption is not really difficult. If there are questions, be sure to discuss them with your tax advisor. There are times, however, that a taxpayer simply does not meet the two-year tests but has no choice but to move now. In those situations, which will be discussed more below, the regulations may allow a partial or fractional portion of the exemption to be taken.

Exceptions to the Two-Year Requirements

The general rule requiring a taxpayer to have owned and lived in the home for two of the last five years is very firm but not set in stone, there are exceptions to the rule. Likewise, there are exceptions to the rule that you not take the primary residence exemption more than once in any two-year period. The regulations provide an exception if you did not meet the ownership and use tests, or your exclusion would have been disallowed because you sold more than one home in a two-year period if your are selling your home due to

1. a change in place of employment,
2. health, or
3. unforeseen circumstances to the extent provided in the regulations.

The first of these three exceptions, a change in place of employment, is the most commonly used and is usually pretty clear in its meaning.

☛ **Example:** Ted and Tish bought their current home about one year ago. They sold their previous home one year ago and used their primary home exemption on that sale. Ted works for a large international corporation and has just been notified that he is being transferred to another state. Ted and Tish's current home will not qualify for a primary residence exemption because they have not met the two-year owner-ship or use test. Additionally, even if they could otherwise meet the ownership and use tests, they would be disqualified from taking the exemption because they have used their exemption on the sale of another property less than two years ago. However, by applying the "change in the place of employment" exception, Ted and Tish will be able to take a reduced exemption.

The "change" does not have to be an involuntary transfer or even have to be with the same company. In the above example, if Ted had simply decided to take a better job in a different area of the country, the exemption would still be applicable. If the change in place of employment is a considerable distance, there is usually no question that the exception can be used. The more difficult question arises when the "change" is close geographically. At the time of this writing, it looks like there is a 50-mile rule, but check with your tax advisor for any recent clarifications.

The "health" exception is more ambiguous. The regulations don't specify which health conditions qualify, so it may be a matter of opinion and the IRS's opinion will control. Obviously, if an illness is well documented in your medical records and your physician writes a supporting letter stating that the change is necessary, your chances of being disallowed on an audit are less. However, if you are trying to use this exception because *you feel* the change will do you good, you are likely to get resistance from the IRS. The best approach is to have good documentation supporting the move as a result of a verifiable medical condition.

The New "Unforeseen Circumstances" Rules

The last exception, "unforeseen circumstances," sounds like a catch-all loophole. After all, just about anything that makes a person want to move twice in less than two years is arguably an "unforeseen circumstance." In practice, however, this exception is useless because it only applies to unforeseen changes . . . "to the extent provided in regulations." The problem was that there were *no* unforeseen circumstances provided in the regulations. In late 2003, however, a new set of rules regarding this issue went into effect. Accordingly, a sale will be considered as occurring primarily because of unforeseen circumstances if any of the following events occur, which "involve" the taxpayer, his or her spouse, a co-owner of the residence, or a member of the taxpayer's household during the taxpayer's period of use and ownership of the residence:

- Death
- Divorce or legal separation
- Becoming eligible for unemployment compensation
- A change in employment that leaves the taxpayer unable to pay the mortgage or reasonable basic living expenses
- Multiple births resulting from the same pregnancy
- Damage to the residence resulting from a natural or manmade disaster, or an act of war or terrorism
- Condemnation, seizure, or other involuntary conversion of the property

The new regulations left open the possibility of additional qualifying situations by giving the IRS commissioner the discretion to determine other circumstances as unforeseen.

How to Calculate a Partial Exclusion

Okay, presuming you do qualify for an exception to the two-year requirement, how do you figure the exclusion to which you *are* entitled? Here's the official version:

Under Reg. Sec. 1.121 3(g)(1), the maximum exclusion is prorated by multiplying it (either $250,000 or $500,000) by a fraction. The numerator of the fraction is the shortest of the following three time periods (expressed in days or months): (1) the ownership period for the "early sale" residence, (2) the use period for the early sale residence, or (3) the time between the sale dates of the two residences. The denominator of the fraction is 730 days (24 months).

Wow, don't you just love the way lawyers and accountants explain things? In plain English, you get a partial exclusion based on how long you were in the home; half the required time would equal half the exclusion and so on.

Fractional Exemption Use for Investment Property

Although the primary residence exclusion is normally associated with single family homes, it does apply to other types of living arrangements. An apartment building with a resident owner can qualify on a percentage basis. If the resident owner meets both the ownership and use tests for the property and has not claimed the exclusion on another property in the past two years, he or she will be able to shield a percentage of the gain on the sale of the apartment building by claiming the primary residence exemption for that portion of the property used as his or her primary residence. The remaining portion will, of course, be taxed as investment property on the sale.

☞ **Example:** Paul owns a four-unit property that consists of a large three-bedroom unit in the front and three smaller units in the rear. Paul lives in the front unit and meets all the other criteria for a main home exclusion. When Paul sells the property he will be able to allocate a portion of the total gain as coming from his primary residence and take the primary residence exclusion. The question is, how much? That depends on how the income taxes for the property have been filed in the past. Presuming Paul has taken all the available depreciation on the investment property portion of the property, he or his accountant has probably already allocated what portion of the property represents primary residence and what part is investment property. If the allocation has not already been made in prior tax returns, Paul will be able to use just about any reasonable allocation method. On a four-unit property the taxpayer could simply allocate 25 percent (one of the four units) of the property as his main home and the remainder as investment property. On the other hand, if the owner's unit is 1,800 square feet and the other three units combined equal 1,800 square feet, Paul could allocate 50 percent of the property as his primary residence. The IRS allows any reasonable allocation and how Paul allocates will be crucial in understanding the future tax consequences. Herein lies a paradox. On one hand, an investor usually wants to maximize depreciation while the property is operational so he or she tends to allocate a higher percentage as investment property. On the other hand, when an owner/resident sells the property he or she will want to claim a higher percentage as primary residence. Remember, the primary residence portion of the gain up to the $250,000/$500,000 limits will be tax-free. The remaining portion allocated as investment property gain will be fully taxable.

Even if an unfavorable allocation was made on prior tax returns, it is possible to back up and refile past tax returns to change the allocation. In the alternative, you can also change the allocation for the current year and wait until the newly allocated portion meets the ownership and use tests as a primary residence. If you are going to change a past allocation, be sure to discuss it with your tax advisor first.

Investment Property Converted to a Primary Residence

One question that always comes up is can a taxpayer "convert" or "recharacterize" an investment property to a primary residence and qualify for the primary residence exemption. The answer is clearly yes, but the owner and the property will have to meet all of the primary residence exclusion tests, meaning that the taxpayer will actually have to use the property as his or her primary residence for the two-year use period. Sometimes that is simply too high a price to pay to qualify the property for the exemption, but other times it is a really smart move.

☞ **Example:** Jack and Barbara live in a suburb of San Francisco. They are both retired and are planning a move to Palm Springs. They also own a triplex within the San Francisco city limits that was left to them many years ago by Barbara's mother and has been fully depreciated since 1999. The triplex was originally built as a single-family house but had been converted over the years to three one-bedroom apartments. The property is very valuable already, but lately there has been tremendous demand for restored San Francisco-style homes and the neighborhood has become very upscale. Single-family homes in the immediate area have been selling for $700,000 to $800,000. Jack and Barbara both like to keep busy and think restoring their property would be a great project and a way to spend some extra time in San Francisco before moving to Palm Springs.

This is a perfect situation for converting an investment property to a primary residence. Jack and Barbara will have to move tenants out to start the restoration project, but if they are willing to move in while working on it, they can convert the property so the whole triplex-restored-to-residence will qualify for the married couple's $500,000 gain exclusion. In California, that will save them approximately $140,000 in combined state and federal capital gains taxes. In addition, the process of living in and restoring the property will probably enhance the property's fair market value. All in all, it seems like a smart move on Jack and Barbara's part.

As you will see in the next section, the downside to converting or recharacterizing investment property to primary residence (or part primary residence) is that some of the depreciation taken might have to be recaptured.

Recapture of Depreciation

As we saw in the previous example, it is possible to convert investment property to a primary residence. That previous example was, however, uncharacteristically perfect because the facts left no doubt that the taxpayer could increase the fair market value while decreasing the tax liability. The facts also stated that the property had been fully depreciated since 1995. In the real world, there usually is not such a large upside potential and the property is usually still being depreciated. This complicates the issue because although the primary residence exemption may apply, it will not shield that portion of the gain equal to the depreciation taken on the property after May 6, 1997 (the effective date of the Taxpayer Reform Act).

☛ **Example:** Joe bought a rental condominium in California in 1996 for $200,000. In 2003, he is considering selling it and is looking at the tax issue. The current market value of the property is $300,000 and the current adjusted basis is approximately $155,000. Joe knows the capital gains tax on the sale is going to be approximately $44,200 if he sells it outright. The idea of writing a check to the IRS for that amount does not sit well with Joe, so he is trying to decide if it would be worthwhile to move into the property for two years to get the primary residence exemption. After doing the math, Joe realizes that he has taken approximately $45,000 in depreciation since May 6, 1997. He knows that none of that depreciation will be shielded by the primary residence exclusion. That means that even if he does move into the property for two years to qualify, he will still have to write a tax check for approximately $15,300.

If Joe is like most people, he is going to give up on the idea of trying to convert the property to a primary residence and look for other alternatives. For most people, moving to a property for two years just to save on taxes is simply too disruptive of their lifestyles to actually do more than merely consider the option. However, it is nice to know that if the tax savings is high enough, or the right situation presents itself, the option is available.

Home Office Tax Issues

The previous section pointed out that any depreciation taken on investment property would not be shielded by the primary residence exemption. The examples used so far have all been about rental or investment property converted to primary residence. However, depreciation is taken not just on rental property, but also on other types of property used for business. One item commonly depreciated is the home office.

If you qualify, you have the right to allocate a portion of your home as a home office and to take expenses associated with that home office including depreciation. The question is whether it is worth it.

☞ **Example:** Victor and Carol live in a small but expensive two-bedroom home. Victor is a real estate broker and does most of his business from home. Victor claims one bedroom of his home as a home office on his taxes and uses it exclusively for business purposes. He has allocated 30 percent of the home as a home office and has taken a depreciation expense of approximately $5,500 on it for the last six years.

Unfortunately, many people do not understand that the amount of depreciation taken on their home office will have to be recaptured and taxed when the home is sold. In the example above, if Victor and Carol sell their home this year, they will have to pay $8,250 in federal taxes and some additional amount to the state. It is possible to do a 1031 exchange on that portion of the house into a corresponding percentage on the new house, but it becomes very complicated and tends to cause problems with mortgage providers. Whether the immediate year-to-year tax advantages of a home office deduction are worthwhile will depend on your own particular tax situation, but keep in mind, the primary residence $250,000/$500,000 exclusion may not protect you from taxes due on recapture of any depreciation taken after May 6, 1997. There are some very recent cases on this that appear to rule out any recapture of depreciation as well. Check with your tax advisor for recent developments.

CHAPTER 16

Stepped-Up Basis

"In this world nothing can be said to be certain but death and taxes."

Benjamin Franklin

In the beginning of this book, we looked at how capital gains taxes are assessed on the difference between the adjusted basis of a property and the net sales price. As such, it makes sense that anything that increases or "steps up" the basis will reduce the overall tax liability. Getting a partial stepped-up basis will reduce taxes and getting a full stepped-up basis may eliminate any taxes by eliminating the gain on the sale of the property. Remember, the taxable "gain" is the difference between the adjusted basis and net sale price, so if the basis is equal to or higher than the net sales price there is no gain to tax.

What Is a Stepped-Up Basis?

The term *stepped-up basis* refers to an adjustment or reallocation made to the basis of an inherited property. The concept of a stepped-up basis is fairly important because it directly impacts the amount of taxes you will face on the sale of inherited property and indirectly impacts the taxes your heirs will face if you pass an appreciated property to them as part of your estate. Let's start with the official definition; IRS Publication 551, *Basis of Assets,* states that:

> Your basis in property you inherit from a decedent is generally one of the following:
>
> 1. The fair market value of the property at the date of the individual's death.
> 2. The fair market value on the alternative valuation date, if the personal representative for the estate chooses to use alternative valuation.
> 3. The value under the special-use valuation method for real property used in farming or other closely held business, if chosen for estate tax purposes.
> 4. The decedent's adjusted basis in land to the extent of the value that is excluded from the decedent's taxable estate as a qualified conservation easement.

For most people who inherit property, either the first or second rule above will apply. Basically, if you inherit property, any gain made by the decedent is simply forgotten. You get the property with a new basis equal to its current fair market value and can sell it immediately without any taxes. If you think this sounds too good to be true, you might be right because there are estate taxes that have to be taken into consideration.

Before estate property passes to the heirs, it is going to be taxed at the estate level. Generally speaking, estate taxes are very high topping out at around 50 percent. So it makes sense that an asset taxed at the estate level should not be taxed again if the heir immediately sells it. To avoid double taxation, the regulations allow a full stepped-up basis for the heirs.

FIGURE 16.1 Federal Estate Tax Exemption

Year	Exempt Amount
2005	$1.5 million
2006	$2 million
2007	$2 million
2008	$2 million
2009	$3.5 million
2010	Unlimited
2011	$1 million (reverts)

☞ **Example:** Ralph owns an apartment building with a current market value of $500,000. His adjusted basis on the property is $100,000. If he sells the property today outright he will have to pay capital gains taxes on a $400,000 gain. If instead, Ralph had passed away and his son, Carl, who inherited it, was immediately selling the property, there would be no taxes because Carl would have received the property with a full stepped-up basis.

The potential problem is that if Ralph's estate was in excess of the estate tax exemption amount for that year, this asset might have been taxed as much as $250,000 (50 percent) at the estate tax level before Carl ever got it. However, the vast majority of people inheriting property receive it from estates valued at less than the estate tax exemption.

At the time of this writing, the estate tax exemption is $1,500,000 per person and the exemption is scheduled to increase as shown in Figure 16.1.

Basically, the estate tax exemption means that there are no federal estate taxes on estates valued at less than the exemption. So, in the previous example, if Ralph passed away in 2005 and his total estate was less than $1,500,000 there would be no estate taxes *and* his son would not face capital gains taxes because he received the apartment building with a full stepped-up basis. This is one of the few situations or "loopholes" where deferred tax liability actually disappears. The IRS is, however, moving to limit the amount of stepped-up basis that can be taken, but for the time being, the advantage is with the taxpayers.

Stepped-Up Basis on Jointly Owned Property

As discussed above, a full stepped-up basis is available on property inherited. But the rules vary a little when the property is jointly owned and the heir already owns a portion of the property. There are different ways or "vestings" possible in joint property ownership. Each vesting has it own survivorship characteristics and tax implications. Perhaps the best known are *joint tenancy, tenants in common,* and *community property.*

Tenants in Common

The vesting tenants in common is the easiest to understand because each of the owners is considered to own a fractional portion of the property and has the right to leave his or her fractional portion of the property to anyone through his or her estate. The tax and stepped-up basis calculations are also very straightforward because the inheriting person gets a full step-up in basis as to that portion of the property.

☛ **Example:** Assume the same facts as the last example, but this time Ralph and Carl co-own the property, 50 percent each, as tenants in common. If Ralph passed away and left his portion to Carl, Carl would receive a step-up in basis for that portion he inherited, but still have his original basis on that portion of the property he already owned. Carl's combined basis on the property after his father's passing would be $300,000 (stepped-up basis of $250,000 on his father's 50 percent plus his own existing $50,000 basis on his 50 percent)

The tenants in common vesting is most often used on partnership or combined ventures where the individual owners want to have the ability to leave their share to someone other than the other co-owner(s).

Joint Tenancy

The concept of joint tenancy is a little hard for some to understand. Joint tenancy is commonly defined as a vesting where each joint tenant owns an equal and undivided interest in the whole property. Joint tenancy is most commonly used in family situations, usually between husband and wife or parents and children. The step-up in basis is very similar to the tenants in common example above, but there may be a need to allocate and deduct some depreciation from the portion getting the step-up in basis. The primary difference between joint tenancy and tenants in common is that in joint tenancy when one joint tenant dies, his or her ownership interest *automatically and instantly* vests to the surviving joint tenant or joint tenants. This means that individual joint tenants do not have the ability to pass their ownership by last will and testament to heirs or whomever they choose. Instead, their portion of the property goes directly to the other surviving joint tenant or joint tenants.

People often mistakenly use a joint tenancy vesting as an estate planning shortcut in an attempt to pass property to heirs and avoid the expenses associated with probating an estate. Unfortunately, this seemingly quick and easy probate avoidance tool usually results in undesirable tax consequences. When joint tenancy heirs do eventually sell the property, they pay significantly more taxes because they only received a partial stepped-up basis. Proper estate planning can avoid the probate expenses and provide the full stepped-up basis.

Community Property

If you live in a community property state (Arizona, California, Idaho, Louisiana, Nevada, New Mexico, Texas, Washington, or Wisconsin) and are married, you have the ability to hold property with your spouse as community property. There are some distinct tax advantages in doing so. Unlike the other forms of joint ownership, the community property vesting allows the surviving spouse to receive a full stepped-up basis on both the deceased spouse's share *and* on the surviving spouse's own share.

☞ **Example:** David and Mona lived in California for most of their lives and were married for over 30 years. They owned two investment properties; an apartment building with a basis of $100,000 and a fair market value of $500,000, and a large parcel of vacant land with a basis of $10,000 and a fair market value of $610,000. Both properties had been in the family for many years. David recently passed away leaving everything to his wife. Mona will receive a full stepped-up basis on both properties to the current fair market value. She can sell both properties and she will pay no capital gains tax.

This is a tremendous advantage over other forms of ownership vesting. In the example above, if David and Mona had held the properties in joint tenancy, Mona would have received only a partial stepped-up basis and the capital gains taxes due would have been approximately $140,000 between federal and state taxes. A devastating result when compared to the zero tax due if stepped up as community property.

This type of vesting mistake is usually pointed out and corrected in any basic estate planning. Unfortunately, most people don't even do basic estate planning. There is a simple rule here, community property avoids taxes, joint tenancy avoids probate, but only proper estate planning (usually a living trust) avoids both.

Filing for a Step-Up in Basis

A step-up in basis does not have to happen immediately. If you inherited property in the past as a joint owner, you may still file for the step-up. You will need to establish the value of the property at the time you inherited it, but the effort and expense is usually well worthwhile. All property appraisers have the ability to give you an appraisal of the property at any particular point in time. You may even be able to get a local real estate agent to provide sufficient information to establish a fair market value on the date of death. However, if you have any reason to believe the valuation may be scrutinized, use an appraiser, not a real estate agent. Once you have your supporting documentation for a date-of-death value, it is a simple matter of having your tax preparer file for the step-up in basis.

Using Fair Market Value to Your Advantage

As you can see, getting a stepped-up basis on a property can greatly affect the tax consequences when the property is eventually sold. Just as important as getting a stepped-up basis is making sure you get the *most favorable* stepped-up basis. From the sections above, it should be clear that a stepped-up basis is always tied to, and based on, the fair market value of the asset at a specific point in time. But what exactly is the fair market value of an asset? Whether you inherited a property ten years ago or if you are inheriting one now, *how* you establish the fair market value may determine your future tax liability. To understand the variables here, we need to start by defining fair market value. According to the IRS, fair market value is "the price the property would sell for on the open market. It is the price that would be agreed on between a willing buyer and a willing seller, with neither being required to act, and both having reasonable knowledge of the relevant facts." By this definition it is going to be necessary to determine what price a willing buyer and seller would agree upon. If you have just inherited a property and are selling it on the open market immediately, the actual sales price in an arms-length transaction will almost always be considered the fair market value. However, if you intend to keep an inherited property for some time before selling, or if you are going back now to file for a stepped-up basis on property you inherited some time ago, you will want to establish a favorable fair market value. The IRS has published rules for determining the value of property. The following is the IRS's appraisal guidelines for determining the value of real estate:

> Because each piece of real estate is unique and its valuation is complicated, a detailed appraisal by a professional appraiser is necessary. The appraiser must be thoroughly trained in the application of appraisal principles and theory. In some instances the opinions of equally qualified appraisers may carry unequal weight, such as when one appraiser has a better knowledge of local conditions. The appraisal report must contain a complete description of the property, such as street address, legal description, and lot and block number, as well as physical features, condition, and dimensions. The use to which the property is put, zoning and permitted uses, and its potential use for other higher and better uses are also relevant. In general, there are three main approaches to the valuation of real estate. An appraisal may require the combined use of two or three methods rather than one method only.
>
> 1. *Comparable sales.* The comparable sales method compares the property with several similar properties that have been sold. The selling prices, after adjustments for differences in date of sale, size, condition, and location, would then indicate the estimated fair market value of the property. If the comparable sales method is used to determine the value of *unimproved real property* (land without significant buildings, structures, or any other im-

provements that add to its value), the appraiser should consider the following factors when comparing the potential comparable property and the property:

a. Location, size, and zoning or use restrictions,

b. Accessibility and road frontage, and available utilities and water rights,

c. Riparian rights (right of access to and use of the water by owners of land on the bank of a river) and existing easements, rights-of-way, leases, etc.,

d. Soil characteristics, vegetative cover, and status of mineral rights, and

e. Other factors affecting value.

For each comparable sale, the appraisal must include the names of the buyer and seller, the deed book and page number, the date of sale and selling price, a property description, the amount and terms of mortgages, property surveys, the assessed value, the tax rate, and the assessor's appraised fair market value. The comparable selling prices must be adjusted to account for differences between the sale property and the property. Because differences of opinion may arise between appraisers as to the degree of comparability and the amount of the adjustment considered necessary for comparison purposes, an appraiser should document each item of adjustment. Only comparable sales having the least adjustments in terms of items and/or total dollar adjustments should be considered as comparable to the property.

2. *Capitalization of income.* This method capitalizes the net income from the property at a rate that represents a fair return on the particular investment at the particular time, considering the risks involved. The key elements are the determination of the income to be capitalized and the rate of capitalization.

3. *Replacement cost new or reproduction cost minus observed depreciation.* This method, used alone, usually

does not result in a determination of fair market value. Instead, it generally tends to set the upper limit of value, particularly in periods of rising costs, because it is reasonable to assume that an informed buyer will not pay more for the real estate than it would cost to reproduce a similar property. Of course, this reasoning does not apply if a similar property cannot be created because of location, unusual construction, or some other reason. Generally, this method serves to support the value determined from other methods. When the replacement cost method is applied to *improved realty,* the land and improvements are valued separately. The replacement cost of a building is figured by considering the materials, the quality of workmanship, and the number of square feet or cubic feet in the building. This cost represents the total cost of labor and material, overhead, and profit. After the replacement cost has been figured, consideration must be given to the following factors:

a. Physical deterioration—the wear and tear on the building itself,

b. Functional obsolescence—usually in older buildings with, for example, inadequate lighting, plumbing, or heating, small rooms, or a poor floor plan, and

c. Economic obsolescence—outside forces causing the whole area to become less desirable.

With this definition in mind, the IRS has told you exactly what they consider a valid appraisal. You may want to make sure your appraisal will conform.

While the above IRS valuation requirements may sound extensive and burdensome, they really are not. Almost all of the requirements are traditionally included in a standard professional property appraisal and in most cases that is all you will need to support your requested stepped-up basis value. However, all appraisers are not alike. Anyone in the real estate industry will tell you there can be a significant difference in "appraised" values on a given piece of real estate. Even in stable market conditions, it is not unusual to get appraisals differing as much as 20 to 25 percent. That variable can make a huge difference in how much you will pay in taxes.

☞ **Example:** Betty and Hal had been married for 30 years before Hal passed away. Hal left everything to Betty including their California home and a sizable piece of vacant land. Hal passed away ten years ago. At the time of Hal's passing, the real estate market was booming, but the year after he died the market slowed down and prices declined about 30 percent on average. Betty really wasn't aware of the downturn in the real estate market because she had no interest in selling. Recently, however, she has decided to move out of state to be near her daughter and grandchildren. Luckily, Betty's timing is good because the real estate cycle has come full circle and market values in her area have climbed back to the previous highs of ten years ago. Betty's home has a current market value of approximately $450,000 and she has recently been offered $400,000 for the vacant land. Both properties were bought almost 40 years ago at $30,000 for the home and $20,000 for the land. She has decided to sell both properties.

If Betty's advisors fail to tell her about filing for the stepped-up basis on these properties, she will face taxes on the approximate $170,000 gain on her home ($450,000 sales price less the $250,000 primary home exemption less the $30,000 original cost basis) and another $380,000 gain on the sale of the land ($400,000 sales price less the $20,000 basis). Combined, Betty's gain would be $550,000 and her tax liability would be approximately $159,000 (15 percent federal and 9.3 percent to California).

However, presuming Betty has good advisors and files for the available step-up in basis, her tax situation will depend on how the properties were vested and how she inherited them. If both properties were held in either community property or in a revocable living trust as community or marital property, Betty will be able to file for a full stepped-up basis on each. Because the properties were inherited ten years ago and the example states that the current values have climbed back to the highs of ten years ago, an appraisal of each property as of Hal's date of death (also ten years ago) should qualify Betty for a full basis step-up to today's values. Presuming valid appraisals did support a step-up to the current values, she could sell both properties and have no taxable gain at all. Even if the properties were both held in Hal and Betty's names as husband and wife as joint tenants, Betty would still be entitled to a stepped-up basis, but only on one half (Hal's half) of each property. If held as joint tenants, her basis on the home would be approximately $240,000 (Hal's half stepped-up to $225,000 plus Betty's half at her original $15,000). After the step-up there would be no tax liability on the sale of the home because the $250,000 primary residence exemption would shield Betty's $210,000 gain. On the land however, there will be some taxes. Betty's new basis would be $210,000 (Hal's half stepped up to $200,000 plus Betty's half at her original $10,000) and the gain on the sale would be $190,000 with a tax liability of approximately $53,100 (15 percent federal and 9.3 percent to California).

All of the calculations above presume one crucial factor—a supporting appraisal that shows the property values on Hal's date of death are approximately equal to today's market values. The example also presumes a real estate market down cycle occurred between the date of death and the sale of the properties. Even if there was no down cycle, a favorable appraisal to support a higher stepped-up basis will save a lot on taxes. Considering the 20 to 25 percent variations commonly seen between appraisers, which one you pick can save you or cost you a lot. In the example above, both of Betty's properties had a combined $950,000 estimated date-of-death value. If an overly conservative appraiser's valuation came in at 25 percent lower, it might cost Betty tens of thousands in additional capital gains taxes.

Some appraisers are naturally more conservative than others. In addition, an appraiser's level of conservativeness may vary dramatically depending on the purpose and use of the appraisal requested. Although it is not discussed often, it is a common practice to look for the most favorable appraiser or "shop" appraisers. Real estate agents do it, mortgage brokers do it, attorneys do it, and it should be no surprise that the IRS will use their "favored" appraisers in a dispute.

If you are going to file for a stepped-up basis either because it is time to sell or to gain a basis advantage on a property you intend to keep a while, you might try to tap into any professional real estate resources you may have. Real estate agents, mortgage brokers, and real estate attorneys may have established relationships with appraisers. If you can use their existing relationships, do so.

Generally speaking, it will usually be to your advantage to establish the highest possible value for stepped-up basis purposes. However, there are times when a high date-of-death valuation is not to your advantage. Case in point, an optimistic or exaggerated value will hurt you if the property is subject to estate taxes.

☞ **Example:** Carl's father passed away a few months ago and left Carl and his sister an estate consisting of the father's home and two small apartment buildings. The father had owned all three properties for many years and Carl and his sister plan to keep all three for a few years before selling them. The approximate value of all three properties is $1,500,000. Carl knows he and his sister are entitled to a stepped-up basis on the properties and he is trying to arrange for the appraisals now. Carl knows there can be some variability in appraisals and wants to make the right decisions to minimize taxes. At the time of the father's death, the federal estate exemption was $1,000,000.

Estate taxes at the time of this writing, start at 37 percent and go up to 50 percent very quickly. In the example above, Carl is going to face some estate tax on his father's estate, but how much? If he hires an appraiser that leans toward a higher valuation, Carl and his sister will receive a higher stepped-up basis, but will have to pay more in estate taxes now. In this situation, it is better to get as conservative a valuation as reasonably possible to minimize the estate taxes (37 percent or higher) at the expense of paying future capital gains tax (15 percent) later.

A second situation where an overly optimistic valuation may backfire is where there are multiple heirs or partners and one heir or partner will be buying out the interests of the others. Obviously, in this situation a balancing of the respective interests will be necessary.

Summary

I am always surprised at how often people overlook or simply don't know about the tax benefits of getting a stepped-up basis on a property. This is one of the last remaining true tax loopholes. If you quality for a step-up in basis, be sure you take advantage of it.

CHAPTER 17

Using Your IRA to Buy Real Estate

"I always imagined that a client needs at least two tax advisors. One tells him what the law is. The other tells him what he wants the law to be. Then he can choose."

Terence Floyd Cuff

Yes, You Can Use Your IRA to Invest in Real Estate

Most people don't know they can use their IRA or IRA-like (401 (k), Keogh, etc.) retirement accounts to invest in real estate. Contrary to what your financial advisor may be telling you, you can. Better yet, if that property investment is made in a Roth IRA, you may never have to pay taxes on the rental income while you own it or taxes on the capital gain when you sell it. This may sound like nonsense, but it's true. The fact is that you can structure or restructure many individual retirement accounts (IRAs) so that you, through your IRA, may buy and sell real estate. Depending on the IRA type, your capital gains and rental income on those investments will be either tax-deferred or, in the case of a Roth IRA, completely tax-free.

Many people today have an IRA, Roth IRA, or some type of other retirement plan (401(k), 403(b)) that can be rolled over to an IRA or Roth IRA. In the case of employer-originated retirement plans, you will not be able to influence the types of investments made by the plan. However, if you have the ability to shift or roll over your retirement funds from a company-originated plan to your own IRA, you can gain a lot more control over how your money is invested.

Most IRAs are administered and invested by one of the big-name investment firms. If you have one of these accounts, the last five years have probably been pretty discouraging. Both the NYSE and the Nasdaq declined significantly after the tech bubble burst, but have more recently been retaking some of the ground lost. Nevertheless, more and more, people are starting to look for ways to have better control over the performance of their investments. And while most stock portfolios have taken it on the chin in the last five years, real estate market investments have been growing steadily.

Real estate investing in IRAs, however, seems to be one of the best-kept secrets around. If you ask a traditional stockbroker or financial advisor, especially ones from big-name investments firms, about using your IRA to invest in real estate, you will probably get stunned silence or a "you can't do that." After all, the most profitable way for the big-name firms to make money from your money is to control it in the financial investment markets. The bottom line is if you take money out of their hands and put it into real estate investments, they lose profits. As such, it is not surprising that the big-name investment firms completely ignore this option. What is surprising, however, is that the real estate industry seems to be missing a lucrative opportunity to promote the use of IRAs for real estate investment.

Today, with the increasing uncertainty of the stock market, investors are actively looking for investment alternatives. The seemingly endless headlines of corporate officers caught using misleading/fraudulent accounting techniques to mislead the investor or outright stealing from the company has brought about prevailing investor skepticism. The everyday investor's blind trust of big-name investment firm recommendations is changing and many individual investors are practicing a more hands-on investment strategy that includes a growing real estate component.

How It Works

The concept of tax-advantaged investments in an IRA is very exciting. Most people invest for the future, and in most cases the *future* means money for retirement or accumulated wealth to pass along to your heirs. If this describes your situation, the concept of IRA real estate investments deserves a closer look. The following are three examples of how a person might benefit from this type of investment.

☛ **Example 1:** Carl has a Roth IRA worth $50,000. His neighbor has a four-unit apartment building he is interested in selling at $400,000. The neighbor has offered it to Carl and is willing to provide 20-year financing on the building (the neighbor's goal is to defer the tax consequences on the sale and create a stream of income, so an installment sale fits his needs). Carl and the neighbor agree on terms of $40,000 down and a 90 percent seller carry-back (note). Carl moves his IRA from his current IRA administrator to one that allows him to self-direct the investments. He then instructs his new IRA administrator to purchase the property in the name of his IRA using funds from his IRA account as the down payment. The IRA becomes the owner of the property. As the tenants make the rent payments to the IRA (through a management company), the IRA makes the mortgage payments. At the end of 20 years, the note is paid in full and Carl, through his IRA, owns the property free and clear. Because Carl used a Roth IRA for the property's purchase, all rental income after the note is paid off will go into the IRA account free of taxes. Likewise, if Carl decides to sell the property somewhere along the way, the sale of the property and any resulting capital gain go into the

IRA tax-free. Most important, because this is a Roth IRA, the distributions to Carl during retirement are also tax-free.

☞ **Example 2:** Pat and Laura live in an area where there is a tremendous amount of growth. Pat and Laura have an opportunity to buy a large parcel of land that they feel is going to be in the path of development. There are many new homes being built in the area and the parcel they are considering is perfect for subdividing and reselling as smaller parcels. Pat and Laura both have IRAs with sufficient funds to purchase and subdivide the parcel. From their self-directed IRA accounts, they instruct the administrator to buy the land and arrange the subdivision process with IRA funds. As the subdivided lots are sold off in the future, all profits will go into their (regular) IRA accounts and continue to grow (shielded from taxes) until distributions begin in their retirement.

☞ **Example 3:** Brad is a contractor who buys run-down houses, fixes them up, and resells them at a profit. He does about two to three houses a year and makes a good living at it. Lately, the market has been very hot and he is sure he could do one or two additional houses a year without much trouble. He has an IRA with sufficient funds to purchase and remodel a house or two per year. Brad converts his IRA to a self-directed IRA and instructs the administrator to purchase an appropriate house he has found. He remodels the house and resells it for a profit. Even though Brad usually pays ordinary income taxes on the profit from his resales, the house owned and resold by his IRA will not. All profits will go tax-free into his IRA account and continue to grow for his retirement.

IRAs—Tax-Free versus Tax-Deferred

In the next section, we are going to look at the mechanics of tax-free and tax-deferred real estate investing in IRAs. But first, it is important to understand the difference between the terms *tax-free* and *tax-deferred*.

- *Tax-deferred.* Most retirement accounts are tax-deferred vehicles that allow the taxpayer to put away money each year for retirement planning. The yearly contributions made to a tax-deferred account are made with pretax dollars, so they have the added advantage of reducing the taxpayer's income tax in the year the contribution is made. The tax-deferred characteristic in this case means that the disbursements from the account made to the taxpayer during retirement will be taxable income in that year.
- *Tax-free.* Roth IRAs on the other hand are tax-free retirement accounts. Yearly contributions made to Roth IRAs are made with after-tax dollars so they offer no tax advantage in the year the contribution is made. However, the big advantage of Roth IRAs is that the investment growth of the retirement account is tax-free and the future disbursements during retirement are also tax-free.

Clearly, if you were now selecting the type of retirement account to use for real estate investing, you would choose the Roth IRA for its tax-free characteristics. But if you were like most others, you probably opted for up-front yearly tax benefits by contributing to a traditional IRA-type account and are now in the tax-deferred investment category rather than tax-free. It is possible to crossover and convert a traditional IRA to a Roth IRA, but the taxes due at the time of the conversion are usually too high to stomach. Whether your IRA investments are tax-deferred or tax-free, real estate investments can be a very smart move.

The first step in being able to do tax-free or tax-deferred real estate investing in an IRA is to set up your IRA as a self-directed IRA.

Where to Start—The Self-Directed IRA

The traditional problem faced by IRA owners is that the financial firm handling their IRA does not offer a way to use IRA funds to invest in real estate. Enter the self-directed IRA. A self-directed IRA is simply one in which the investor has greater control over how the IRA funds are invested. You can buy and sell investments, including real estate, within your self-directed IRA while deferring taxes. Today, there are literally hundreds of companies that offer self-directed IRAs, but not all self-directed IRAs are alike. Some of the bigger investment firms have recently started offering "pseudo" self-directed IRAs that allow the investor to "choose" from a number of preselected investment options. Many times the options offered are the same ones that were used by the firm before the repackaging and remarketing of their service/product as a "self-directed" IRA. Again, as mentioned above, the investment firms are most profitable if they control your money, so the option for real estate investment will be unavailable. Usually the dividing line between the pseudo self-directed IRA and a true self-directed IRA is whether the company is simply acting as a custodian of the account (your money) or if they act more as the administrator. Custodians generally do not have the paperwork and accounting systems in place to facilitate real estate investments, but many IRA administrators now do.

A small but growing number of companies have started to spring up across the country offering self-directed IRA administration services. Likewise, many independent financial advisors who have begun to embrace the idea of diversifying their client's IRA holdings to include a real estate component are looking to the true self-directed IRA.

The first step in moving toward an IRA with real estate investment ability is to move or roll over existing retirements accounts to one of the administrators who offer the real estate investment option.

Generally, any traditional IRA, Roth IRA, Simple, or Keogh-type of retirement account can be converted into a self-directed IRA. Employer-sponsored plans can sometimes also be converted. To find out about the process, contact the IRA administrator of your choice for assistance.

How to Buy Real Estate within Your Self-Directed IRA

Once you have established your self-directed IRA, your administrator will have a procedure for you to follow in directing funds to a property investment. The ordinary transactional process of offer and acceptance, escrow, title insurance, and so on will be the same, however, your IRA administrator will be the purchasing (or selling) party on behalf of your IRA. Each of the various IRA administrators will have their own specific process, but in each case you will be directing their actions by use of a buy or sell order of some type. There will be charges and fees associated with each transaction you do, so be sure to investigate the costs involved before you settle on a particular administrator.

There are also IRA advisors out there if you want more than just an administrator. IRA advisors generally provide a full range of assistance including helping you find the investments and showing you how to work with the administrators.

Self-Dealing and Other Prohibited Transactions

Before you get too excited about the possibilities of real estate investing in your self-directed IRA, you need to eliminate some types of transactions and property uses from your thought process. The following are some transactions that will not qualify for IRA advantaged tax treatment:

- The sale, exchange, or leasing of any property between the IRA and a disqualified person
- The lending of money or other extension of credit between the IRA and a disqualified person
- The furnishing of goods, services, or facilities between the IRA and a disqualified person
- The transfer to, or use by or for, the benefit of a disqualified person of the income or assets of the IRA

- Any act by a disqualified person who is a fiduciary whereby he or she deals with the income or assets of an IRA in his or her own interest or for his or her own account
- The receipt of any consideration for his or her own personal account by any disqualified person who is a fiduciary from any party dealing with the IRA in connection with the transaction involving the income or assets of the IRA

For purposes of the prohibited transaction rules, the definition of a "disqualified person" includes yourself and any persons or entities (corporations, trusts, estates, or partnerships) that stand in close relationship to you.

Unrelated Business Income Tax (UBIT) Issues

There is no dispute that an IRA may invest in real estate outright. However, an issue arises when you leverage or finance property within your IRA. The best way to maximize IRA real estate investments is usually going to be by leveraging the property, so this is an issue for most IRA real estate investors. The problem is that a somewhat obscure IRS rule regarding *unrelated business income* (UBI) comes into play. IRS Publication 598 defines UBI as:

The income from a trade or business that is regularly carried on by an exempt organization and that is not substantially related to the performance by the organization of its exempt purpose or function, except that the organization uses the profits derived from this activity.

In this case, the exempt organization they are referring to is your IRA. As such, income that would otherwise be tax-free in your IRA may be taxed if it is defined as UBI. The publication goes on to specifically state that income from *debt-financed* property is considered UBI.

Thus, if you own an asset in your retirement account that generates UBI, your account may be subject to taxation on that income. Generally, the rules say that IRAs that receive $1,000 or more of UBI during a single tax year must file a special form before the tax filing deadline and pay taxes on that amount of income. IRAs that receive less than $1,000 of UBI are not required to file.

As you can imagine, this UBI rule puts a bit of a damper on what would otherwise have been tax-deferred or tax-free income and investment. So if you are a leverage-minded investor (like most people) the challenge becomes finding a way to have leveraged property in your IRA, but not having it earn over the yearly $1,000 UBI limit.

There are a number of ways to structure real estate purchases within self-directed IRAs that would seem to solve or at least lessen the impact of this UBIT obstacle. Resolving the UBIT issue is a topic beyond the scope of this book, but there is a wealth of additional information on the Internet at the Web sites listed below.

Summary

Using your IRA for real estate investment seems like it will be a big part of diversifying retirement funds in the future. Eventually, the real estate community will catch on to this potentially limitless source of investment funds. Once they do, the public will hear a lot more about it and many more IRA administrators will spring up to handle a growing number of these types of IRA investments.

A number of these companies can be located right now on the Internet with a simple search for "self-directed IRA." Names you are sure to find include Entrust Administration at http://www.entrustadmin.com, Sterling Trust Services at http://www.sterling-trust.com, and Equity Trust Company at http://www.trustetc.com. Each of these companies, especially Entrust Administration, has an extensive Web site with lots of good information.

CONCLUSION

"Today is the first day of the rest of your taxable year."

Jeffery L. Yablon

In this book, I have tried to explain the majority of tools and techniques used by millionaire real estate investors in tax planning. But the fact is you don't have to be a millionaire real estate investor to want to avoid taxes when possible. Most of the exchanges and installment sales done in this country year in and year out are not done by millionaires, but by everyday real estate investors. For every multimillion-dollar property that changes hands, there will be hundreds of rental houses, duplexes, and a host of other small investment properties sold. So, while the title of this book is *Tax Secrets of Millionaire Real Estate Investors,* the tools and techniques described herein are for everyone to use. With that said, it is important for all real estate investors to understand the tax options and alternatives available to them. Likewise, it is also important that all investors understand that these tax rules are complicated and always changing.

My hope is that this book has been a good starting place—a way to get you thinking about tax planning and to give you a glimpse of some of the strategies used by sophisticated investors. However, neither this book nor any other book written can be a substitute for the person-to-person guidance of a knowledgeable accountant or attorney. The advice you get can only be a good as the advisor you choose.

Form: 45-Day Identification of Replacement Property

The taxpayer(s) identified below (hereinafter "Exchangers) are in the process of doing a like-kind exchange of property under the provisions of the Internal Revenue Code Section 1031. In accordance with the 45-day replacement property requirements, the Exchangers hereby identify the following properties:

- Property 1 _____ Value _____
- Property 2 _____ Value _____
- Property 3 _____ Value _____

IDENTIFICATION REQUIREMENTS: Under the provisions of IRC Section 1031, replacement property is identified only if it is designated as replacement property in a written document signed by the taxpayer and hand delivered, mailed, faxed, or otherwise sent before the end of the identification period to either: (a) The person obligated to transfer the replacement property to the taxpayer (regardless of whether that person is a disqualified person); or, (b) Any other person involved in the exchange other than the taxpayer or a disqualified person.

ALTERNATIVE AND MULTIPLE PROPERTIES: The taxpayer may identify more than one replacement property. Regardless of the number of relinquished properties transferred by the taxpayer as part of the same deferred exchange, the maximum number of replacement properties that the taxpayer may identify is: (a) Three properties without regard to the fair market values of the properties (the three-property rule); or (b) Any number of properties as long as their aggregate fair market value as of the end of the identification period does not exceed 200 percent of the aggregate fair market value of all the relinquished properties as of the date the relinquished properties were transferred by the taxpayer (the 200-percent rule). If you intend to identify more than three properties, consult your qualified intermediary or exchange advisor before doing so.

IDENTIFICATION CANNOT BE MADE LATE: Identification must be made within the 45-day requirement. The IRS does not allow any extension for holidays or weekends. If the 45th day of your identification period falls on a holiday or a weekend, your identification must be properly made on the ordinary business day BEFORE the holiday or weekend.

Date _____

_____   _____
EXCHANGER   EXCHANGER

_____   _____
EXCHANGER   EXCHANGER

APPENDIX B

Revenue Procedure 2000-37

Exchange of property held for productive use or investment—treatment of deferred exchanges—"qualified exchange accommodation arrangement."

IRS won't challenge qualification of property as either "replacement property" or "relinquished property" for purposes of applying non-recognition rules of Code Sec. 1031, or treatment of accommodation party as property owner, if property is held in qualified exchange accommodation arrangement (QEAA). Regs issued in 1991 didn't apply to exchanges where replacement property is acquired before relinquished property is transferred. Since regs were published, taxpayers engaged in various transactions to facilitate reverse like-kind exchanges, and IRS believed establishment of "safe harbor" would enable taxpayers who had genuine intent to accomplish like-kind exchange to qualify. Requirements are specified for QEAAs, and permissible agreements, regardless of whether their terms result from arms' length bargaining, were also provided. Safe harbor applies to QEAAs entered into by qualified exchange accommodation titleholder on or after 9/15/2000.

1. Purpose

This revenue procedure provides a safe harbor under which the Internal Revenue Service will not challenge (a) the qualification of property as either "replacement property" or "relinquished property" (as defined in section 1.1031(k)-1(a) of the Income Tax Regulations) for purposes of section 1031 of the Internal Revenue Code and the regulations thereunder or (b) the treatment of the "exchange accommodation titleholder" as the beneficial owner of such property for federal income tax purposes, if the property is held in a "qualified exchange accommodation arrangement" (QEAA), as defined in section 4.02 of this revenue procedure.

2. Background

01.   Section 1031(a)(1) provides that no gain or loss is recognized on the exchange of property held for productive use in a trade or business or for investment if the property is exchanged solely for property of like kind that is to be held either for productive use in a trade or business or for investment.

02.   Section 1031(a)(3) provides that property received by the taxpayer is not treated as like-kind property if it: (a) is not identified as property to be received in the exchange on or before the day that is 45 days after the date on which the taxpayer transfers the relinquished property; or (b) is received after the earlier of the date that is 180 days after the date on which the taxpayer transfers the relinquished property, or the due date (determined with regard to extension) for the transferor's federal income tax return for the year in which the transfer of the relinquished property occurs.

03.   Determining the owner of property for federal income tax purposes requires an analysis of all of the facts and circumstances. As a general rule, the party that bears the economic burdens and benefits of ownership will be considered the owner of property for federal income tax purposes. See Rev. Rul. 82-144, 1982-2 C.B. 34.

04.   On April 25, 1991, the Treasury Department and the Service promulgated final regulations under section 1.1031(k)-1 providing rules for deferred like-kind exchanges under section 1031(a)(3). The preamble to the final regulations states that the deferred exchange rules under section 1031(a)(3) do not apply to reverse-Starker exchanges (i.e., exchanges where the replacement property

is acquired before the relinquished property is transferred) and consequently that the final regulations do not apply to such exchanges. T.D. 8346, 1991-1 C.B. 150, 151; see *Starker v. United States,* 602 F.2d 1341 (9th Cir. 1979). However, the preamble indicates that Treasury and the Service will continue to study the applicability of the general rule of section 1031(a)(1) to these transactions. T.D. 8346, 1991-1 C.B. 150, 151.

05. Since the promulgation of the final regulations under section 1.1031(k)-1, taxpayers have engaged in a wide variety of transactions, including so-called "parking" transactions, to facilitate reverse like-kind exchanges. Parking transactions typically are designed to "park" the desired replacement property with an accommodation party until such time as the taxpayer arranges for the transfer of the relinquished property to the ultimate transferee in a simultaneous or deferred exchange. Once such a transfer is arranged, the taxpayer transfers the relinquished property to the accommodation party in exchange for the replacement property, and the accommodation party then transfers the relinquished property to the ultimate transferee. In other situations, an accommodation party may acquire the desired replacement property on behalf of the taxpayer and immediately exchange such property with the taxpayer for the relinquished property, thereafter holding the relinquished property until the taxpayer arranges for a transfer of such property to the ultimate transferee. In the parking arrangements, taxpayers attempt to arrange the transaction so that the accommodation party has enough of the benefits and burdens relating to the property so that the accommodation party will be treated as the owner for federal income tax purposes.

06. Treasury and the Service have determined that it is in the best interest of sound tax administration to provide taxpayers with a workable means of qualifying their transactions under section 1031 in situations where the taxpayer has a genuine intent to accomplish a like-kind exchange at the time that it arranges for the acquisition of the replacement property and actually accomplishes the exchange within a short time thereafter. Accordingly, this revenue procedure provides a safe harbor that allows a taxpayer to treat the accommodation party as the owner of the property for federal income tax purposes, thereby enabling the taxpayer to accomplish a qualifying like-kind exchange.

3. Scope

01. EXCLUSIVITY. This revenue procedure provides a safe harbor for the qualification under section 1031 of certain arrangements between taxpayers and exchange accommodation titleholders and provides for the treatment of the exchange accommodation titleholder as the beneficial owner of the property for federal income tax purposes. These provisions apply only in the limited context described in this revenue procedure. The principles set forth in this revenue procedure have no application to any federal income tax determinations other than determinations that involve arrangements qualifying for the safe harbor.

02. NO INFERENCE. No inference is intended with respect to the federal income tax treatment of arrangements similar to those described in this revenue procedure that were entered into prior to the effective date of this revenue procedure. Further, the Service recognizes that "parking" transactions can be accomplished outside of the safe harbor provided in this revenue procedure. Accordingly, no inference is intended with respect to the federal income tax treatment of "parking" transactions that do not satisfy the terms of the safe harbor provided in this revenue procedure, whether entered into prior to or after the effective date of this revenue procedure.

03. OTHER ISSUES. Services for the taxpayer in connection with a person's role as the exchange accommodation titleholder in a QEAA shall not be taken into account in determining whether that person or a related person is a disqualified person (as defined in section 1.1031(k)-1(k)). Even though property will not fail to be treated as being held in a QEAA as a result of one or more arrangements described in section 4.03 of this revenue procedure, the Service still may recast an amount paid pursuant to such an arrangement as a fee paid to the exchange accommodation titleholder for acting as an exchange accommodation titleholder to the extent necessary to reflect the true economic substance of the arrangement. Other federal income tax issues implicated, but not addressed, in this revenue procedure include the treatment, for federal income tax purposes, of payments described in section 4.03(7) and whether an exchange accommodation titleholder may be precluded from claim-

ing depreciation deductions (e.g., as a dealer) with respect to the relinquished property or the replacement property.

04. EFFECT OF NONCOMPLIANCE. If the requirements of this revenue procedure are not satisfied (for example, the property subject to a QEAA is not transferred within the time period provided), then this revenue procedure does not apply. Accordingly, the determination of whether the taxpayer or the exchange accommodation titleholder is the owner of the property for federal income tax purposes, and the proper treatment of any transactions entered into by or between the parties, will be made without regard to the provisions of this revenue procedure.

4. Qualified Exchange Accommodation Arrangements

01. GENERALLY. The Service will not challenge the qualification of property as either "replacement property" or "relinquished property" (as defined in section 1.1031(k)-1(a)) for purposes of section 1031 and the regulations thereunder, or the treatment of the exchange accommodation titleholder as the beneficial owner of such property for federal income tax purposes, if the property is held in a QEAA.

02. QUALIFIED EXCHANGE ACCOMMODATION ARRANGEMENTS. For purposes of this revenue procedure, property is held in a QEAA if all of the following requirements are met:

(1) Qualified indicia of ownership of the property is held by a person (the "exchange accommodation titleholder") who is not the taxpayer or a disqualified person and either such person is subject to federal income tax or, if such person is treated as a partnership or S corporation for federal income tax purposes, more than 90 percent of its interests or stock are owned by partners or shareholders who are subject to federal income tax. Such qualified indicia of ownership must be held by the exchange accommodation titleholder at all times from the date of acquisition by the exchange accommodation titleholder until the property is transferred as described in section 4.02(5) of this revenue procedure. For this purpose, "qualified indicia of ownership" means legal title to the property, other indicia of ownership of the property that are treated as beneficial ownership

of the property under applicable principles of commercial law (e.g., a contract for deed), or interests in an entity that is disregarded as an entity separate from its owner for federal income tax purposes (e.g., a single member limited liability company) and that holds either legal title to the property or such other indicia of ownership;

(2)   At the time the qualified indicia of ownership of the property is transferred to the exchange accommodation titleholder, it is the taxpayer's bona fide intent that the property held by the exchange accommodation titleholder represent either replacement property or relinquished property in an exchange that is intended to qualify for non-recognition of gain (in whole or in part) or loss under section 1031;

(3)   No later than five business days after the transfer of qualified indicia of ownership of the property to the exchange accommodation titleholder, the taxpayer and the exchange accommodation titleholder enter into a written agreement (the "qualified exchange accommodation agreement") that provides that the exchange accommodation titleholder is holding the property for the benefit of the taxpayer in order to facilitate an exchange under section 1031 and this revenue procedure, and that the taxpayer and the exchange accommodation titleholder agree to report the acquisition, holding, and disposition of the property as provided in this revenue procedure. The agreement must specify that the exchange accommodation titleholder will be treated as the beneficial owner of the property for all federal income tax purposes. Both parties must report the federal income tax attributes of the property on their federal income tax returns in a manner consistent with this agreement;

(4)   No later than 45 days after the transfer of qualified indicia of ownership of the replacement property to the exchange accommodation titleholder, the relinquished property is properly identified. Identification must be made in a manner consistent with the principles described in section 1.1031(k)-1(c). For purposes of this section, the taxpayer may properly identify alternative and multiple properties, as described in section 1.1031(k)-1(c)(4);

(5) No later than 180 days after the transfer of qualified indicia of ownership of the property to the exchange accommodation titleholder, (a) the property is transferred (either directly or indirectly through a qualified intermediary (as defined in section 1.1031(k)-1(g)(4)) to the taxpayer as replacement property; or (b) the property is transferred to a person who is not the taxpayer or a disqualified person as relinquished property; and

(6) The combined time period that the relinquished property and the replacement property are held in a QEAA does not exceed 180 days.

03. PERMISSIBLE AGREEMENTS. Property will not fail to be treated as being held in a QEAA as a result of any one or more of the following legal or contractual arrangements, regardless of whether such arrangements contain terms that typically would result from arm's length bargaining between unrelated parties with respect to such arrangements:

(1) An exchange accommodation titleholder that satisfies the requirements of the qualified intermediary safe harbor set forth in section 1.1031(k)-1(g)(4) may enter into an exchange agreement with the taxpayer to serve as the qualified intermediary in a simultaneous or deferred exchange of the property under section 1031;

(2) The taxpayer or a disqualified person guarantees some or all of the obligations of the exchange accommodation titleholder, including secured or unsecured debt incurred to acquire the property, or indemnifies the exchange accommodation titleholder against costs and expenses;

(3) The taxpayer or a disqualified person loans or advances funds to the exchange accommodation titleholder or guarantees a loan or advance to the exchange accommodation titleholder;

(4) The property is leased by the exchange accommodation titleholder to the taxpayer or a disqualified person;

(5) The taxpayer or a disqualified person manages the property, supervises improvement of the property, acts as a contractor,

or otherwise provides services to the exchange accommodation titleholder with respect to the property;

(6) The taxpayer and the exchange accommodation titleholder enter into agreements or arrangements relating to the purchase or sale of the property, including puts and calls at fixed or formula prices, effective for a period not in excess of 185 days from the date the property is acquired by the exchange accommodation titleholder; and

(7) The taxpayer and the exchange accommodation titleholder enter into agreements or arrangements providing that any variation in the value of a relinquished property from the estimated value on the date of the exchange accommodation titleholder's receipt of the property be taken into account upon the exchange accommodation titleholder's disposition of the relinquished property through the taxpayer's advance of funds to, or receipt of funds from, the exchange accommodation titleholder.

04. PERMISSIBLE TREATMENT. Property will not fail to be treated as being held in a QEAA merely because the accounting, regulatory, or state, local, or foreign tax treatment of the arrangement between the taxpayer and the exchange accommodation titleholder is different from the treatment required by section 4.02(3) of this revenue procedure.

Revenue Procedure 2002-22

SECTION 1. PURPOSE

This revenue procedure specifies the conditions under which the Internal Revenue Service will consider a request for a ruling that an undivided fractional interest in rental real property (other than a mineral property as defined in section 614) is not an interest in a business entity, within the meaning of §301.7701-2(a) of the Procedure and Administration Regulations.

This revenue procedure supersedes Rev. Proc. 2000-46, 2002-2 C.B. 438, which provides that the Service will not issue advance rulings or determination letters on the questions of whether an undivided fractional interest in real property is an interest in an entity that is not eligible for tax-free exchange under §1031(a)(1) of the Internal Revenue Code and whether arrangements where taxpayers acquire undivided fractional interests in real property constitute separate entities for federal tax purposes under §7701. This revenue procedure also modifies Rev. Proc. 2002-3, 2002-1 I.R.B. 117, by removing these issues from the list of subjects on which the Service will not rule. Requests for advance rulings described in Rev. Proc. 2000-46 that are not covered by this revenue procedure, such as rulings concerning mineral property, will be considered under procedures set forth in Rev. Proc. 2002-1, 2002-1 I.R.B. 1 (or its successor).

SECTION 2. BACKGROUND

Section 301.7701-1(a)(1) provides that whether an organization is an entity separate from its owners for federal tax purposes is a matter of federal law and does not depend on whether the entity is recognized as an entity under local law. Section 301.7701-1(a)(2) provides that a joint venture or other contractual arrangement may create a separate entity for federal tax purposes if the participants carry on a trade, business, financial operation, or venture and divide the profits therefrom, but the mere co-ownership of property that is maintained, kept in repair, and rented or leased does not constitute a separate entity for federal tax purposes.

Section 301.7701-2(a) provides that a business entity is any entity recognized for federal tax purposes (including an entity with a single owner that may be disregarded as an entity separate from its owner under §301.7701-3) that is not properly classified as a trust under §301.7701-4 or otherwise subject to special treatment under the Internal Revenue Code. A business entity with two or more members is classified for federal tax purposes as either a corporation or a partnership.

Section 761(a) provides that the term "partnership" includes a syndicate, group, pool, joint venture, or other unincorporated organization through or by means of which any business, financial operation, or venture is carried on, and that is not a corporation or a trust or estate.

Section 1.761-1(a) of the Income Tax Regulations provides that the term "partnership" means a partnership as determined under §301.7701-1, 301.7701-2, and 301.7701-3.

The central characteristic of a tenancy in common, one of the traditional concurrent estates in land, is that each owner is deemed to own individually a physically undivided part of the entire parcel of property. Each tenant in common is entitled to share with the other tenants the possession of the whole parcel and has the associated rights to a proportionate share of rents or profits from the property, to transfer the interest, and to demand a partition of the property. These rights generally provide a tenant in common the benefits of ownership of the property within the constraint that no rights may be exercised to the detriment of the other tenants in common. Richard R. Powell, Powell on Real Property 50.01-50.07 (Michael Allan Wolf ed., 2000).

Rev. Rul. 75-374, 1975-2 C.B. 261, concludes that a two-person co-ownership of an apartment building that was rented to tenants did not constitute a partnership for federal tax purposes. In the revenue ruling, the co-owners employed an agent to manage the apartments on their behalf; the agent collected rents, paid property taxes, insurance premiums, repair and maintenance expenses, and provided the tenants with customary services, such as heat, air conditioning, trash removal, unattended parking, and maintenance of public areas. The ruling concludes that the agent's activities in providing customary services to the tenants, although imputed to the co-owners, were not sufficiently extensive to cause the co-ownership to be characterized as a partnership. See also Rev. Rul. 79-77, 1979-1 C.B. 448, which did not find a business entity where three individuals transferred ownership of a commercial building subject to a net lease to a trust with the three individuals as beneficiaries.

Where a sponsor packages co-ownership interests for sale by acquiring property, negotiating a master lease on the property, and arranging for financing, the courts have looked at the relationships not only among the co-owners, but also between the sponsor (or persons related to the sponsor) and the co-owners in determining whether the co-ownership gives rise to a partnership. For example, in Bergford v. Commissioner, 12 F.3d 166 (9th Cir. 1993), 78 investors purchased "co-ownership" interests in computer equipment that was subject to a 7-year net lease. As part of the purchase, the co-owners authorized the manager to arrange financing and refinancing, purchase and lease the equipment, collect rents and apply those rents to the notes used to finance the equipment, prepare statements, and advance funds to participants on an interest-free basis to meet cash flow. The agreement allowed the co-owners to decide by majority vote whether to sell or lease the equipment at the end of the lease. Absent a majority vote, the manager could make that decision. In addition, the manager was entitled to a remarketing fee of 10 percent of the equipment's selling price or lease rental whether or not a co-owner terminated the agreement or the manager performed any remarketing. A co-owner could assign an interest in the co-ownership only after fulfilling numerous conditions and obtaining the manager's consent.

The court held that the co-ownership arrangement constituted a partnership for federal tax purposes. Among the factors that influenced the court's decision were the limitations on the co-owners' ability to sell, lease, or encumber either the co-ownership interest or the underlying property, and the manager's effective participation in both profits (through the remarketing fee) and losses (through the advances). Bergford, 12 , 88 T.C. 449 (1987), F.3d at 169-170. Accord Bussing v. Commissioneraff_d on reh_g, 89 T.C. 1050 (1987); Alhouse v. Commissioner, T.C. Memo. 1991-652.

Under § 1.761-1(a) and § 301.7701-1 through 301.7701-3, a federal tax partnership does not include mere co-ownership of property where the owners' activities are limited to keeping the property maintained, in repair, rented, or leased. However, as the above authorities demonstrate, a partnership for federal tax purposes is broader in scope than the common law meaning of partnership and may include groups not classified by state law as partnerships. Bergford, 12 F.3d at 169. Where the parties to a venture join together capital or services with the intent of conducting a business or enterprise and of sharing the profits and losses from the venture, a partnership (or other business entity) is created. Bussing, 88 T.C. at 460. Furthermore, where the economic benefits to the individual participants are not derivative of their co-ownership, but rather come from their joint relationship toward a common goal, the co-ownership arrangement will be characterized as a partnership (or other business entity) for federal tax purposes. Bergford, 12 F.3d at 169.

SECTION 3. SCOPE

This revenue procedure applies to co-ownership of rental real property (other than mineral interests) (the Property) in an arrangement classified under local law as a tenancy-in-common. This revenue procedure provides guidelines for requesting advance rulings solely to assist taxpayers in preparing ruling requests and the Service in issuing advance ruling letters as promptly as practicable. The guidelines set forth in this revenue procedure are not intended to be substantive rules and are not to be used for audit purposes.

SECTION 4. GUIDELINES FOR SUBMITTING RULING REQUESTS

The Service ordinarily will not consider a request for a ruling under this revenue procedure unless the information described in section 5 of this revenue procedure is included in the ruling request and the conditions described in section 6 of this revenue procedure are satisfied. Even if sections 5 and 6 of this revenue procedure are satisfied, however, the Service may decline to issue a ruling under this revenue procedure whenever warranted by the facts and circumstances of a particular case and whenever appropriate in the interest of sound tax administration.

Where multiple parcels of property owned by the co-owners are leased to a single tenant pursuant to a single lease agreement and any debt of one or more co-owners is secured by all of the parcels, the Service will generally treat all of the parcels as a single "Property." In such a case, the Service will generally not consider a ruling request under this revenue procedure unless: (1) each co-owner's percentage interest in each parcel is identical to that co-owner's percentage interest in every other parcel, (2) each co-owner's percentage interests in the parcels cannot be separated and traded independently, and (3) the parcels of property are properly viewed as a single business unit. The Service will generally treat contiguous parcels as comprising a single business unit. Even if the parcels are not contiguous, however, the Service may treat multiple parcels as comprising a single business unit where there is a close connection between the business use of one parcel and the business use of another parcel. For example, an office building and a garage that services the tenants of the office building may be treated as a single business unit even if the office building and the garage are not contiguous.

For purposes of this revenue procedure, the following definitions apply. The term "co-owner" means any person that owns an interest in the Property as a tenant in common. The term "sponsor" means any person who divides a single interest in the Property into multiple co-ownership interests for the purpose of offering those interests for sale. The term "related person" means a person bearing a relationship described in §267(b) or 707(b)(1), except that in applying §267(b) or 707(b)(1), the co-ownership will be treated as a partnership and each co-owner will be treated as a partner. The term "disregarded entity" means an entity that is disregarded as an entity separate from its owner for federal tax purposes. Examples of disregarded entities include qualified REIT subsidiaries (within the meaning of §856(i)(2)), qualified subchapter S subsidiaries (within the meaning of §1361(b)(3)(B)), and business entities that have only one owner and do not elect to be classified as corporations. The term "blanket lien" means any mortgage or trust deed that is recorded against the Property as a whole.

SECTION 5. INFORMATION TO BE SUBMITTED

.01 Section 8 of Rev. Proc. 2002-1 outlines general requirements concerning the information to be submitted as part of a ruling request, including advance rulings under this revenue procedure. For example, any ruling request must contain a complete statement of all facts relating to the co-ownership, including those relating to promoting, financing, and managing the Property. Among the information to be included are the items of information specified in this revenue procedure; therefore, the ruling request must provide all items of information and conditions specified below and in section 6 of this revenue procedure, or at least account for all of the items. For example, if a co-ownership arrangement has no brokerage agreement permitted in section 6.12 of this revenue procedure, the ruling request should so state. Furthermore, merely submitting documents and supplementary materials required by section 5.02 of this revenue procedure does not satisfy all of the information requirements contained in section 5.02 of this revenue procedure or in section 8 of Rev. Proc. 2002-1; all material facts in the documents submitted must be explained in the ruling request and may not be merely incorporated by reference. All submitted documents and supplementary materials must contain applicable exhibits, attachments, and amendments. The ruling request must identify and explain any information or documents required in section 5 of this revenue procedure that are not included and any conditions in section 6 of this revenue procedure that are or are not satisfied.

.02 <u>Required General Information and Copies of Documents and Supplementary Materials</u>. Generally the following information and copies of documents and materials must be submitted with the ruling request:

(1) The name, taxpayer identification number, and percentage fractional interest in Property of each co-owner;

(2) The name, taxpayer identification number, ownership of, and any relationship among, all persons involved in the acquisition, sale, lease and other use of Property, including the sponsor, lessee, manager, and lender;

(3) A full description of the Property;

(4) A representation that each of the co-owners holds title to the Property (including each of multiple parcels of property treated as a single Property under this revenue procedure) as a tenant in common under local law;

(5) All promotional documents relating to the sale of fractional interests in the Property;

(6) All lending agreements relating to the Property;

(7) All agreements among the co-owners relating to the Property;

(8) Any lease agreement relating to the Property;

(9) Any purchase and sale agreement relating to the Property;

(10) Any property management or brokerage agreement relating to the Property; and

(11) Any other agreement relating to the Property not specified in this section, including agreements relating to any debt secured by the Property (such as guarantees or indemnity agreements) and any call and put options relating to the Property.

SECTION 6. CONDITIONS FOR OBTAINING RULINGS

The Service ordinarily will not consider a request for a ruling under this revenue procedure unless the conditions described below are satisfied. Nevertheless, where the conditions described below are not satisfied, the Service may consider a request for a ruling under this revenue procedure where the facts and circumstances clearly establish that such a ruling is appropriate.

.01 <u>Tenancy in Common Ownership</u>. Each of the co-owners must hold title to the Property (either directly or through a disregarded entity) as a tenant in common under local law. Thus, title to the Property as a whole may not be held by an entity recognized under local law.

.02 <u>Number of Co-Owners</u>. The number of co-owners must be limited to no more than 35 persons. For this purpose, "person" is defined as in §7701(a)(1), except that a husband and wife are treated as a single person and all persons who acquire interests from a co-owner by inheritance are treated as a single person.

.03 <u>No Treatment of Co-Ownership as an Entity</u>. The co-ownership may not file a partnership or corporate tax return, conduct business under a common name, execute an agreement identifying any or all of the co-owners as partners, shareholders, or members of a business entity, or otherwise hold itself out as a partnership or other form of business entity (nor may the co-owners hold themselves out as partners, shareholders, or members of a business entity). The Service generally will not issue a ruling under this revenue procedure if the co-owners held interests in the Property through a partnership or corporation immediately prior to the formation of the co-ownership.

.04 <u>Co-Ownership Agreement</u>. The co-owners may enter into a limited co-ownership agreement that may run with the land. For example, a co-ownership agreement may provide that a co-owner must offer the co-ownership interest for sale to the other co-owners, the sponsor, or the lessee at fair market value (determined as of the time the partition right is exercised) before exercising any right to partition (see section 6.06 of this revenue procedure for conditions relating to restrictions on alienation); or that certain actions on behalf of the co-ownership require the vote of co-owners holding more than 50 percent of the undivided interests in the Property (see section 6.05 of this revenue procedure for conditions relating to voting).

.05 <u>Voting</u>. The co-owners must retain the right to approve the hiring of any manager, the sale or other disposition of the Property, any leases of a portion or all of the Property, or the creation or modification of a blanket lien. Any sale, lease, or re-lease of a portion or all of the Property, any negotiation or renegotiation of indebtedness secured by a blanket lien, the hiring of any manager, or the negotiation of any management contract (or any extension or renewal of such contract) must be by unanimous approval of the co-owners. For all other actions on behalf of the co-ownership, the co-owners may agree to be bound by the vote of those holding more than 50 percent of the undivided interests in the Property. A co-owner who has consented to an action in conformance with this section 6.05 may provide the manager or other person a power of attorney to execute a specific document with respect to that action, but may not provide the manager or other person with a global power of attorney.

.06 <u>Restrictions on Alienation</u>. In general, each co-owner must have the rights to transfer, partition, and encumber the co-owner's undivided interest in the Property without the agreement or approval of any person. However, restrictions on the right to transfer, partition, or encumber interests in the Property that are required by a lender and that are consistent with customary commercial lending practices are not prohibited. See section 6.14 of this revenue procedure for restrictions on who may be a lender. Moreover, the co-owners, the sponsor, or the lessee may have a right of first offer (the right to have the first opportunity to offer to purchase the co-ownership interest) with respect to any co-owner's exercise of the right to transfer the co-ownership interest in the Property. In addition, a co-owner may agree to offer the co-ownership interest for sale to the other co-owners, the sponsor, or the lessee at fair market value (determined as of the time the partition right is exercised) before exercising any right to partition.

.07 <u>Sharing Proceeds and Liabilities upon Sale of Property</u>. If the Property is sold, any debt secured by a blanket lien must be satisfied and the remaining sales proceeds must be distributed to the co-owners.

.08 <u>Proportionate Sharing of Profits and Losses</u>. Each co-owner must share in all revenues generated by the Property and all costs associated with the Property in proportion to the co-owner's undivided interest in the Property. Neither the other co-owners, nor the sponsor, nor the manager may advance funds to a co-owner to meet expenses associated with the co-ownership interest, unless the advance is recourse to the co-owner (and, where the co-owner is a disregarded entity, the owner of the co-owner) and is not for a period exceeding 31 days.

.09 <u>Proportionate Sharing of Debt</u>. The co-owners must share in any indebtedness secured by a blanket lien in proportion to their undivided interests.

.10 <u>Options</u>. A co-owner may issue an option to purchase the co-owner's undivided interest (call option), provided that the exercise price for the call option reflects the fair market value of the Property determined as of the time the option is exercised.

For this purpose, the fair market value of an undivided interest in the Property is equal to the co-owner's percentage interest in the Property multiplied by the fair market value of the Property as a whole. A co-owner may not acquire an option to sell the co-owner's undivided interest (put option) to the sponsor, the lessee, another co-owner, or the lender, or any person related to the sponsor, the lessee, another co-owner, or the lender.

.11 <u>No Business Activities</u>. The co-owners' activities must be limited to those customarily performed in connection with the maintenance and repair of rental real property (customary activities). See Rev. Rul. 75-374, 1975-2 C.B. 261. Activities will be treated as customary activities for this purpose if the activities would not prevent an amount received by an organization described in §511(a)(2) from qualifying as rent under §512(b)(3)(A) and the regulations thereunder. In determining the co-owners' activities, all activities of the co-owners, their agents, and any persons related to the co-owners with respect to the Property will be taken into account, whether or not those activities are performed by the co-owners in their capacities as co-owners. For example, if the sponsor or a lessee is a co-owner, then all of the activities of the sponsor or lessee (or any person related to the sponsor or lessee) with respect to the Property will be taken into account in determining whether the co-owners' activities are customary activities. However, activities of a co-owner or a related person with respect to the Property (other than in the co-owner's capacity as a co-owner) will not be taken into account if the co-owner owns an undivided interest in the Property for less than 6 months.

.12 <u>Management and Brokerage Agreements</u>. The co-owners may enter into management or brokerage agreements, which must be renewable no less frequently than annually, with an agent who may be the sponsor or a co-owner (or any person related to the sponsor or a co-owner), but who may not be a lessee. The management agreement may authorize the manager to maintain a common bank account for the collection and deposit of rents and to offset expenses associated with the Property against any revenues before disbursing each co-owner's share of net revenues. In all events, however, the manager must disburse to the co-owners their shares of net revenues within 3 months from the date of receipt of those revenues. The management agreement may also authorize the manager to prepare statements for the co-owners showing their shares of revenue and costs from the Property. In addition, the management agreement may authorize the manager to obtain or modify insurance on the Property, and to negotiate modifications of the terms of any lease or any indebtedness encumbering the Property, subject to the approval of the co-owners. (See section 6.05 of this revenue procedure for conditions relating to the approval of lease and debt modifications.) The determination of any fees paid by the co-ownership to the manager must not depend in whole or in part on the income or profits derived by any person from the Property and may not exceed the fair market value of the manager's services. Any fee paid by the co-ownership to a broker must be comparable to fees paid by unrelated parties to brokers for similar services.

.13 <u>Leasing Agreements</u>. All leasing arrangements must be bona fide leases for federal tax purposes. Rents paid by a lessee must reflect the fair market value for the use of the Property. The determination of the amount of the rent must not depend, in whole or in part, on the income or profits derived by any person from the Property leased (other than an amount based on a fixed percentage or percentages of receipts or sales). See section 856(d)(2)(A) and the regulations thereunder. Thus, for example, the amount of rent paid by a lessee may not be based on a percentage of net income from the Property, cash flow, increases in equity, or similar arrangements.

.14 <u>Loan Agreements</u>. The lender with respect to any debt that encumbers the Property or with respect to any debt incurred to acquire an undivided interest in the Property may not be a related person to any co-owner, the sponsor, the manager, or any lessee of the Property.

.15 <u>Payments to Sponsor</u>. Except as otherwise provided in this revenue procedure, the amount of any payment to the sponsor for the acquisition of the co-ownership interest (and the amount of any fees paid to the sponsor for services) must reflect the fair market value of the acquired co-ownership interest (or the services rendered) and may not depend, in whole or in part, on the income or profits derived by any person from the Property.

GLOSSARY

1031 exchange an exchange of properties under the tax-deferral provisions of Internal Revenue Code Section 1031.

180-day period The provisions of IRC Section 1031 give the exchanger 180 days from the closing of the relinquished property to complete the acquisition of the replacement property.

200 percent rule An alternative to the commonly followed three-property rule, the 200 percent rule permits an exchanger to identify more than three properties if the total value of all identified properties does not exceed 200 percent of the value of the relinquished property.

95 percent rule An alternative to the commonly followed three-property identification rule, the 95 percent rule allows the exchanger to identify as many properties as he or she desires as long as 95 percent of those identified properties are ultimately acquired as replacement property.

accelerated cost recovery system (ACRS) A statutory method of depreciation allowing accelerated rates for real estate used in business and/or held for investment during the years 1981 through 1986. This method allowed assets to be depreciated at a faster rate than had been allowed previously. It has been replaced by modified accelerated cost recovery system (MACRS) for real estate placed in service after 1986.

accelerated depreciation A method of depreciation that produces larger deductions for depreciation in the early years of an asset's life versus spreading the cost evenly over the life of the asset, as with the straight-line depreciation method. For most business property, except real estate, the law allows you to depreciate the cost at a rate faster than would be allowed under straight-line depreciation.

acceleration clause A clause within the mortgage agreement or trust deed that requires the buyer to pay off the note if the property is resold or transferred. This is commonly referred to as a "due on transfer" clause.

accommodator A person or company hired to facilitate a 1031 exchange by creating the necessary supporting documentation and holding the proceeds from the sale of the relinquished property on behalf of the exchanging taxpayer until the completion of the purchase of the replacement property. Also known as a qualified intermediary, middleman, or facilitator.

active income Income from wages, tips, salaries, commissions, or from a trade or business in which you materially participate.

active participation The level of involvement that real estate investors must meet to qualify for the $25,000 passive loss deduction. The full passive loss deduction may only be taken by taxpayers having an adjusted gross income (AGI) less than $100,000. A partial (shrinking) passive loss deduction is available on AGIs from $100,000 to $150,000. Thereafter, the deduction is completely phased out.

adjusted basis The starting point for determining taxable gain or loss. It is generally your original cost increased by capital improvements and decreased by depreciation.

adjusted gross income (AGI) Your gross income *less* allowable adjustments.

alternative minimum tax (AMT) A special tax designed primarily to prevent high-income taxpayers from using so many tax breaks that their regular tax bill is reduced to little or nothing.

annuity An annual payment of money by a company or individual to a person called the annuitant. The payment is for a fixed period or the life of the annuitant. The payments you receive include the return of your investment in the contract plus interest or other return on your invested capital.

applicable federal rate The interest rate fixed by the U.S. Treasury Department for determining imputed interest. If you are receiving or making payments for a loan or installment sale but little or no interest is stated on the contract, the IRS assumes a rate of interest based on the published applicable federal rate.

assumption clause A clause within the mortgage note that details the conditions under which another person may assume the note. In some cases the seller may not want the note to be assumable at all. In that case, the note must be paid in full if the property is sold or transferred (if there is a due-on-sale or transfer clause). A note should contain either an assumption clause, or in the alternative, a due-on-sale clause.

balloon payment A lump sum payment that is larger than the regularly scheduled monthly payments. A balloon payment is usually used in the note to reduce some portion of the principal or for a required early payoff of the whole note.

basis Usually the original acquisition cost if the property was purchased. Gifts and inherited property, however, will have an assumed or stepped-up basis. The word *basis* is commonly used interchangeably with *adjusted basis* which usually refers to the original cost plus any capital improvements, less any depreciation taken.

boot In a like-kind exchange any money or other nonqualifying property transferred or received by the taxpayer is known as boot and is taxable to the extent of the gain.

burden of proof A legal doctrine that places the burden of proving an issue on one party or the other. In income tax law, it is the responsibility of the taxpayer to prove that his or her tax return is accurate, rather than the IRS having to provide convincing evidence that it is inaccurate. In most cases, the burden of proof remains on the taxpayer's shoulders.

capital gain The difference between the amounts realized and adjusted basis on the sale or exchange of capital assets like real estate. The federal capital gains tax rate at the time of this writing (2004) is a flat 15 percent. However, that portion representing recapture of depreciation is federally taxed at 25 percent (see Chapter 2). State capital gains tax rates vary from state to state.

constructive receipt An exchanger is not allowed to have receipt of the sale proceeds at any time during the exchange process or the exchange will fail. The proceeds are considered "constructively received" by the exchanger if at any time the exchanger has unfettered use of or access to them. Funds need to be transferred to a qualified intermediary and held there in trust for the exchanger's purchase of the replacement property.

deferred exchange A nonsimultaneous exchange of property under the tax-deferral provisions of Internal Revenue Code Section 1031.

depreciation A deduction to reflect the gradual loss of value of business property—such as office equipment, vehicles, buildings, and furniture—as it wears out or becomes obsolete. The tax law assigns a life to various types of property and your basis in such property is deducted over that period of time. The tax law specifies the depreciation term for specific types of assets.

depreciation recapture An amount of prior depreciation that must be recaptured as ordinary income upon the sale of the property. Recapture is computed on Form 4797.

direct deeding The IRS now allows the respective titleholders in an exchange to deed directly to the ultimate owner. Before direct deeding was approved, both properties had to first be deeded to the qualified intermediary and then from the qualified intermediary to the ultimate owner.

disqualified person One who cannot act as an exchanger's intermediary.

down-leg Out-of-date (slang) terminology referring to the sale of the relinquished property.

due-on-sale clause or due-on-transfer clause A clause within the mortgage agreement or note and deed of trust that requires the buyer to pay off the note if the property is resold or transferred. This is commonly also referred to as an "acceleration" clause.

EAT An exchange accommodation titleholder (see below).

estate tax The federal taxes levied on the transfer of property from the deceased to his or her heirs, legatees, or devisees. It is based on the fair market value of the decedent's property at death less his or her liabilities.

exchange accommodation titleholder (EAT) One who holds title to the properties and acts as a parking entity during a reverse exchange.

exchange agreement The agreement between the exchanger and the qualified intermediary that sets out the duties and responsibilities of each. The exchange agreement is normally passed through the escrow or closing agent and supplements the escrow or closing instructions.

exchange period The 180 days allowed by IRC Section 1031 to complete the acquisition of the replacement property. The clock starts running at the close of the sale on the relinquished property.

exchanger The taxpayer using the provisions of IRC Section 1031 to exchange one property for another while deferring capital gains taxes.

fair market value The price at which a willing seller will sell and a willing buyer will buy in an arm's length transaction when neither is under compulsion to sell or buy and both have reasonable knowledge of the relevant facts. To establish fair market value, it is common to compare other similar properties sold near the same time as your property.

identification period The 45-day replacement property identification period specified in IRC Section 1031. The exchanger must identify a replacement property within this period or risk a failed exchange.

interest-only note A note or mortgage that provides for monthly payments consisting only of the interest on the principal. Usually this is done to lower the buyer's payments for a period of time or to simplify the calculations for the seller when principal payments are made or pay-off calculations are needed.

IRC Section 1031 The section of the Internal Revenue Code pertaining to like-kind exchanges.

joint tenants Ownership by two persons. Under joint tenancy, when one of the joint tenants dies the decedent's interest passes to the survivor by act of law.

like-kind exchange An exchange of properties under the tax deferral provisions of Internal Revenue Code Section 1031.

like-kind property In real estate, all real estate used for business or held for investment is considered to be like-kind. The exception is that foreign real estate is not like-kind to domestic real estate.

loan-to-value ratio (LTV) A measure of the amount of total financing in relation to the fair market value or sales price of the property. A $160,000 loan on a $200,000 property has an 80 percent LTV.

mortgage boot One of the primary conditions to be met in a fully tax-deferred exchange is to have a mortgage on the replacement property equal to or higher than the mortgage that existed on the relinquished property. If this condition is not met, the net mortgage relief is considered "mortgage boot" and is taxed to the extent of the gain.

passive activity An activity defined in the Internal Revenue Code as one or more trade, business, or rental activities that the taxpayer does not materially participate in managing or running. Real estate rentals and limited partnerships are examples of passive activities. Passive loss rules apply to losses from passive activities. All income and losses from passive activities are grouped together on an income tax return, and generally, loss deductions are limited to income or suspended until the passive activity that generated them is disposed of in its entirety.

passive income Income from a passive activity. You can offset a passive loss against your passive income. You cannot offset a passive loss against ordinary income.

passive loss Loss from a passive activity. Passive activities are investments in which you do not materially participate. Deduction of losses from passive activities is limited to the total of income from other passive activities. Passive losses generally can't be deducted against other kinds of income, such as your salary or income from interest, dividends, or capital gains. Generally, all real estate and limited partnership investments are considered passive activities but there is a limited exception for rental real estate in which you actively participate. There is a $25,000-per-year exception for rental real estate activities subject to limitations for high-income taxpayers. Losses you can't use because you have no passive income to offset can be carried over to future years or until you sell or dispose of your interest.

prepayment penalty A provision in a mortgage note that requires the borrower to pay a monetary penalty if the note is paid off before a specified amount of time. Each state has its own laws restricting the use of prepayment penalties. See Chapter 11 for more information.

qualified intermediary A person or company hired to facilitate a 1031 exchange by creating the necessary supporting documentation and holding the proceeds from the sale of the relinquished property on behalf of the exchanging taxpayer until the completion of the purchase of the replacement property. Also known as an accommodator, middleman, or facilitator.

realized gain The difference between the amounts received upon the sale or other disposition of property and the adjusted basis of the property.

recognized gain The portion of realized gain or loss that is subject to income taxation.

related persons There are special rules that apply to exchanges between "related persons." Generally, related persons include family members (siblings, spouse, ancestors, and lineal descendants) or entities (corporations, partnerships, estates, trusts, etc.) where a family member owns more than 50 percent in value of the entity directly or indirectly.

relinquished property The property given up in the exchange.

replacement property The property received in the exchange.

reverse exchange An exchange of properties under the tax-deferral provisions of Internal Revenue Code Section 1031. However, in a reverse exchange the replacement property is acquired prior to the sale of the relinquished property.

Roth IRA An IRA in which contributions are not deductible. However, if you meet the qualifications, your withdrawals, including interest and gains, are completely tax-free. Withdrawals must be taken after you reach age 59½ and at least four calendar years after the year in which the account was opened. Up to $2,000 a year can be contributed to a Roth IRA as long as your adjusted gross income is under $150,000.

S corporation A corporation that is taxed much like a partnership. The corporation generally pays no tax because profits and losses and other tax items are passed on and taxed to the shareholders. S corporations provide the legal liability protection of a corporation to its shareholders while avoiding corporate double taxation.

safe harbor A method of doing something that is expressly approved by the IRS. In exchanges, the term *safe harbor* refers to the use of a qualified intermediary, or in the case of reverse exchanges, an exchange accommodation titleholder.

Section 1231 property Long-term depreciable property used in a trade or business, such as equipment, vehicles, and rental real estate. Provided Section 1231 assets are held for the required period of time, capital gains treatment is available on a profit upon the sale of the asset while a loss is deductible as an ordinary loss.

Section 1245 property Depreciable personal property such as business equipment and vehicles. Any gain on the sale in excess of depreciation may qualify for favorable capital gains tax treatment under certain conditions.

Section 1250 property Depreciable real estate.

Seller in a 1031 exchange In exchange discussions, the "seller" usually refers to the person who owns the replacement property before the exchange occurs, although the exchanger is commonly mistakenly referred to as the "seller" of the relinquished property.

sequential deeding The process of deeding title of the exchange properties first to the qualified intermediary who then in-turn deeds title to the respective new owners. Sequential deeding is rarely used in ordinary exchanges; most exchanges now involve direct deeding.

short-term capital gain or loss The profit or loss from the sale or exchange of a capital asset that you held for one year or less.

simultaneous exchange A properly documented 1031 exchange of property in which the completion of the sale of the relinquished property and the completion of the purchase of the replacement property occur concurrently.

Starker exchange Starker was the name of two landmark court cases allowing a deferral period or delay between the relinquished property sale and the replacement property purchase. Prior to the Starker court decisions, all 1031 exchanges were thought to require simultaneous closings.

stepped-up basis The basis of inherited property. The basis is stepped up to its value on the date of the death of the owner, or a date nine months later if chosen by the executor of the estate. The tax on any appreciation during the decedent's lifetime is not taxable. The heir uses the higher basis to figure his or her gain when the property is sold.

straight-line depreciation method A depreciation method that spreads the cost or other basis of an asset on a pro rata basis over its useful life.

tax deferral Postponement of taxes to a later year. Shifting income to a later year. Investments in qualified retirement plans provide tax deferral.

tax shelter An investment designed to result in favorable tax treatment.

tax-deferred exchange A properly documented 1031 exchange. The term *tax-deferred* refers to the fact that taxes will not be triggered, as would otherwise be the case in an ordinary sale and subsequent purchase.

tax-free exchange A properly documented 1031 exchange. The term *tax-free* refers to the fact that taxes will not be triggered, as would otherwise be the case in an ordinary sale and subsequent purchase.

tenants in common Two or more persons who have undivided ownership rights in property. If one owner dies, the other does not automatically take the entire estate. Whoever is designated in the decedent's will inherits the decedent's share of the property.

three-property rule IRC Section 1031 requires that an exchanger identify the potential replacement property within 45 days after the closing of the relinquished property. The exchanger is allowed to identify three potential properties, at least one of which must be acquired within the 180-day exchange period.

up-leg Out-of-date (slang) terminology referring to the purchase of the replacement property.

RECOMMENDED ADVISORS

Finding good advisors in the area of capital gains tax planning is difficult. Many real estate agents and accountants tend to steer you away from some types of tax-deferral devices simply because they don't understand them. Advice is only as good as the advisor you choose. Many of the tax strategies in this book will not be known by your local real estate agents and tax preparers.

The following two people are recommended because of their knowledge and experience in handling investment properties and developing capital gains tax planning strategies. Both of these advisors are located in Southern California.

Real Estate Broker and Investment Property Specialist:

Ed Dowd
Coldwell Banker
5540 7th Street
Long Beach, CA 90804
562-961-1305

Ed Dowd handles marketing and sales of investment properties anywhere in Los Angeles and Orange Counties. He has hands-on experience with every tax-deferral strategy in this book. He is also an expert on tenant-in-common (TIC) exchanges.

Accountant and Financial Planner:

Matthew Crammer
Crammer Accountancy
8141 E. 2nd Street, Ste. 340
Downey, CA 90241
562-923-9436

Matt is a tax advisor and financial planner. He has an in-depth knowledge of the various capital gains tax strategies. Matt provides all accounting services from filing tax returns to advising clients on tax strategies and financial investments.

271

INDEX

A

Accelerated cost recovery system (ACRS), 29, 30
Accelerated depreciation, 29, 36
Acceleration clause, 135–36
Accommodator. *See* Qualified intermediary
Achong v. Comr., 24
Acquisition expenses, 70
Acquisition period, 81–83
ACRS. *See* Accelerated cost recovery system
Active participation
  exception, 44–47
  requirements, 49–50
Adjusted basis
  calculation of, 8
  installment sale issues, 127–28
  return of, 140–46
  tax liability and, 12
  1031 exchange, 63–64
Administrator, 234–35
Advertising, 21
Alienation, 112
Annuity contract, 153–54
Appraisal, 222–24
Appreciation, 3
Assignment, 132
Assumption, 135–36
Assumption clause, 132
Attorney's fees, 131

B

Balloon payment, 130
Beneficial owner, 99
Best security, 133
Biedenharn Realty Co., Inc. v. U.S., 24, 25
Bloomington Coca-Cola v. Commissioner, 104
Brokerage agreement, 113
Build-to-suit exchange
  financing issues, 107
  insurance issues, 108
  process, 104–6
  property construction, 97
  timelines, 107
  types, 103–4
Burden of proof, 19–20
Business activity, 113
Business entities, 22–23
Business use, 69, 84
Buy-to-hold. *See* Investor
Buy-to-sell. *See* Dealer

C

Capital asset
  IRS definition of, 2–3
  sale of, 3
  1031 exchange, 67
  useful life, 27–28
  variables, 4
Capital gain
  calculation of, 8
  charitable remainder trust, 186

  components, 8
  deferral tools, 59–60
  depreciation's impact on, 10
  growth planning, 5
  installment sale, 121
  long-term, 3
  primary residence exemption, 90–91, 201–2
  private annuity trust and, 154–55
  reporting, 140–46
  short-term, 3
  state tax, 2
  tax deferral, 5–6, 121
  tax lia3bility, 7–14
  tax planning, 4–5
  tax rate, 2, 3, 10
Capitalization of income method, 223
Carry-back financing, 123–28
Cash boot, 71–72
Cash flow, 38
Charitable remainder annuity trust (CRAT), 188
Charitable remainder trust
  charity selection, 199
  disadvantages, 194–99
  family inheritance considerations, 195–99
  income stream, 180–82
  income tax deduction, 181–84
  irrevocability requirements, 194–95
  legal issues, 190–94

Charitable remainder
trust *continued*
    mortgage issues, 191–92
    overview, 179–80
    restrictions, 192–94
    structure, 184–87
    trustee, 192
    types, 187–90
Charitable remainder unitrust
(CRUT), 188–90
Commercial annuity, 164–65
Commercial property
    prepayment penalty, 125,
      138–40
    triple-net lease, 109–10
    useful life, 28, 30
Community property, 220
Comparable sales, 222–23
Construction exchange. *See*
Build-to-suit exchange
Co-ownership, 85–87, 112
Cost segregation
    considerations, 38–39
    disadvantages, 41
    example, 39–40
    expense, 41
    purpose, 35
    studies, 36–38
    time strategy, 39–42
Crammer, Matthew, 178, 200
CRAT. *See* Charitable
remainder annuity trust
CRUT. *See* Charitable
remainder unitrust

D

Dealer
    business entities, 22
    court decisions, 24–25
    definition of, 16
    determination criteria,
      20–21
    intent, 19–20

investor versus, 15–25
    tax consequences, 17–21
Debt
    early pay-off, 125–26
    forgiveness, 2
    proportionate sharing of,
      113
Declining balance method,
    29, 30
Default, 124
Depreciation, 3
    benefit of, 27–33
    bonus deduction, 40
    concept, 27–28, 63
    cost segregation, 35–42
    effects, 30–31
    investor versus dealer, 21
    IRS Publication 527, 28
    land-to-improvement
      ratio, 29
    maximization of, 31–33
    methods, 29
    on paper expense, 63
    recapture of. *See*
      Recapture of
      depreciation
    recovery periods, 28
    1031 exchange, 63–64
Developer, 16
Die-on-transfer clause, 132
Direct deeding, 75
Discount point, 123
Disqualified persons, 74, 78,
    235–36
Distressed property, 97
Distribution, 193
Dowd, Ed, 117
Down payment, 130, 133–34
Due-on-(further)-
    encumbrance clause, 132
Due-on-sale clause, 132,
    135–36
Due-on-transfer clause,
    135–36

E

EAT. *See* Exchange
accommodation titleholder
Entrust Administration, 237
Equity Trust Company, 237
Estate tax, 1–2
    exemption, 157, 217–18
    property values and,
      227–28
    rate, 4
    wealth replacement trust
      and, 196–98
Exchange accommodation
titleholder (EAT)
    build-to-suit exchange,
      105
    financing issues, 107
    Revenue Procedure
      2002–37, 99
    reverse build-to-suit
      exchange, 107
Exchange agreement, 57, 74,
    75

F

Fair market value, 32, 221–28
Family limited partnership,
    23
Financing agreement, 120
FLIP CRUT, 189
Foreclosure, 124
Forward build-to-suit
    exchange, 103–8
Fully taxable disposition, 52

G

Gain, 8
Gault v. Comr., 24
Generation-skipping tax, 157
Gift tax, 1, 4
Goods and services, 105
Gross profit ratio, 141–42,
    144, 148–50
Growth planning, 5

H

Higher price rule, 69–71
Holding entity, 105
Holding period, 20, 83–85, 89
Home office, 212–13
Hospital Corp. of America, et al. v. Commissioner, 36

I

Identification period, 76–79
Improvement
    cost segregation, 35–42
    depreciation schedule, 37
    exchange. *See* Build-to-suit exchange
    ratio, 29, 31–33
    types of, 20
Income accumulation account, 198–99
Income stream
    charitable remainder annuity trust, 188
    charitable remainder trust, 180–82, 193
    charitable remainder unitrust, 188–90
    installment sale, 121–22
    private annuity trust, 159–60
Income tax, 1–2
    charitable gift deduction, 181–84
    rate, 3–4
    shelter, 43–44
Independent economic viability, 171
Individual retirement account (IRA), 229–37
Inheritance tax, 197–98
Inherited property, 215–28
Inspection, 132
Installment sale, 59
    adjusted basis issues, 127–28

advantages of, 121–23
concept, 120
definition of, 119–20
disadvantages of, 123–28
down payment, 133–34
early pay-off, 125–26
exchange combination, 147–52
financing agreement, 120
foreclosure, 124
Form 6252, 143, 145
interest rate considerations, 134–35
liquidity issues, 128
loan-to-value ratio, 129–30
note provisions, 131–33
prepayment penalties, 136–40
private annuity trust combination, 166–67
private annuity trust versus, 173–74
reallocation rule, 149–51
risk management, 129–33
taxes, 140–46
Insurance
    build-to-suit exchange issues, 108
    installment sale requirements, 132
Intent, 19–20, 92–93
Interest income, 140–46
Interest-only note, 121, 131
Interest rale
    installment sale issues, 134–35
    private annuity, 171
Internal Revenue Service (IRS)
    appraisal guidelines, 222–24
    audit, 18–19
    burden of proof, 20
    dealer issues, 21

fair market value, 221–22
Form 6252, 143, 145
installment sale definition, 119–20
installment sale/ exchange combination rules, 148–52
private annuity trust requirements, 170–71
Publication 527, 28, 32, 44
Publication 537, 148–49
Publication 551, 210
Publication 598, 236
Publication 925, 50–52
reallocation rule, 149–51
Revenue Procedure 2000-37, 98–100
Revenue Procedure 2002-22, 111–14
useful life, 27–28
Investment
    categories of, 16
    cycles, 4–5
    relocating, 66–67
    tax on, 7–8
Investment property
    definition of, 138
    fractional exemption, 208–10
    prepayment penalty, 138–40
    primary residence conversion, 210–11
    tax-free exchange, 69, 84
Investor
    business entities, 22–23
    court decisions, 24–25
    dealer versus, 15–25
    intent, 19–20
    material participation, 51–52
    tax consequences, 17–21
    workload reduction, 64–66

Irrevocable trust. *See* Charitable remainder trust; Private annuity trust
IRA. *See* Individual retirement account
IRS. *See* Internal Revenue Service

J

Jobs and Growth Act of 2003, 40
Joint tenancy, 219
Joint venture, 85–87

L

Land value, 32
Land-to-improvement ratio, 29, 31–33
Late fees, 131
Leasing agreement, 113
Leverage, 62–63, 122
Liability, 112
Life expectancy, 171, 175
Like-kind exchange. *See* 1031 exchange
Limited liability company (LLC), 22–23
Limited partnership, 23
Liquidity, 128
LLC. *See* Limited liability company
Loan agreement, 113
Loan-to-value ratio, 129–30
Loan-to-value ratio clause, 132
Long-term capital gain, 3

M

MACRS. *See* Modified accelerated cost recovery system
Maintenance provisions, 132
Malat v. Riddell, 25
Management agreement, 113
Margolis v. Commissioner, 25

Material participation, 49–51
Modified accelerated cost recovery system (MACRS), 29, 30, 37
Modified adjusted gross income, 46–47
Mortgage
boot, 71–72
charitable remainder trust issues, 191–92
relief, 71

N

Net income or income only CRUT (NICRUT), 189
Net income with make-up CRUT (NIMCRUT), 189
NICRUT. *See* Net income or income only CRUT
NIMCRUT. *See* Net income with make-up CRUT
NNN. *See* Triple net interest
Nonpassive income, 44–45
No-receipt-of-funds rule, 72–73

O

On-paper expense, 63
Options, 113
Owner-occupied property, 137
Ownership test, 202–6

P

Parking arrangements, 98–99
Parking intermediary, 100–101
Partnership, 85–87
Passive investment
disposition of, 52–53
rules, 43–43
Passive loss
active participation exception, 44–47
carry forward, 52

phase-out levels, 47
real estate professional exception, 44, 47–52
Personal property, 41
Personal service activity, 50–51
PMA. *See* Project management agreement
Prepayment penalty, 125, 132, 137–40
Primary residence exclusion
fractional exemption, 208–10
home office tax issues, 212–13
investment property conversion, 210–11
overview, 201–2
ownership test, 202–6
rule exceptions, 206
time period calculations, 203–5
unforeseen circumstances rule, 207
use test, 202–6
Private annuity trust, 59
accounting expense, 173
advantages, 154–55, 157–59
components, 156–57
concept, 153
costs, 171–73, 176
establishment of, 160–62, 176
estate tax liability, 157–58
frequently asked questions, 174–77
income stream, 159–60
installment sale combination, 166–67
installment sale versus, 173–74
investments, 164–65, 167–68, 176

IRS requirements,
170–71
legal issues, 169–73
overview, 174
payment deferral, 176,
177
property transfer/sale,
162
reinvestment, 164
structure, 159–60
tax deferral, 163–64
tax liability, 154
trustee, 169–70
Profit
proportionate sharing,
112
ratio, 141–42, 144
reporting of, 17
taking of, 18
tax consequences, 22
Project management
agreement (PMA), 105
Property
basis, 3
deterioration, 127
marketability, 123
recharacterization,
87–88
Purchase money, 137

Q

QEAA. *See* Qualified
exchange accommodation
arrangement
Qualified assumption clause,
136
Qualified exchange
accommodation
arrangement (QEAA), 99,
100
Qualified intermediary
build-to-suit exchange,
104–5
disqualified persons, 74
function, 56, 57, 74
process, 75

safe harbor, 74
use of, 73–75
Qualified property, 40
Quality indicia of ownership,
99

R

Real estate
dealer. *See* Dealer
depreciation, 28–29
investment cycles, 4–5
investor. *See* Investor
IRA purchase of, 229–37
partnership, 110–11
useful life, 28
Real estate investment trust
(REIT), 110–11
Real estate professional
passive loss exception,
44, 47–52
requirements, 48
Reallocation rule, 149–51
Real property trade/business,
48–49
Recapture of depreciation
capital gain and, 8–9
considerations, 10
cost segregation issues,
41
home office issues,
212–13
installment sale, 121
primary residence
conversion, 211–12
private annuity trust and,
154
tax liability, 11–14
tax rate, 9–11, 28
tax reporting, 140–46
REIT. *See* Real estate
investment trust
Related parties, 53, 89
Relinquished property
adjusted basis, 63–64
build-to-suit exchange,
104–5
contingencies, 77

holding period, 83–85
mortgage rule, 71–72
price requirement, 69–71
reallocation rules,
149–51
safe harbor, 98
sale collapse, 97
sale, 56–58, 97
tenants-in-common
exchange, 115
time requirements,
81–83, 107
Rent, 132
Replacement cost method,
223–24
Replacement property, 67
adjusted basis, 64
build-to-suit exchange,
105
contingencies, 77
holding period, 83–85
identification period,
76–79, 107
like-kind requirement,
67–68
mortgage rule, 71–72
parking arrangements,
98–99
price requirement, 69–71
proper identification of,
78–79
purchase of, 58–59
reallocation rules,
149–51
safe harbor, 98
tenants-in-common
exchange, 115
three-property-
identification rule, 79
time requirement, 76–79,
81–83
Residential property
prepayment penalty, 125,
137–38
useful life of, 28, 30
Reverse build-to-suit
exchange, 103–8

Reverse exchange
    cost of, 100
    legal issues, 97–102
    opportunities, 96–97
    process, 100–101
Risk management, 129–33
Roth IRA, 229–37

S

Safe harbor, 74, 98
Sales
    frequency of, 24, 25
    of inherited property,
        215–18
    number of, 20
    passive property interest,
        52–53
    patterns, 24
    proceeds, 112
    of relinquished property,
        56–58
    tax, 41
Schedule C, 17
Schedule D, 17
Schedule E, 17, 30
Scheuber v. Comr., 25
S corporation, 22–23
Section 1245 property, 41
Section 1250 property, 41
Self-dealing, 235–36
Self-directed IRA, 233–36
Self-employment, 18, 22
Seller financing, 120
    advantage to buyer, 123
    down payment, 133–34
    interest rate issues,
        134–35
    prepayment penalties,
        136–40
    qualified assumption
        clause, 136
    risk management,
        129–36
    taxes, 140–46

terms, 130–31
Separate entities, 22–23
Short-term capital gain, 3
Significant participation
    activity, 50
Simultaneous exchange,
    72–73, 76
Special use components,
    35–36
Specialty property, 37–38
Sponsor, 113
Spouse, 49, 51
Standard CRUT, 188–89
Starker exchange. *See* 1031
    exchange
Starker v. U.S., 56, 70
State tax, 2
Stepped-up basis
    fair market value, 221–28
    jointly-owned property,
        218–20
    overview, 215–18
Sterling Trust Services, 237
Straight-line depreciation, 29,
    30
Structured leasehold build-to-
    suit exchange, 104
Subdivider, 16
Suburban Realty Co. v. U.S.,
    25
Suspended loss, 52–53

T

Tax-deferred account, 233
Tax-free account, 233
Tax-free exchange. *See* 1031
    exchange
Tax liability, 11–14
Taxpayer Reform Act of 1997,
    90
Tax planning, 4–5
Tax Reform Act of 1997, 201
Tax service, 132

1031 exchange
    adjusted basis, 64
    advantages, 59–68
    advice/guidance, 80–81
    business use
        requirement, 69
    capital gain on, 59–60
    cost segregation and, 41
    counteroffer, 57
    deferred gain, 5–6
    depreciation, 63–64
    future of, 94
    higher price rule, 69–71
    holding period
        requirements, 83–85
    identification period,
        76–79
    installment sale
        combination, 147–52
    investor versus dealer, 18
    leveraging, 62–63
    like-kind requirement,
        67–68
    mortgage rule, 71–72
    no-receipt-of-funds rule,
        72–73
    original, 55–56
    partnership dissolution,
        85–87
    primary residence issues,
        89–93
    process, 56–58
    property
        recharacterization,
        87–88
    property type, 67–68
    provisions, 57
    qualified intermediaries,
        73–75
    reallocation rule, 149–51
    related parties rule, 89
    relocating investment,
        66–67
    requirements, 68–73,
        76–79

safe harbor, 74
to TIC exchange, 114–15
time requirements,
    76–79, 81–83
trading up, 61–62
use of, 6
wealth building with,
    60–61
workload reduction,
    64–66
Tenancy in common
    ownership, 112
Tenant-in-common (TIC)
    advisor/broker, 116–17
    exchange, 109–11, 114
    property selection,
        115–16
    Revenue Procedure
        2002-22, 111–14
    sponsors, 116–17
    stepped-up basis, 218–19

1031 exchange to 114–15
TIC. *See* Tenant-in-common
Time allowances, 72–73
Trade up, 61–62
Trading property. *See* 1031
    exchange
Traditional build-to-suit
    exchange, 103–8
Triple net (NNN) interest,
    110–11
Triple-net lease, 109–10
Trust accounting, 173
Trustee
    asset management fees,
        172–73
    charitable remainder
        trust, 186–87, 192
    influence over, 171
    requirements, 169–70,
        175
    responsibilities, 162, 164

U

UBIT. *See* Unrelated business
    income tax
UFI. *See* Undivided fractional
    interest
Undivided fractional interest
    (UFI), 110–11, 114
Unrelated business income
    tax (UBIT), 236–37
Unrelated parties, 52
Useful life, 27–28
Use test, 202–6
U.S. v. Winthrop, 20

V–W

Voting rights, 112
Wealth building, 60–61
Wealth replacement trust,
    195–98
Winthrop, U.S. v., 20

Share the message!

Bulk discounts
Discounts start at only 10 copies and range from 30% to 55% off retail price based on quantity.

Custom publishing
Private label a cover with your organization's name and logo. Or, tailor information to your needs with a custom pamphlet that highlights specific chapters.

Ancillaries
Workshop outlines, videos, and other products are available on select titles.

Dynamic speakers
Engaging authors are available to share their expertise and insight at your event.

**Call Dearborn Trade Special Sales at
1-800-621-9621, ext. 4444,
or e-mail trade@dearborn.com**

Dearborn™
Trade Publishing
A **Kaplan Professional** Company